IMPERTINENT
VOICES

IMPERTINENT VOICES

Subversive strategies in contemporary women's poetry

Liz Yorke

London and New York

First published 1991
by Routledge
11 New Fetter Lane, London EC4P 4EE

Simultaneously published in the USA and Canada
by Routledge
a division of Routledge, Chapman and Hall, Inc.
29 West 35th Street, New York, NY 10001

Set in 10/12pt Baskerville by Witwell Ltd, Southport
Printed and bound in Great Britain by Clays Ltd., St Ives plc

British Library Cataloguing in Publication Data
Yorke, Liz
Impertinent voices: subversive strategies in contemporary
women's poetry
1. American and English poetry. Authors. Women
I. Title
821.914099287

Library of Congress Cataloging in Publication Data
Yorke, Liz
Impertinent voices: subversive strategies in contemporary women's
poetry/Liz Yorke.
p.   cm.
Includes bibliographical references.
1. American and English poetry – Women authors – History and
criticism.
2. Feminism and literature – United States – History – 20th century.
3. Women and literature – United States – History – 20th century.
4. American poetry – 20th century – History and criticism. 5. Sex
role in literature.
I. Title.
PS310.F45Y67   1991
811'.54099287–dc20 91–10062

ISBN 0-415-05204-1
ISBN 0-415-05205-X pbk

For my grandmother Mabel, of whom I know little, for my mother Marjorie who, had circumstances been different, might have been a writer, and for my daughter, Susannah, who weaves her own future, a shawl, a rainbow – with my love.

CONTENTS

CONTENTS

ACKNOWLEDGEMENTS

I would like here to acknowledge with heartfelt thanks the many people whose thoughtful support and sustaining encouragement has been crucial to the development of this book. Diana Collecott, of Durham University; Margaret Beetham and Jeffrey Wainwright of Manchester Polytechnic, have each in their different ways been dear friends, exemplary teachers and counsellors of wisdom through the years of thinking and writing. I could not have found more caring supervision or more insightful criticism: I cannot thank them enough.

I owe much to those who have read, commented on and laboured over the work at various stages of completion – especially Linda Anderson, Joseph Bristow, Valerie Hannegan, Jan Montefiore, Sue Roe, Moira Taylor and Janet Tyrrell. I am greatly indebted to Elaine Hobby and Chris White for their careful editing of 'Primary Intensities'. I thank Jan Berry especially for her help in reading the final typescript and for the generous support she has given me in so many ways.

My debt to the work of other feminists – critics, writers, students, friends, the members of Network and all those others I have not named – cannot be measured. I would like to thank all those whose chance conversations, comments, encouragement and friendship have contributed to this book in less obvious ways.

The work of Rachel Blau DuPlessis, Susan Stanford Friedman, Alicia Suskin Ostriker, Diana Collecott, Julia Kristeva, Luce Irigaray, Hélène Cixous, Rosalind Coward, Jacqueline Rose, Juliet Mitchell, Susan Sellers, Elizabeth Grosz has been especially valuable to me in profound and formative ways.

But most of all, I want to thank the poets whose work has taught so many women so much: H.D., Sylvia Plath, Adrienne

Rich, Audre Lorde, Susan Griffin, Olga Broumas.

I acknowledge with thanks the help, tuition and library resources made available to me at Manchester Polytechnic. I am also grateful to The British Academy for the Major State Studentship Award which financed me through three years of work for the Doctoral thesis out of which this book is drawn. This award enabled me to go to the USA for a month to visit the Schlesinger Library at Harvard University, Boston; the Beineke Library at Yale, New Haven and the Library of Congress, Washington. My thanks especially to Diana Kealey and Pip Cotterill for their help in organising the travel and accommodation and for putting me in touch with their American friends.

I want to say a very big thank-you to Jonathan, Stephen and Susannah for putting up with an abstracted writing mother who so often did not tune in to their needs of the moment, yet despite this are still prepared to gather me to them in love.

And, my very deep thanks to Mantz Yorke for the years of support, encouragement and sustaining love that made this writing possible.

Finally, I make grateful acknowledgement for permission to reprint the following:

Excerpts from 'Twelve Aspects of God': 'Leda and Her Swan', 'Artemis'; and 'Innocence': 'Innocence', 'Rumpelstiltskin', 'Snow White'; in Olga Broumas, Beginning With O, copyright © 1977 by Olga Broumas, reprinted by permission of Yale University Press, New Haven and London.

Excerpts from H.D., Helen in Egypt, New Directions, New York, 1961, copyright © 1961 by Norman Holmes Pearson, reprinted by permission of New Directions Publishing Corporation, New York, and Carcanet Press Limited, Manchester.

Excerpts from 'The Master' and 'The Dancer', in H.D.: Collected Poems, 1912–1944, copyright © 1982 by the Estate of Hilda Doolittle, reprinted by permission of New Directions Publishing Corporation, New York, and Carcanet Press Limited, Manchester.

Excerpts from 'Deer Skull' and 'The Woman Who Swims in Her Tears', Susan Griffin, in Made From This Earth: Selections from Her Writing 1967–1982, copyright © 1982 by Susan Griffin, published by The Women's Press, London, 1982. 'The Woman

ACKNOWLEDGEMENTS

Who Swims in Her Tears' first appeared in *Like the Iris*, copyright © 1976, Harper & Row, New York. Reprinted by permission of Susan Griffin, author.

Excerpts from 'Ceremony' by Johari Kunjufu in *Black Sister: Poetry by Black American Women: 1746–1980*, ed. Erlene Stetson, copyright © 1981 by Erlene Stetson, reprinted by Indiana University Press, Bloomington, Indiana.

Excerpts from 'Dahomey', 'Recreation', 'Black Mother Woman' in *The Black Unicorn: Poems*, copyright © 1978 by Audre Lorde, and 'Love Poem' in *Chosen Poems – Old and New*, copyright © 1982 by Audre Lorde, reprinted by permission of W. W. Norton & Co., New York and London.

Excerpts from 'A Life', copyright © 1960 by Ted Hughes, 'Stillborn', copyright © 1971 by Ted Hughes, 'Facelift', copyright © 1962 by Ted Hughes, 'Magi', copyright © 1971 by Ted Hughes, 'In Plaster', copyright © 1971 by Ted Hughes, 'Ariel', copyright © 1965 by Ted Hughes, 'Medusa', copyright © 1965 by Ted Hughes, 'Tulips', copyright © 1962 by Ted Hughes, 'Elm', copyright © 1963 by Ted Hughes, 'Stings', copyright © 1963 by Ted Hughes, 'Daddy', copyright © 1963 by Ted Hughes, 'Wintering', copyright © 1963 by Ted Hughes, 'Lady Lazarus', copyright © 1963 by Ted Hughes, 'Contusion', copyright © 1963 by Ted Hughes, 'Three Women', copyright © 1963 by Ted Hughes, 'Purdah', copyright © 1963 by Ted Hughes, 'Old Ladies Home', copyright © 1981 by the Estate of Sylvia Plath, 'Barren Woman', copyright © 1961 by Ted Hughes, 'Poems Potatoes', copyright © 1958 by Ted Hughes, 'The Swarm', copyright © 1981 by the Estate of Sylvia Plath 1981: all from *Sylvia Plath: Collected Poems*, ed. Ted Hughes, Faber and Faber, London 1981, reprinted by permission of Harper Collins Inc., New York and Faber and Faber Ltd., London. 'Moonrise', 'Frog Autumn', 'I Want, I Want', 'Point Shirley', 'All the Dead Dears', 'The Disquieting Muses', from *The Colossus*, copyright © 1962 by Sylvia Plath, reprinted by permission of Alfred A. Knopf Inc., New York. Excerpts from *The Journals of Sylvia Plath*, ed. Ted Hughes and Frances McCullough (not yet published in the UK), printed by kind permission of the Sylvia Plath Estate and Faber and Faber Ltd, London; also © 1982 by Ted Hughes as Executor of the Estate of Sylvia Plath. Used by permission of Doubleday, a division of Doubleday Dell Publishing Group, Inc.

Excerpts from 'To a Poet', 'Origins and History of Consciousness', 'Transcendental Etude', 'Hunger', 'Natural Resources', 'Twenty-One Love Poems' in *The Dream of a Common Language: Poems 1974-1977*, copyright © 1978 by Adrienne Rich, 'Frame', in *A Wild Patience Has Taken Me This Far: Poems 1978-1981*, copyright © 1981 by Adrienne Rich; 'Contradictions: Tracking Poems', in *Your Native Land, Your Life*, copyright © 1986 by Adrienne Rich, reprinted by permission of W. W. Norton & Co., New York and London.

INTRODUCTION
The re-visionary task

Women poets today often write poetry that is rooted in the material realities of women's lives. Feminist poets may present to readers a *politically pertinent* and possibly disturbing articulation of women's experience. In daring to speak freely, impudently, even presumptuously about their bodies, their sexuality and their relationship to cultural forms, women poets are seriously calling into question the conventional logic of patriarchal discourses. Their objectionable *impertinent* voices, voices which are more than a nuisance to 'fathers', strive to bring to articulation words for experiences that may have been suppressed in lonely silence, words for what cannot or dare not be said, words for the grief and anger of thwarted desire.

The re-visionary task of reminiscence and retrieval also involves *re-inscription*, a process in which the old narratives, stories, scripts, mythologies become transvalued, re-presented in different terms. In drawing attention to the work of transvaluation being done by women poets, I seek in this book to make overt some of the poetic strategies that characterise this transgressive work of re-vision.

I have found it productive to negotiate the difficult margin between French feminist theory and Anglo-American feminist criticism in making my critical approach to re-visionary poetry. Wendy Martin, in her book *An American Triptych*, includes a section on Adrienne Rich. Writing from a non-Lacanian position, she sees the work of (lesbian) feminist poetry as requiring 'a re-structuring or re-forming, a seeing again or revisioning, of the social matrix and the linguistic generalisations that sustain symbolic and metaphysical assumptions – the very definitions of reality'.[1] Her extrapolation of Adrienne Rich's 1977 re-visionary poetic, together with the emphasis in *Of Woman Born*, on 'the

1

repossession by women of our bodies',[2] closely parallels the Irigarayan post-Lacanian project of 'active, creative coding or inscription, a positive marking of women's bodies, which may produce a female body whose sexuality is lived in other, different terms than the limiting possibilities available to women in patriarchy'.[3] Juxtaposing these two formulations helps to clarify the strategic project of re-visionary mythmaking that is common to both approaches. If the search for the *authenticity* of our experience within poetry turns out to be a limited project, so too does the search for the *authenticity* of the female body's language. As Mary Jacobus so succinctly put it, the acts of recuperation and re-vision of women's writing

> involve a recognition that all attempts to inscribe female differences within writing are a matter of inscribing women within fictions of one kind or another (whether literary, critical, or psychoanalytic); and hence, that what is at stake for both women writing and writing about women is the rewriting of these fictions – the work of revision which makes 'the difference of view' a question rather than an answer, and a question to be asked not simply of women, but of writing too.[4]

Fictions that may not be true, but need not be false either. 'Writing the experience' and 'writing the body' are both re-visionary projects, and both are essential strategies for a feminist poetic. The questions I have asked of the poets whose work I have examined here, have related to that crucial 'difference of view' that is bound up with being a woman and a writer seeking to construct a new relation between women and women, and between women and men – as well as a new relation to our mothers, to our bodies and to society. I argue that re-visionary mythmaking, as a poetic of disruption, involves a thorough-going critique of established definitions, values and ethics relating to the representation of women – in theory, as in artistic representation. Through its pleasurable rehabilitation of what is heterogeneous to patriarchal systems of meaning, poetry can be thoroughly undermining to the logic of the social contract.

Women poets have concerned themselves with the making of new mythic constructs, constructs which I have wanted to see as informing the making of new subjectivities for women, *that is, as working to produce a new status for the female subject-in-process* within discourse. But women poets are more and less consciously engaged in an even larger project, that of constructing *a new symbolic which would re-organise the social socio-symbolic systems of patriarchy.* Women poets are working towards creating alternative fields of signification within which we all, women and men, may identify ourselves. The creation of this new symbolic – which may take decades – is a most important project for all concerned women or men who work within the field of language. The feminist desire for a whole (holistic) new poetry emerges from the desire for vast cultural change, not only of the phallogocentric symbolic, but also of social, religious, political, sexual and psychical structures in the real world. All these projects for change are inextricably interrelated: changes in thought/language go hand in hand with changes in social and political structures in the world.

It will be clear that, in my reading of the French feminist writers, I have not privileged one theoretical approach over another. This is because I have found that each vision presents an aspect of the truth which can be considered a valid trajectory of thought in its own terms. Yet each in itself is not enough. Feminist criticism is not to be limited by the ideological position of one person or of one school of thought, however strong! Thus, I give attention to the specificity of women's biological difference from men, to the complexities of the mother–daughter bond, to the erotics of a decensored writing of the body. In studying the innovative strategies employed by poets, I move between women's material and historical (socio-economic) oppression and their construction as subjects. In so doing, I construct a both/and model for criticism in which both psychoanalytic/mystic/intuitive and rational/historical/materialist approaches are held in tension. I identify multiple modes whereby women may come to language and subjectivity. Overall, I construct an intertextual matrix in which many different poets' work may find a legitimate place. I approach the poet's work with a loving attentiveness involving 'the adoption of a state of "active receptivity" in which the reader tries to "hear" what the text is consciously and unconsciously saying'.[5] Hélène Cixous stresses that this faithfulness to the other requires close, respectful reading, an openness and a willingness to work with a multiplicity of readings, and a preparedness to adopt a whole range of approaches to the text. 'Learning to love the other' in this way may begin to bring us into community with each other. Despite this empathic approach, I have none the less tried to weigh the political implications of each gesture of interpretation.

The different fields of historical experience and its mediation within language I see as equally inseparable. Women writers and poets are creating fictional work – stories, myths, tales – that are rooted in the historical body, in the materiality of women's existence in real life. In doing so, they are giving voice to a largely unlistened-to dimension of experience, one that has been denied validity and legitimation in a culture still very much dominated by men. The historical specificity and the complex interplay of differing levels of this lived experience, including the act of remembrance/reminiscence – as a mode whereby that experience may be re-interpreted – come together in the mythic constructs of the poetry. The complexity inherent in experience, when it is further informed by a diversity of feminist insights, becomes mediated in the fictional constructions of writers and has the power to transform a woman's relation to the symbolic. However, big questions remain: how far are we made by what we read? How far can we see the text as also a writer, as also marking the palimpsest of social, historical and personal experience? Indeed, how far can we see the poem as actually playing a part in the creative construction of codes that will affirm women in their social and political relation to others?

Despite these questions, I do see the possiblity of constructing a non-patriarchal symbolic which could set itself against phallogocentric logic. Opening up the potential for the transformation of the symbolic – as well as the redefinition of the status of women and others – involves the poets in a sustained critique of classical dualism and of its binary oppositions. In poetry, the task of constructing a language and a mythic world that seeks to move beyond the frames of patriarchal thought has already begun. I have as yet no clear conception of what this 'unthinkable' non-patriarchal symbolic would entail for non-poetic language, yet I am becoming increasingly convinced that it can and will be constructed. Women are refusing to imagine themselves as men imagine them and are already breaking out of the silence, becoming visible: they are increasingly articulate and much more ready to tune in to their own desires. Surely, the massively obvious presence of embodied, lively, strong, sexual, self-defined women who refuse to consider themselves as absent, decapitated, dead – not non-men but positively inspiring women – will find an acceptable and accepted place within the logic of cultural forms!

Because, in particular, I consider the theoretical and poetic writings of women who have rejected macho-masculinist modes of thought, who refuse patriarchal codes of value and ethical practice, and who seek to inscribe their own position, I recognise that small but growing pockets of such alternative symbolisation do already exist. These texts have initiated and sustained representations out of which women might transform both themselves and their relation to social codes. That the social codes themselves also change as a result of this knowledge becoming more and more collectively available is encouraging some women to press harder and shout louder for an equitable vision of social justice for all. I remind myself, for instance, that the pressure for changes in the law that have been articulated around the issues of rape and male violence towards women has been intense and the changes achieved do not yet go far enough, but things have changed and are changing in ways that seemed inconceivable, 'unthinkable' even as recently as the sixties. I remind myself that what is 'unthinkable' now may eventually become acceptable ways of thinking for the future – for both women and men. This work of construction, though slow and at times agonisingly obstructed by those who are antagonistic to women's liberation, is of vital importance.

This work of reminiscence is crucial. The retrieval of women's experience in history through the re-visionary telling of women's stories enables us to clarify our differences from one another. It enables us to recognise the injustices and the intransigence of systems of oppression as they affect ourselves and others in different situations. The importance of those politically assertive inscriptions which bring the voices of oppressed women out of their isolated, resourceless state cannot be overstressed. Whether women who are oppressed write for themselves or whether another woman or man assumes that responsibility, their receptivity and fidelity to damaging experiences of oppression will alert those who have power to work for change to protest and demand that action be taken.

Like the projects of psychoanalysis, the work of reminiscence involves the unfixing of the stereotyped associations that cluster around the traditional thought-forms, the myths and stories of western patriarchal cultures. For the critic or the reader it involves the construction of a new logic for interpretation (this being the project of this book, as it has evolved over time). For the woman poet, it involves the creation of alternative truths that are time and context bound, and constructed in the different light of understanding from a woman's point of view. Such unfixing of stereotypic associations often means giving attention to scenarios that we would often prefer to forget: the painful frustrations of thwarted desire, the experiences of poverty, abuse, separation or rejection. It means daring to feel to the full the angry, passionate resentments banked up in the body, held in the muscles and indicated unconsciously in the gestures, in the hostile stances – which we, as women, as lovers and as mothers and/or daughters, have been led to believe we should not feel. Something more of the unconscious world of repressed representation will gradually become revealed as women poets and writers take that risk and begin to make their passionate, im/pertinent voices heard in the global movement that is feminism today.

Part I

RETHINKING WOMANKIND

1

A SONG OUT OF SILENCE

What would happen to logocentrism, to the great philoso-
phical systems, to the order of the world in general if the
rock upon which they founded this church should crumble?
   . . . all the history, all the stories would be there to retell
differently; the future would be incalculable; the historic
forces would and will change hands and change body –
another thought which is yet unthinkable – will transform
the functioning of all society. We are living in an age where
the conceptual foundation of an ancient culture is in the
process of being undermined by millions of species of mole
(Topoi, ground mines) never known before.
   When they wake up from among the dead, from among
words, from among laws.
                Hélène Cixous and Catherine Clément, 'Sorties'[1]

*Counting myself, a feminist critic, as one among many of these
species of moles, I mine the dark, subterranean passages of
theory, half blind, trying to think unthinkable thoughts, surfac-
ing occasionally, necessarily, to face the world. And returning,
with a renewed sense of dire urgency, to dig more and more
furiously into library shelves. These are beginning now, in the
early nineties, to make room for women's books. All those
women's words telling their stories, speaking their poems: the
awakened, the undead – the incalculable future! The functioning
of society transformed, the rock crumbling before my eyes. The
stories transformed, actively transforming culture. I am begin-
ning to see more clearly as 'the new day' approaches that the
future is in the hands that dig, here, now, everywhere – and
return to my particular tunnel to trace a path, criss-crossed by
other women's work, a network of paths, interconnecting . . . .*

This book addresses questions relating to the cultural construction and the status of the woman as subject within poetic discourses. It also explores the potential of the language of poetry to transform women's relation to myth, to history, and to representation generally, through a retelling of the histories, the stories – undertaken when women 'wake up from among the dead'.

It is a feminist imperative to propose new ways of conceptualising women's relation to each other and to men; to call into question unhelpful assumptions and to denaturalise the terms within which such relations are currently thought. Given the fundamental differences that exist between people, this must be an essential project for feminism. Ethically and tactically, interventions which highlight these differences are crucial. Women writers have also struggled towards affirming and validating other women in their multiform differences from each other – and whether those differences are spelt out in terms of age, race, sexual orientation, colour, culture, class, ability, religion, caste, or clan – whether they re-present women when they are at work, or at home, in the streets, or in the rice fields – what 'women' have *in common* is that we live and work and play and have sex in our (various) anatomically female bodies. Living in a biologically female body is at the centre of our existence as women.

As Adrienne Rich comments in her book, *Blood, Bread and Poetry*, 'to write "my body" plunges me into lived experience, particularity . . . . To locate myself in my body means more than understanding what it has meant to me to have a vulva and clitoris and uterus and breasts. It means recognizing this white skin, the places it has taken me, the places it has not let me go.' [2] She calls for each of us to recognise our point of location in the system, our whiteness, our class, our religion, our ability, our work or our inability to get work, our sexuality, our sexual orientation, as a point of location for which we each have to take responsibility wherever we are in the system. For Rich, her location as a white middle-class woman poet is more acceptable within patriarchy than her location as a Jewish lesbian feminist. To claim that identity within patriarchal systems has meant courageously breaking through a culturally imposed silence and identifying herself as the despised Jewess, the unspeakable lesbian, the marginalised feminist. We all, women and men, speak from a particular location within the structures and hierarchies of a patriarchal system. My own point of location has certainly played a part in influencing my perspective and approach.

My opinions and ideas about poetry were formed predominantly by reading female poets and women critics. I am perhaps to be considered a woman-identified reader, that is, a reader who has looked to the words of other women poets and critics for meanings in which to identify and validate my own position. As critic, I am concerned with producing a politically strategic analysis which encourages the emergence of marginalised voices, especially lesbian and black voices, from the silences of self-censorship and/or cultural exclusion.

Despite the given-ness of male traditions, and women's unavoidable engagement with their poetic and literary conventions, it is the trajectory of the specifically female quest for personal, social and spiritual change that I wish to underline as crucial to my project. I choose to approach women's poetry as a distinct genre, a term which traditionally denotes a type, kind or species of literature. A genre which is inclusive and wide-ranging – and which spans cultures and continents. Like men, women too have many traditions, many points of location within different social systems, many political movements and many kinds of poetry. Alicia Suskin Ostriker has stressed that

> Without a sense of the multiple and complex patterns of thought, feeling, verbal resonance, and even vocabulary shared by women writers, we cannot read any woman adequately. Time and again we will overlook some central shaping principle not only in a Rich or a Plath but in a Marianne Moore or an Elizabeth Bishop, in the same way as critics have misread Emily Dickinson. For writers necessarily articulate gendered experience just as they necessarily articulate the spirit of a nationality, an age, a language.[3]

Increasingly, women writers are looking to each other to discover how other women have managed to confront and/or subvert the patriarchal saturation of western languages and cultures. In their refusal to collaborate with (heterosexual) patriarchal ideology, language and law, many contemporary women poets are transforming the history of poetry. Ostriker has justifiably argued that 'they constitute a literary movement comparable to

11

romanticism or modernism in our literary past' (p. 7). Women poets are indeed worthy of study in their own right as a movement, as a genre, as a collectivity of diverse voices sharing in common only various experiences of living in biologically female bodies. The poets I have chosen to read for this study also share a common project – that of formulating restitutive *poetic mythologies* to set against perceived injustices of various kinds. Thus, I am not necessarily attempting to reinstate the concept of difference-as-opposition, but, rather, prefer to stress the multiplicity, ambiguity and heterogeneity of the term 'woman' in relation to, and in its difference from, the term, 'man' – that is to say, in contrary rather than oppositional terms.

Some women poets have, quite deliberately and with much forethought, worked to produce strategic fictions in which they attempt to grasp the specificity and integrity of living in a biologically female body. But how far is this writing which explores female specificity to be condemned as biologistic and essentialist, unhelpful to the cause of women? I argue that if we are to break out of our complicity with patriarchal systems of thought, we must take the risk of essentialism, for the woman-as-subject is located in a specific body, and that same body is positioned within language – in relation to the social/political world – as well as in psychological relation to others. We should not, therefore, view our subjective or poetic conceptualisation of our own bodies as some sort of essence or fixed absolute, but rather recognise it as a construct, a mythology, whose meanings may, for well or ill, be culturally engendered and sustained. As Rosa Braidotti suggests in her astute essay, 'The Politics of Ontological Difference':

> one should start politically with the assertion of the need for the presence of real-life women in positions of discursive subjecthood, and theoretically with the recognition of the primacy of the bodily roots of subjectivity, rejecting both the traditional vision of the subject as universal, neutral, or gender-free and the binary logic that sustains it.[4]

The female body is always already mediated in and through language. How a woman understands her own body is perpetually being shaped by the psychical and social meanings circulating in the culture, just as her view of herself is constructed in relation to specific temporal and geographic contexts.

12

Women frequently internalise disparaging and harassing messages from apparently perennially available misogynist myths. However, 'the body' as such is far from being a conception 'beyond the reaches of historical change, something immutable and consequently outside the field of political intervention' (p. 92). To take such a view is itself ultimately reductive and deterministic in that it refuses the very possibility of political intervention. In Braidotti's words, 'a feminist woman theoretician who is interested in thinking about sexual difference and the feminine today cannot afford not to be essentialist' (p. 93). Neither can we afford to disembody sexual difference in any project 'aiming to redefine female subjectivity'. As the 'threshold of subjectivity' and 'the point of intersection, as the interface between the biological and the social', the 'body' is the site or location for the construction of the subject in relation to other subjects (p. 97). Little wonder that poets and theorists alike have returned and returned to the body of woman to engage in what Braidotti calls 'the positive project of turning difference into a strength, of affirming its positivity' (p. 101). My task then, is to explore some of the poetic possibilities and practice opened up within that difference.

My study deliberately places itself at the difficult margin between French feminist theory and Anglo-American feminist criticism, since both are concerned with challenging the 'hidden agendas concealed in the texture of language' (Daly) [5] and both see language as 'the precursory movement of a transformation of social and cultural structures' (Cixous). [6] Both groups of writers, in different ways, see language – especially the symbolic language of myth and poetry – as potentially subversive and profoundly political. Many women theorists and poets have been concerned with examining critically those patriarchal cultural presuppositions which are encoded in 'myth'. I use the term 'myth' here to denote those messages emitting from patriarchal sources, whether religious, historical, classical or cultural, which have functioned to organise our perceptions of reality. I suggest that every myth, every history, every reality, may be mediated anew by the poet: such myth may be re-envisioned, re-presented or re-written using the powerful transformational medium of poetry. Further, each new *reading* of such re-visionary poems may be seen as contributing to an ongoing process of re-vision and re-interpretation within cultural forms.

This quest to construct new meaning I will call *re-visionary*

13

mythmaking. It is a term which owes much to both Adrienne Rich and Mary Daly but should not be limited to their conceptual frameworks. The complex process of re-vision involves both the reworking of old histories, old mythologies, old stories – as well as the fabrication or making of new living myths which draw both from the past and project forward into the future. Rich's essay, 'When We Dead Awaken: Writing as Re-Vision' (1971), illuminates one aspect of the term re-vision as I will use it.[7] In that essay, she challenges 'the sacredness of the gentlemanly canon' and calls for the urgent retrieval of 'buried works by women' writers: asking women's questions, seeing with women's eyes is crucially important to this aspect of re-vision. Rich defines 're-vision' as 'the act of looking back, of seeing with fresh eyes, of entering an old text from a new critical direction'. Restoring women to history and history to women has been a major and valuable project for feminism.

Rachel Blau DuPlessis, in her essay, 'The Critique of Consciousness and Myth in Levertov, Rich, and Rukeyser', which was included in Gilbert and Gubar's groundbreaking collection *Shakespeare's Sisters*, points to the work of cultural and ideological critique that is a major characteristic of re-visionary poetry:

> The act of critique guides the central acts of perception in the poems. Their poems analyze women's assumptions and patterns of action, revealing the cultural norms that uphold traditional consciousness of women. The poets discuss the role of the individual in history, especially in the creation of social change. Their myths have an unusual dimension, for critique becomes the heart of the myth. Their myths are critical of prior mythic thought; they are historically specific rather than eternal; they replace archetypes by prototypes.[8]

The poet's critique is directed at the cultural norms carried in and through patriarchal language – and her task may be defined in terms of constructing 'prototypes' which have the potential to produce social change. Some poems may be seen as directly calling into question women's long-held assumptions and related habitual behaviour. Re-visionary mythmaking is also to be seen as *pro*-visional in that it is constructed to meet the political and spiritual necessities of its historical context. The

14

revisionary myth has always had its place and moment in history, but its effects are thrown forward into the future. Whatever cultural critique, visionary or spiritual insight, guidance or projection into past or future the re-visionary myth offers, its 'prototypes' are necessarily provisional. In its pro-visionality, the re-visionary myth is never fixed, never universal: the understandings conveyed are temporary and are always subject to change or transformation as further evidence or insight becomes available.

The concept of *re-vision* also carries suggestive possibilities for the construction within culture of an alternative field of identification, inviting a new attitude or exploring a fresh perspective for 'real-life women'. Subjective change might occur most dramatically where the poetic text works to break through culture-wide censorship, silencing and exclusion to bring the reader to a new clarity of vision in relation to its themes. As a tactical strategy for intervention within hostile cultural forms, re-visionary mythmaking is especially relevant to lesbian women. Bonnie Zimmerman has spoken of the 'speechlessness, invisibility and inauthenticity' that are the 'unique oppression' of lesbians who are excluded from the cultural symbolic order.[9] Situated at the margins, veiled in silence as the 'dispossessed of language', the 'unspeakable' lesbian, once she becomes able to tell her story, may begin to define herself and her community through naming experience in her own terms. Her disruptive words, barred from the consciousness of conventional discursive practice, manifestly exceed the limits of the permitted within patriarchy. For, in speaking of 'women together, of women alone, of women as anything but the fantasies of men', lesbian poetry significantly disturbs conventional patriarchal patterns.[10] In that lesbian poets have, to some considerable extent, begun to emerge out of a hostile and repressive discursive practice, they have a particular importance in this study overall.

In terms of writing poetry, the work of re-vision involves the important task of bringing what has been silenced into speech, but even more crucial is the transformation of language itself. The language we use must be held up to scrutiny, criticised, revised, rewritten, spoken, acted upon. Here, Judith McDaniel argues that for her, language and action are not separate modes, but a locus or focus of cultural change in itself:

Language for me is action. To speak words that have been

15

unspoken, to imagine that which is unimaginable, is to create the place in which change (action) occurs. I do believe our acts are limited – ultimately – only by what we fail or succeed in conceptualising. To imagine a changed universe will not cause it to come into being, that is a more complex affair; but to fail to imagine it, the consequences of that are clear.[11]

Black and lesbian poets have played an important role in producing poetic re-visionary mythologies. Their work has shown that dispossessed groups, however they are marginalised, may devise specific strategies of writing to break against, through, out of those essentialist definitions and mythic models which still oppress, stifle and subdue them.

Adrienne Rich's comments have been especially instructive to me, in that she tells us how her woman-centred poetry works toward producing the disruptive, critical or transformational re-visionary mythology:

Poetry is, among other things, a criticism of language. In setting words together in new configurations, in the mere, immense shift from male to female pronouns, in the relationships between words created through echo, repetition, rhythm, rhyme, it lets us hear and see our words in a new dimension.[12]

Rich details many problems for the woman writer working, as she must, within the boundaries of a patriarchal language: 'problems of contact with herself, problems of language and style, problems of energy and survival'. She refers particularly to the work of Virginia Woolf, and her sense that Woolf struggled against the spectre of male judgement: 'It is the tone of a woman almost in touch with her anger, who is determined not to appear angry, who is *willing* herself to be calm, detached, and even charming in a roomful of men where things have been said which are attacks on her very integrity.'[13]

But the articulate poet, when she speaks as a woman towards other women, invokes a new context for the creation of significance. Feminist publishing and criticism has created a new climate for reception of her work. In defining her readership as female, the woman writer has enabled herself to write free of 'the spectre of male judgement'. The woman-identified poet may now speak out of a transformed personal experience to a receptive readership more able to 'hear' what she is saying. Permitted such freedom from censure, the opportunity arises for the release of suppressed (repressed) representations: she may create a poetry in which 'words . . . identical with the old become new in a semantic context that arises from qualitatively new experience'.[14]

Poets may also construct mythic configurations out of the particular historical, psychological and social *experiences* specific to black, poor, physically challenged, or lesbian women marginalised under patriarchy. They are not left by the poet to suffer in silence: many poems testify to their suffering, explore their *unspeakable* realities. Adrienne Rich, recognising that many groups of underprivileged or denied women may lack the skills needed to bear witness for themselves, frequently takes on this communal responsibility. She refers us to the words of Simone Weil: 'those who suffer from injustice most are the least able to articulate their suffering; and . . . the silent majority, if released into language, would not be content with a perpetuation of the conditions which have betrayed them.'[15] Rich speaks of one role of the poet as being the one 'endowed to speak for those who do not have the gift of language, or to see for those who – for whatever reasons – are less conscious of what they are living through'.[16] The poet, here, assumes a communal responsibility to find words for less articulate women, whose words may not be heard or listened to, whose experience may be individual or of a larger group but which, since it is not made public, is not available. To articulate such *difference* (here seen as what has been repressed in the signifying practices of western culture) is to speak out of the 'silences' of culture. The subversive power of the re-visionary poet in finding words to articulate the intrapsychic repressed, as well as bearing witness to social oppression (since these dimensions interconnect, are inseparable), provides the impetus and the means whereby the 'not-said' may become audible and public. Where patriarchy has pronounced and (mis-) judged, each ideologically pernicious version of what has gone before may be transformed by the poet as it is re-produced in language.

Perhaps it would be of value at this point to offer a reading to show in detail this re-visionary strategy at work in a specific text. In Rich's poem, 'To a Poet', we find the articulate poet speaking for and to the woman whose experience of being a mother within patriarchy has denied her any chance to become articulate:

> I write this   not for you
> who fight to write your own
> words   fighting up the falls
> but for another woman   dumb
> with loneliness   dust   seeping plastic bags
> with children   in a house
> where language floats and spins
> *abortion* in
> the bowl[17]

Whilst Rich speaks on behalf of the emptied, silenced woman who, taken over and totally preoccupied as maternal nurturer/ housewife, is 'landlocked', 'dragged down', she also speaks *to* her (and the reader), offering her words in which she may recognise herself, in which she may assess her position, and through which she may realise how angry she is. The poem may well put her in touch with her desire for change. The traditional experience of mothering, as it exists within the systems of patriarchy, has allowed this woman little chance to hear her own voice, even less to develop her own voice as a poet. None the less, she still fights to write her own words 'fighting up the falls': poetry is for her still, if barely, possible.

The other woman is so trapped in her situation she will not ever have any chance to write. She is perhaps poor, disabled, blind, deaf, or relatively uneducated. Perhaps she is denied the class advantage or the skin privilege of the first woman. In any case, she has no possible access at all to writing poetry. In her multiform poverty, she is rendered 'dumb' – 'dumb/ with loneliness dust   seeping   plastic bags' – her potential for using language has, in Rich's bitter and grieving terms, been aborted. In addressing her poem 'To a Poet', Rich leaves open the possibility that either woman, indeed any woman, is potentially a poet. She addresses both women, using a somehow composite 'you' – 'your life/ wrapped round you in your twenties/ an old bathrobe'. Though neither of the women has current access to her own or to any public voice as a poet as such, both are would-be poets.

In writing the poem for a female readership, Rich also confronts women themselves with what might be their own situation. She offers a 'mythic mirror' in which a woman might 'know herself'. In spelling out this reality *as it is*, Rich points all too sharply the contradictions between women's actual position as mothers in patriarchy, and the glorified cultural image, haloed and sanctified, of familiar, ideal forms of patriarchal mother-hood:

Scraping eggcrust from the child's
dried dish   skimming the skin
from cooled milk   wringing diapers
Language floats at the vanishing-point
incarnate   breathes the fluorescent bulb
primary   states the scarred grain of the floor
and on the ceiling in torn plaster laughs   *imago*

> *and I have fears that you will cease to be*
> *before your pen has glean'd your teeming brain*

for you are not a suicide but no-one calls this murder
Small mouths, needy, suck you: *This is love.*

The template for patriarchal motherhood requires a woman to learn 'through painful self-discipline and self-cauterisation, those qualities which are supposed to be "innate" in us: patience, self-sacrifice, the willingness to repeat endlessly the small, routine chores of socialising a human being'.[18] The poem finds its focus in this almost unnameable conflict between the 'central ambiguity at the heart of patriarchy: the ideas of the sacredness of motherhood and the redemptive power of woman' – and what is many women's experience of mothering within white western patriarchal forms (p. 83). Rich brings out of the silence and the darkness, the other side of the dichotomy: the experience of class or race or ability-bound poverty. Such poverty can lead to experiences of profound despair, depression, anxiety, loneliness – compounded by being surrounded by dependent and needy young children. The poem directly challenges ideologies that propose/preserve notions of the sanctified mother, in posing the question: is this self-annihilating form of maternal giving 'love', or is it 'murder'? It is a question that reaches deeply and painfully into a mother's inner life, as well as revealing outer, patriarchally wardened 'territory', opening up to consciousness and culture a contradictory space of significance where 'anger and tenderness', in a crisis of non-resolution, are opposed.

Tenderness is acceptable, anger is not. Censor and censure can combine to produce shame, guilt, resentment, self-recrimination in a besieged woman, for anger plays no part in beatific motherhood. A woman's self-respect may depend on countering this debilitating form of inner chastisement, that forbidden anger turned inward. Her survival may depend on directing attention towards this profoundly difficult psycho-social tangle of meaning that ties her in knots, keeps her preoccupied by naming her as 'a bad mother', condemns her, refuses her meanings, keeps her subdued, alienated from herself and from writing. The revisionary poem must invoke a situational context that many women are likely to share, if is to be successful in its mission. It must speak to an experienced reality – if it is to overcome resistance and flood consciousness with revelatory comprehension. Forbidden female desire, anger, distress, and other psychological dimensions of what, socially, cannot and 'should' not be said may indeed be lent words by the poet.

Margaret Homans locates the poem in relation to the 'grand and abstract' transcendent sublime of Romantic theory, noting its relation to Keats' lines: 'When I have fears that I may cease to be/ Before my pen has gleaned my teeming brain.'[19] She valuably points to the reactive strategy Rich employs in 'translating' Keats' words into her own. But the words *'incarnate'*, *'primary'*, *'imago'* relate to the lexicons of religion, biology and psychoanalysis. These orienting words lend themselves to a very different reading, one that sees language as 'at the vanishing point' between flesh and voice – (incarnate: to embody in flesh). Language is in a sense *'primary'*, that is, in a state of being primitive or elementary (as a substance that cannot be resolved into a simpler formulation), or belonging to the first stages. The term *'imago'* is from psychoanalysis and refers to an internalised aggressive image founded on a parent or other, persisting in the unconscious as an uncontrollable influence – this is the hostile *imago* which mocks her with derisory laughter from 'the ceiling in torn plaster'. These various references, in complex ways, cut across Homans' somewhat over-literal reading.

My reading views these images as contributing to a metaphor of the body-as-preceding-language. The material oppression of the woman maintains her language in a state of relative undevelopment; it continues to exist only in a primitive form. For the more oppressed woman language-as-poetry ultimately fails to survive. To me this is a valid figuration of the profound and tragic loss of women's creativity to culture, which is also a psychological loss felt deep in the body as a kind of death, mutilation or 'abortion', a cutting off of creative life even before pen is put to paper. This is a loss incurred by too many women, prevented by the material circumstances of their lives from writing of any kind.

The articulation of the repressed dimensions of language is crucially important, for if repression is not seen as a question of repressed emotion but of repressed representation, then poetry can play an important part in articulating, for poet or reader, what may have previously been refused entry into consciousness. The woman of Rich's poem has little chance of reading, of writing, or, even, of listening to her own voice. Plainly, as in the experience of her counterpart in real life, this woman's experience is manifestly tied to her biology – as a predictable outcome of her particular (class, gender, biologically-bound) location within patriarchal systems. Homans' critique of what she sees as Rich's essentialism, in the end, loses that all-important sense of the ground or location of women's oppression in the physical and biological *body*. The basis of the anatomical division between the sexes – which underpins the oppressive systems of patriarchal ideology – is biological. Setting women free from this biologically-bound existence will take more than denying that women have bodies, more than condemning women's writing for its 'essentialist' use of female body imagery. We must move on from this ultimately limited and limiting argument.

2

THE POET AS WITNESS
Im/pertinence, fidelity, respect

What are the words you do not yet have? What do you need to say? What are the tyrannies you swallow day by day and attempt to make your own, until you will sicken and die of them, still in silence?

Each of us is here now because in one way or another we share a commitment to language and to the power of language, and to the reclaiming of that language which has been made to work against us. In the transformation of silence into language and action, it is vitally necessary for each one of us to establish or examine her function in that transformation and to recognise her role as vital within that transformation.

Audre Lorde, *Sister Outsider*[1]

Our understanding of experience may become fixed and framed by the written word and thus may be rendered static and conventionalised – held in place by the sentence, by language which limits and constrains our thought. Stereotyped scenarios, repeatedly confirmed, may become deeply engraved in the memory. Unless these are challenged, they will remain a permanent influence on behaviour. The buttressing of male power through reiterating and confirming the centrality of the masculine is now recognised to be an integral part of most of our institutional forms. But we must also recognise more fully that patriarchal control over meaning and behaviour is never absolute. When the patriarchally inscribed framing of experience is no longer felt to be valid it can be replaced, its earlier representations, whether circulating in the individual consciousness or in cultural forms, can be criticised and vigorously challenged.

Feminists may create and develop many alternative modes of representation. These new representations may even put memory itself into question. *Anywhere that experience, memory, fantasy or dream can be retrieved, whether in words or images, it may be revalued, and re-presented. This effort of retrieval may permit different textures, colours, aspects, lights and shadings to be heard, seen and felt: such feminist transvaluation is a continual re-processing.*

Adrienne Rich's 'documentary' poem 'Frame' invites feminists to make an evaluative scrutiny of hegemonic structures of control – to imagine just such a displacement of the centrality of the masculine.[2] This poem in effect urges us carefully to evaluate even the information that seems to come to us directly through the senses. As with the act of remembrance, the act of perception itself needs to be examined, its apparent insights challenged. In this poem, the poet negotiates the deep divide between self and other: she portrays the antagonisms between white and black, male and female, powerful and powerless. In doing so, she reveals the gap between conventional interpretation and a feminist interpretation of 'what really happened'. As critic I must give detailed and *faithful* attention to the language used by the poet. Equally, I must explore the transfigurations and im/pertinencies of her interpretation of this unsavoury drama, which occurs all too frequently in the real patriarchal world.

Fidelity to the author must lie with the reader/critic. The integrity of the reader's act of deciphering depends utterly on her positive receptivity and dedication to the other. The quality of her criticism depends on her capacity to be attentive to the other (author, person, poem): to validate her; to come to know her situation as if she were inside it herself, in her time and place and being, and in that way to learn to respect her negotiations within that specific context. To ask: how does the critic become able to enter into another's personal and social reality – without knowingly misapprehending, misappropriating or misrepresenting her – is to ask ourselves 'how to love the other, the strange, the unknown, the not-me-at-all?'[3]

In order to legitimate the perceptions of the black woman of the poem and to validate her understandings, the white poet and white readers must at least begin to imagine 'the possibility of being the other'. Not to say, 'I am not black, not there, not her', but to say 'I am not her but I could be her.' In Cixous' words:

> I am not, I could be her, as we advance along the most
> powerful path of meditation that we can possibly pursue
> while thinking of the other. In general, when we think of
> the other, it is in terms of negative non-identification, of
> exclusion, whereas here there is a recognition of the differ-
> ence of the other, but accompanied by the continual raising
> of the possibility of being the other.   (p. 33)

In a sense, though Cixous here seems to spell out the task for the
critical reader, it is also the task for the poet who sees herself as
bearing witness to an other's situation of oppression. In this
powerful yet meditative poem, Rich accepts the distance and
difference between herself, a white woman, and a (black) woman
charged by white police with assault, trespass and battery: *'I
don't know her. I am/ standing though somewhere just outside
the frame/ of all this, trying to see.'* The act of bearing witness
requires the poet to enter into the reality of the other and to seek
to know the other in her difference, as if she were herself actually
in the position of the other.

The poem targets for critique white males in positions of
power, whose racism and sexism combine to negate a black
female student's intellectual, social and bodily presence. Neither
the professor with the 'coldest eyes' nor 'the other policeman'
acknowledge her as she is to herself, both are represented as blind
to her other reality. The female student is manifestly 'present' yet
pointedly wonders 'which of the faces/ can she trust to see her at
all, either today/ or in any future'. Pernicious ideological
construals, embedded or encoded in the behaviour and actions of
the males within the text – as they so frequently are in experience
– are *shown*, rather than spelt out, that is, they are implicitly
rendered in the situation enacted in silence. The dramatic action
is shared by both male and female participants, but each per-
ceives and construes from a different centre of attention: his
version, her version silently compete, unequally.

The student, in the eyes of the male protagonists, is inevitably
and unquestionably guilty. Holding power, they seem not to
have to account for their actions towards this insignificant black
woman. Their actions speak louder than words:

the policeman is going to work, the handcuffs are on her

wrists he is throwing her down his knee has gone into
her breast he is dragging her down the stairs

Her *mind* – in their minds – is not recognised: it is absent, is not
significant. Yet, at another level, her body, her sex, is construed by
them to be 'available'. With peculiar ease, the policemen split her
body from her mind and, in further pursuing their 'interpre-
tation', develop the presumptuous logic that ultimately leads to
the 'implied charges' of prostitution. This familiar and stereo-
typic masculist pattern of construal leads them sadistically to
despise the black woman's 'whorish' body. They then draw on
racist hatred to justify the physical abuse they mete out: 'in silence
that he twists the flesh of her thigh/ with his nails in silence . . .'.

In this pernicious racist and masculist viewpoint then, the
black woman is reduced to a mindless absence. Or, if she is
perceived as a presence, it is as a bodily presence, a permitted
object of sexual use/abuse, as a valid target for their sadistic
attention. The woman's own perception of her self is hardly
represented in their conscious apprehension. The white males,
the white police officer, evidence a total failure of empathic
identification, a total lack of other-directed feeling or under-
standing. They are depicted, in their macho-masculinity, as so
firmly boundaried as to be incapable of any relational respect for
the other. The men successfully possess their version of 'truth',
but they are individually isolated and alone, locked in a heavily
defended fortress. The masculist male is here shown as seriously
limited by his lack of vision. He seems unwilling and unable to
emerge from the circularity of repeated conflicts of power. To
generalise, I think fairly, machismo-racist males seem to be
endlessly compelled to construct aggressive strategies of defence
against the female other's destabilising visions or versions of
'truth'.

Rich dramatises, in her depiction of this situation, the racist
and sexist codes as a social pattern that informs white patriarchal
masculist behaviour. In writing the poem, however, Rich uses
the language of poetry to render invalid and unjustified the
rationale that has institutionalised such behaviour as acceptable,
or condonable, within the structures of society. In writing the
poem, she offers an alternative *interpretation* of the woman's
experience to that which the dominant male voice of 1980,
policing meaning, would have perpetuated. The woman charged

with trespass, assault and battery is, in the poem's constructs, demonstrably innocent – merely waiting for a bus and not soliciting.

The poem highlights the all-important moment of *construal*: an aggressive androcentric *meaning* 'overpowers' that of the woman. The male seizes truth, determines meaning – and makes that particular meaning stick by wiping out other meanings. The macho-male is shown as controlling meaning by physical force, and as being socially supported in this by the instituted power of law. A male-centred language *and* focus of attention may have interpreted experience, but it has done so by forcefully excluding other interpretations, rendering them occult, invalid. The male is able to reinforce his meanings through bringing the mechanisms of ridicule, dismissal, non-recognition and physical force into play. *In patriarchal culture, through time, women's words have not been respected.*

Black women have, throughout history, found themselves punitively subjected to these and similar tyrannies; they have also been socialised to respect fear 'more than our own needs for language and definition'. Audre Lorde, here, stresses the necessity for her own writing:

> Primarily, I write for those women who do not speak; who do not have verbalization because they, we, are so terrified, because we are taught to respect fear more than ourselves. We've been taught to respect our fears, but we *must* learn to respect ourselves and our needs.[4]

In the fidelity of her writing, Rich, too, strives to speak words that give meaning to black women's experience, respecting their realities, and profoundly dedicating her writing to the other woman in her racial difference. In my further analysis of this poem, I show how Rich negotiates the woman poet's task of transforming silence into language through im/pertinent disclosure. The perceiving poet, as witness, describes events which she can only 'see', in a limited way and which she cannot hear:

> *I am unable*
> *to hear a sound of all this all that I know is what*
> *I can see from this position there is no soundtrack*
> *to go with this and I understand at once*
> *it is meant to be in silence that this happens*

The events and actions described the poet cannot ever fully know about. She is not 'supposed' to know about them, for they are 'meant' to be hidden in the silences of suppression. The poet is forced to stand 'just outside the frame' – and she must struggle to 'make sense' of what she can only ever partially and vicariously experience.

We are easily persuaded that this 'I' voice is close to the subjectivity of Rich herself. The voice is personal and direct, and apparently unmediated by a masking persona. Rich deliberately avoids the use of the distancing techniques of reportage when this voice is 'speaking': it is a voice which presents itself as the subjective voice of honest, unpunctuated, urgent and direct inner speech. We are meant to hear this as the interior monologue of a white woman, *'who they will say/ was never there'*. Yet, in this transcription, this voice, this 'person' engaged in her perceptions, her thoughts, shows every sign of becoming increasingly disturbed by what she is seeing. The poet makes repeated positive assertions which insist that this intelligent woman is, in fact, physically present *in the body*: *'I am standing'*; *'I can see her'*; *'I can hear nothing'*; *'I understand at once'* and, with emphatic surety, *'I say I am there'*. In its modes of presentation this writing asserts full presence and virtually proclaims that this intimate personal voice, reliably, tells the truth. It also signals that the poet's 'seeing' is not simply passively receptive: she becomes actively and emotionally engaged in what is happening, and becomes less and less objective and detached from the events being witnessed.

This personalised subjective voice is inset within another form of writing that also claims the authoritative knowledge of empirical truth. The voice speaking in the third person offers precise, specific, descriptive narrative detail. This voice uses the indirect speech of reportage, marking the writing as again coming from an eye-witness, who is giving a commentary on the actual process of an event:

Winter twilight. She comes out of the lab-
oratory, last class of the day
a pile of notebooks slung in her knapsack, coat
zipped high against the already swirling
evening sleet. The wind is wicked and the
busses slower than usual. On her mind

is organic chemistry and the issue
of next month's rent

The scene is represented as it is happening, and as if in its natural duration: the narrative structure of the poem traces a linear chronological movement through time and space. We are told exactly when: it is winter, twilight – and getting darker. It is the moment of leaving the laboratory, after the 'last class of the day'. The present tense signals immediacy, here and now: 'she comes out', 'on her mind is. . . .'. We are told what the weather is like: 'the wind is wicked'. We are told how she moves her body, where she looks, where she stands as she waits for the bus – even of 'the crystals of sleet about to melt/ on her hair'. We vicariously experience textures, weight, movement. The poet gives us material, concrete details and takes us through moment by moment. The action is precisely temporally and geographically located: 'This is Boston, 1979.'

This voice presents itself as that of an initially emotionally uninvolved observer, who, we gradually realise, is speaking from an identical perspective to the intimate personal voice of the white woman. She watches and reports. Not, however, as the eye/lens of the camera would record, but, rather, as if she were a telepath or clairvoyant, able to receive inner thought processes – for how else could she 'know' this student's preoccupations in such fine nuance! This writing, in its structures of omniscience, claims to refer to a specific reality, that it is familiar with all aspects of the real, that it 'knows' everything as it happens, in all its spatial, temporal, and psychological complexity, that it is in possession of the authoritative empirical truth. An objective truth spoken in a voice which, despite the initial formality and distance of this mode of writing, also becomes increasingly subjective. The breathless syntax signals a sense of urgency, distress and agitation as the action proceeds. Even this supposedly detached reporter/perceiver cannot remain objective: the distracted onrush of lines that are barely punctuated, capitalised, or measured; the heavy insistent repetitions of 'in silence that'; the speed and momentum of the narrative action; the cumulative descriptive detail – all indicate a concerned, anguished participant, one who becomes more and more intensely agitated, even hysterical:

in silence that he pushes her into the car
banging her head in silence that she cries out

in silence that she tries to explain she was only
waiting for a bus . . .

    . . . in silence that she sinks her teeth
into his hand in silence that she is charged
with trespass assault and battery . . .

Two very different voices, but both bear witness to the same story
being enacted before their eyes. We are not being asked whose
voice we believe, or told whose voice possesses truth. Rather, the
truth effect is compounded by this holistic representation. Both
voices convey different aspects of the perception of this ugly
incident.

However, the important dimension of this overwriting is not
that it represents 'truth' as such, nor that it reveals what has not
been written, or what cannot be known *for sure*. Its real
importance lies in the recognition that if the political reality
evoked by the poem, if the situation and context is one that is
shared by a great many other women, then the poem will have
succeeded in heightening collective awareness of the issues
raised. Out of the silences, out of the blank spaces, this poem will
have brought to consciousness the manifold, unspoken, hidden
degradations experienced by black women, many of which are
implicit in the *action* described. The poem will also have focused
the concerned attention of both male and female readers, and
reframed those political urgencies motivating current action,
towards a goal that can now be shared by others. In this sense, the
poem could be said to carry feminist revolutionary potential in
that it substantiates and makes specific and concrete previously
concealed injustices. It focuses with clarity and urgency on a
particular issue of concern: the racist abuse of the white police
against the body and integrity of the black woman.

The poet does not satisfyingly propose solutions or resolve the
questions raised: the responsibility for such restitution lies in the
choices made by the concerned reader. More importantly, how-
ever, the hypothetical situation, plausibly regenerated in the
poem, may be matched in many black women's personal exper-
iences. Indeed, if this writing spells out an experienced reality or
a terrifying fantasy of the *reader*, traced sometime in the past, the
poem can offer a means to facilitate retrieval, and allow re-
interpretation, of the memory, dream or fantasy trace. Women
may be enabled to recall painful events or anxieties which have

been wiped out of consciousness through repression or denial, they may more deeply recognise the character of their fears, and realise why they have held their behaviour in check. If the writing revives the memory, dream or fantasy, and thus enables detailed recall and re-evaluation, if it allows *a reader* a more accurate comprehension of her/his own experiences, whether past, present or future, then the poem is *a revelation*: 'the most commonplace truth when it floods the *whole soul*, is like a revelation.'[5]

The poet, in voicing her counter-proposal to the patriarchally coerced meaning, may be seen as an assertive thinking and *feeling* presence. She has entered language as an embodied (if somewhat handicapped) 'I', in that she assumes the validity and integrity of her own meanings. Yet she is, individually, relatively powerless in the face of legal and social systems that have for centuries supported the white man in his forceful supremacy. The poet, with some despair, predicts that her words will be denied validity: '*What I am telling you/ is told by a white woman who they will say/ was never there.*' Despite this, she repeats her assertion of full presence, of possessing truth: '*I say I am there*'. This bitterly ironic statement of presence turns back on itself reflexively, for she and we all *know* these are just words.

I have made a detailed examination of the meaningful patterns of this poetry, identifying not only the patterns of racist logic, of conventional masculist social codes, of the modes of appropriation of the female body, but also those codes relating to the power differential between female and male protagonists. I have focused on bodily behaviour, actions through time, silence, speech, sensory and intellectual perception, presence, absence. The material differentials – of class, race, gender, education, location – come into play very clearly in making this examination of the language of the poem.

To pay attention to these very different patterns means to construct a very different critical practice for approaching the reading of poetry to those inherited from male-dominated traditions. I have sought to show one way a feminist critic might, in practice, approach the material and ideological patterns of a poem. I have looked carefully at how Rich has used language to construct a different version of reality. Not as self-expression, or as perpetuating any kind of unity of consciousness, but, rather, to stress the splits and divisions both within each consciousness represented, and between the protagonists, all of the actors and the acted upon, within this framing reconstruction.

Rich is, as a poet, more than usually aware of the importance of *grammar* in the ideological shaping of meaning. The positional and structural relations between the words are as important in her work as the words she has chosen. If the focusing of the concerned attention – of poet and reader – is important, so too is the poet's discerning selection of words. It is not only who tells the tale, but also how the tale is told and what part the words themselves play in constructing the story. This story is spoken by the woman poet as an articulate 'witness' *who takes the woman's part*. It is a (black) feminist commonplace that without collective womanly support, any lone (black) woman's story will not be believed against that constructed, or construed, from a white, middle-class, male-centred viewpoint. Black women know that, if it is allowed to go unchallenged and uncontested, white androcentric language will retain its power – and that too many black women will remain silenced victims.

What Rich's poem 'Frame' does, is offer the reader a transposed configuration of meaning. She creates a new version of events that, through its politically assertive inscription, its legitimation of the (black) woman's viewpoint, expands the horizon of possible meanings circulating in the culture. It also seeks to bring the voice of oppressed women out of their isolated, *resourceless* state, out of the depressing void of non- or distorted representation, of non- or mis-recognition. Achieving respect involves, indeed depends on, collective recognition of the woman's 'story', as well as on support from other women. Rich's desire is for women to move out of victim status into a position where they can defend/assert themselves. Where they can speak out *and be heard*. Where the black woman's construal is no longer ridiculed 'out of court' – her meaningful presence no longer 'set upon' by the power of the patriarchal word, but collectively and publicly respected in society.

For poets to create woman-centred meaning has required a continual negotiation between powerful, that is, culturally sanctified or justified instituted meanings, and those insurgent gynocentric meanings, only partially silenced, which break through the boundaries of patriarchal thought so subversively. Constant, vigilant, defensive policing is required by those whose psychic and monetary economy depends on perpetuating the myth of the woman as frightened, fragmented, dejected and dependent – *other*. Keeping women censored, subdued, depressed, alienated from their own meanings, requires a constant effort, just as challenging those meanings requires sustained activist interpretative intervention from feminists. The making of culturally significant myths which relate to the experiential situations in which women find themselves, is political.

I am aware that, in offering readings of poems, I identify and thus temporarily fix meaning. This, in effect, privileges one reading out of many possible readings. To present a reading necessarily represses other readings I or others might have made. Indeed, to take up any kind of position within language is to exclude other positions. At the same time, in re-interpreting, I also participate in a chain of readerly activity which is founded on lack, on the infinite interpretation and uncertainty of the play of language. The process of endless interpretation can only be interrupted by taking an ethical stance in the face of the ultimate absence of meaning, of finding any absolute truth residing in the text. The interpretations I offer are therefore of a kind that could always be otherwise: they are always and inevitably incomplete, open-ended, time-bound and specific to the moment. They can usefully be viewed as a means radically to open up the text to new, perhaps conflicting and contradictory interpretations and commentaries by other critics. The readings I offer can only be considered tentative, exploratory, part of an ongoing dialogue or intertextual exchange within a community of other readers – and are in no sense the final word.

Words can and do lose their historical context in the passing of time, and inevitably do become open to limitless interpretation by subsequent readers. The author herself cannot foresee the future history of interpretations: once published and made public, her words are rendered completely out of her control. In this contradictory way, the live author may well be a powerful inscriber of her own meanings, but since her authority over her own writing is not constant, the meanings encoded within her text can only ever be present and absent at the same time, just as, in Derrida's terms, the trace of writing, as of experience, is always crossed through, is legible, and yet is always 'under erasure'.[6] Her writing is constantly under threat of (mis- or re-) interpretation by critics and readers: *their interpretation is always both a framing reconstruction and an im/pertinent erasure – their reading always producing a transfiguration into an other-text. Which is their responsibility.*

In interpreting poetry in this way, I do not risk denying the character of poetry. I fully acknowledge the techniques the poet uses. But, in offering my framing reconstruction, pertinent or im/pertinent, do I pass too easily over the fact that the manipulations and illusions of poetic language prevent any easy slippage from poem to poet, to the real, the historical, the true? How justifiable is it for the critic to make this attempt to reduce the heterogeneity of the text? For her to try to fit its polysemic generosity into an interpretive frame? Reducing a poem's anarchy of associations to a particular limited and limiting coherence may create a message out of the fictional construct of the poem that is in line with a critic's own unconscious, or her consciously held political position. If so, what status can be ascribed to such a project?

At the same time, I have to ask: do *historical lived experience* and *truth* disappear so irrevocably, so irretrievably? And from whence does this urge to decode, to demystify, to interpret, come? Does it, at bottom, emerge out of a sense that the message it bears for the responsible reader of a live poet's work, is crucially important *because of the imperative political need to act on such understandings*? It seems likely.

3

UNSETTLING RATIONAL VIOLENCE
Susan Griffin's holistic 'knowing'

To free ourselves, to recover our power-from-within, the power to feel, to heal, to love, to create, to shape our futures, to change our social structures, we may have to do battle with our own thought-forms. We may have to change the inner territory as well as the outer, confront the forms of authority that we carry within. For we shape culture in our own image, just as it shapes us. If we are unwilling to confront ourselves, we risk reproducing the landscape of domination in the very structures we create to challenge authority.

Starhawk, *Dreaming the Dark*[1]

The poet is like a walker. She walks in the sand, and while she walks, she leaves her footprints. In the process of writing a poem, one is moved and is moving, and moves. The words one writes find feelings in oneself, and these feelings find words of their own, which in turn locate other feelings. In this way, slowly, step by step, a knowledge buried in the body comes to consciousness. This is a healing process.

Susan Griffin, 'Poetry as a Way of Knowledge'[2]

I have argued that the poem must invoke a situational context that many women are likely to share, must speak to an experienced reality, if it is to overcome resistance or denial and allow 'a knowledge buried in the body' to come to consciousness. Reading/experiencing the poem may bring a reader's understanding of her own experiences, and those of others, into flux and play. She may be enabled to reach more deeply into her own meanings, as she creatively interprets the patterns given her by the poem. In

34

the dynamic interrelationship between text and reader, there is the potential to bring about a rethinking, a reframing, a reconstrual.

Susan Griffin writes her poetry out of a conviction that to free the feeling is to free the words that heal; to free the passion is to hear 'the silence on which the music is grounded'.[3] Yet she also acknowledges that the world of the feelings cannot be dissociated from reason: 'we cannot live without reason, but reason can become too muscular and thus insensitive and incapable of knowing' (p. 248). In the reasonable world of popular science, there has been a widespread failure to acknowledge the interrelation between the knowing subject, and knowledge of the object, even though this interrelation is accepted within the field of 'serious' science. Evelyn Fox Keller views this pseudo-scientific stance of subjective separation from the object world as typically masculine, as a particular mode of perceiving: nature is objectified and any interrelation between knower and known is denied.

The pressure exerted by dominant modes of 'scientific' thought can lead women as well as men to reproduce 'the landscape of domination in the very structures we create to challenge authority'.[4] In Keller's view, the autonomy, separation and distancing inherent in the mode of objectivity characteristic of much scientific investigation, services the need to master and dominate the world. Jessica Benjamin takes this condemnation even further, in linking this objectivising mentality with male dominance, terming the scientific stance, 'rational violence':

> male rationality and individuality are culturally hegemonic. . . . Further . . . male rationality and violence are linked within institutions that appear to be sexless and genderless, but which exhibit the same tendencies to control and objectify the other out of existence that we find in the erotic form of domination. That is, the male posture in our culture is embodied in exceedingly powerful and dangerous forms of destructiveness and objectification.[5]

How does the poet construct a different kind of knowledge within language? Is it necessary for women's language to be intuitive, poetic, of the feeling, of the body? Is this the way for women to free themselves of the constructs of a controlling rationalist patriarchy, concerned above all with establishing the data of objective truth?

Griffin, rather, points to the fundamental interconnectedness of all things – past and present, nature and culture, objective and subjective:

> Language itself contains a memory of past and original meanings. If we have believed that culture can be separated from nature, language tells us otherwise. For the word 'culture' itself is built upon a metaphor for our connection to the earth: to cultivate, to cultivate the soil.[6]

In this extract from 'Deer Skull', a poem that embodies this different way of knowing, knower and known interrelate: autonomy, detachment and separation are refused. A mother has been asked by her daughter to clean a deer skull found in the woods and tell her a story about it. The mother's attention is depicted by the poet as lovingly reaching out for full feeling and thinking connection, physically, sensually, emotionally. The poet cares for, cleans and touches the deer skull's textures and surfaces, wanting to know more, and to know it differently –

> I wanted to see the lines of it
> what it would be if it had been
> polished by the wind, the water
> and my hands this agent making
> the skull more itself.
> Slowly I was not afraid at all
> and my fingers went into the deepest
> holes of this thing, not afraid
> for myself or it, feeling
> suddenly as if my cleaning this
> small fragment of earth away
> from the crevices inside was
> like loving.[7]

The mother's loving yet fearless hands intimately search into the deepest holes, the absences, of this thing: a sensual, very intimate *knowing*. Knowing more, feeling more, she understands the life of the deer as being inseparable from its death; its presence as inseparable from its absence:

> I knew
> this was the shell of the deer that had
> lived here, this was this deer

and not this deer, her home and
now empty of her, but not
empty of her, I knew also, not
empty of her, as my hands
trembled.

Creative reminiscence must play an important part in enabling
the poet 'to connect' to the deer that had once lived. The poet's
dedicated and faithful attention to the otherness of the skull, her
respect for its difference (animal/human, life/death, past/pre-
sent), and her love for 'the strange, the unknown, the not-me-at-
all' enables us to conceive of the deer skull in different terms: it
can no longer be considered an emptied-out, dead object of study.
The poet in effect bears witness to its previous unspoken life,
explores the holistic totality of its absence/presence, and refuses
to exclude or objectify any aspect of its existence, past, present or
future. We have to imagine such knowing as a giving of the
fullest attention to the object in all its dimensions. It is a form of
knowing which exceeds the limits of the rational and the
objective. The knower allows the thing known to be experienced
in and through the senses and the body, rather than holding it at
a distance intellectually. Distance between subject and object
disappears allowing no act of mastery or control and, far from
being confirmed as commanding subject-of-conquest, the
knower becomes absorbed in that which is known:

> Imagine knowing as an act of love . . . a giving of self to the
> subject matter, rather than an 'objective' standing at a
> distance. As one allows the known to suffuse one's being,
> one takes it in, envelops and is enveloped by it. The knower,
> as Aristotle said, becomes the known; but it too becomes
> transformed, though not fixated, by being known. As on the
> traditional model, the distance between subject and object is
> closed, but it is not by an act of mastery or conquest, and,
> far from being affirmed in subjectivity, the knower becomes
> literally absorbed by that which is known.[8]

In the structures of this language, the skull becomes person-
alised, is addressed as 'you', a 'you' that is also, reflexively, the
'mother' whose being is centred in this imaginative process of
knowing, an experience of process that is likened to the proc-
esses of birth or death. She addresses herself/the deer skull

meditatively: 'what/ does it feel like to be a deer/ dying, the death consumes/ you like birth, you are/ nowhere else but in the centre.' The poet is moved to weep, as the knowledge of her body comes to consciousness:

> Remembering those gentle deer
> that watched me as I wept,
> or the deer that leapt as if
> out of my mind, when I saw
> speaking there in that green place
> the authority of the heart,
> and the deer of the woods where
> my feet stood stared at me until
> I whispered to her and cried
> at her presence.

Conscious of the risks of reproducing the patterns of Romantic Idealism in her poetry, Griffin complexly links the 'authority of the heart' to 'my mind', to 'that green place' and to the 'presence' of the deer: heart, mind, earth, creature – all are interrelated. She is careful not to give the imagination absolute power over the rational mind: rationality has its place alongside the intuitive, neither is paramount. In this poem, Griffin constructs her vision around all important indicators of the presence of rational thinking: the weight of *as if* must be balanced against the many assertions of imagined presence. The mother tells the daughter the *story* of the deer, and in doing so gives her objective facts about the deer. She passes on, woman to woman, this 'gentle' way of knowing, which is transmitted through the words of the story inscribed 'on this thin paper/ as fragile and as tough/ as knowledge'. Susan Griffin's fragile and temporary yet tough words of 'knowledge' and 'authority' directly counter the objectivising codes of 'rational violence'. The processes of knowing the skull are intimately linked to her knowing of her own body and its bony skull: 'And when I cleaned the skull/ I washed myself and sat/ my body half out of the water/ and put my hands again over/ my face, my fingers edging the/ bone over my eyes'. Griffin's truths as constructed within the poem are of the body, of the mind and of the feeling, and these are all one with nature:

> *We know ourselves to be made from this earth. We know this earth is made from our bodies. For we see ourselves.*

*And we are nature. We are nature seeing nature. We are
nature with a concept of nature. Nature weeping.*[9]

In her preface to *Woman and Nature*, Griffin informs us that this
'we' voice is 'my voice but was quickly joined by the voices of
other women', and that 'the book is not so much utopian as a
description of a different way of seeing'. I see her work in poetry
as also being an attempt to encode another way of seeing – one in
which an ecologically aware identification with and observation
of nature's processes is linked to a recognition of the always
temporary fixity of knowledge.

The woman's process of knowing involves a concerned,
participatory, *relational* connection between woman/nature,
nature/woman. In the language of the poem, objective 'man'
who has considered himself superior, autonomous, separate from
nature, as if set apart from its process, is implicitly criticised by
the woman/mother who knows that we (all) *are* nature. It seems
that the desire or goal of this poetic is to transform the language
and thought forms of 'masculine' rationality by exceeding it:
sensitivity and feeling, intuition and bodily awareness of the
traditional feminine must not be excluded in any holistic view of
the world. Rational science and, by extension, culture, if it
accepted the validity of integrating subjective and objective,
might then be enabled to become genuinely 'human' rather than
detached from feeling and emotion and thereby able to be
callously inhuman.

The primacy of the rational scientific subject as a commanding
autonomous centre of knowledge, an origin of meaning, a white
(-coated), self-identified, coolly reasonable self viewing the object
world, controlling it through the authority of definition, gives
way, in this re-visionary story, to a non-authoritarian, apparently
non-dualist interrelation established between subject and object.
The poet acknowledges that as natural beings we experience
feelings, pain, loss, vulnerability, death, that we all participate in
the uncontrollable life energies of nature.

Unhappily though, it seems to be from the *patriarchal* tem-
plate that Susan Griffin has derived her ideology of maternal
empathy that focuses women's energy towards the 'attentive love
– and the loving attention' of 'Deer Skull'. It is out of *patriarchal*
maternal practice that this holistic mode of valuing, ordering
and conceptualising arises. It is within patriarchal mothering

practice that we can most clearly locate the 'vocabulary and logic of connection', and the value that insists that 'intellectual activities are distinguishable but not separable from disciplines of feeling' – and feminists have long recognised that this feminine logic can be both a lure and a snare.[10]

In addition, can this voice be seen as truly non-dualist, if the male voice is replaced by the female? Has 'he' not become the enemy, the other, in this re-visionary story? Does Griffin's inclusive gynocentric 'we', her assertion of the primacy of woman–body–vision, and therefore the moral superiority of her powers – render the male as absent from the scene of re-vision? At another level, does this poetic also risk an idealist transcendence of history? Does it risk moving to a space beyond or above gender difference in an all-female world of *semi-rational* relation? If this is a new 'way of knowing', is it too dismissive of the positive values of science? And, despite Susan Griffin's disclaimer, is not any writing that posits the woman's vision as central, utopian? These difficulties are compounded when we consider that this woman = nature symbolic parallel seems to affirm old essentialist stereotypes. Is this not perilously close to returning woman to the old essentialist frame that sees all women as intuitive, feeling, sensitive, maternal, caring – by nature?

Often, the use of the collective pronoun, that all-inclusive, somehow totalitarian 'we' of woman-knowing, seems to deny diversity and difference among women. Are 'we' as feminists happy with this transcending 'we' of gynocentric synthesis? Does it not risk committing the same sin as the transcending, universalising controlling subject of patriarchal discourse? Is there a way forward for feminism in substituting a generic 'she' for the generic 'he' – in a reversal of sexist ideology (or pseudo-reversal, since women do not generally have the economic or military or physical power to oppress, sexually harrass or otherwise abuse men)?

I want to suggest, despite these theoretical anxieties, that the movement towards a more holistic mode of perception must sometimes require a reactive oppositional posture as part of the dialectical process (hence my own use of a generic 'she' in my writing). In discovering and writing the contradictory countervoice to patriarchy, I see the woman writer as having to define herself as, at least initially, in opposition. Perhaps there is a necessary *passage through* in the trajectory of a writing that

desires to heal the wounds of patriarchal tyranny? At least it
might make it possible for women to restore enough confidence
and capability to enable us to face challenge more confidently
and courageously? Perhaps. This poetic, however, attempts to do
more than that. More than a mere 'affirmation of the difference',
it constitutes an attempt to regenerate, enrich or exceed the limits
of the patriarchal feminine. The poet seeks to transmute the
cultural networks that keep women in their place, that is, in
bondage to the interlocking chain of contemptuous, dualistic,
patriarchal metaphors that consign them to otherness, darkness,
death. Disobeying the injunctions of the father and reorganising
value around the symbolic mother may also be strategically
useful in challenging the discipline of the patriarchal word, the
patristic organisation of value and the social codes organised
around the Law of the Father. Such a transgressive poetic
practice can reframe and rewrite those dualistic patterns of
opposition within which patriarchal meaning is constructed –
those

> metaphors that organise culture . . . ever her moon to the
> masculine sun, nature to culture, concavity to masculine
> convexity, matter to form, immobility/inertia to the march
> of progress, terrain trod by the masculine footstep, vessel
> . . . . While man is obviously the active, the upright, the
> productive . . . and besides, that's how it happens in
> History.[11]

To transform the *relation* between the hierarchies of opposit-
ional dualities – subject/object; man/woman; masculine/femi-
nine; active/passive – is the goal of this poetic. Griffin has chosen
to focus her energies towards the disruption of value within these
rhetorical codes that have come to seem natural to our language
and thought-forms: metaphoric codes which have systematised
our hierarchies of value and acceptability into specific patterns,
always with the active male in the superior, dominant position –
on top.

Disordering meaning, unsettling significance: this woman
poet has situated herself in the place of mystery, of the mystic: the
place of almost boundary-less relational connection, a place
unpoliced by the 'phallus' of conventional mythic codes. She
'gets out from under' patriarchal meaning by radically destabilis-
ing the metaphoric terrain of cultural struggle. She experiments

with new positions; she strives to dismantle patriarchal hierarchies of metaphor and desires woman-as-sign or woman-as-symbol to open and expand into a new space of significance.

Time moves us on, and Susan Griffin's quest for deeper levels of understanding continues its movement 'towards'. She does not remain ideologically fixed, or closed to new recognitions, even when these radically disturb earlier frames. Working through the tensions, the contradictions and disjuncts of her theory, she continually revises her earlier ideological positions. In a later, astutely self-aware critical essay, 'The Way of All Ideology', written in 1982, she curves into yet another plane of thought, in writing of her difficult struggle to reconcile the warring voices within her. One voice is that of 'the dreamer, the seeker, the poet, the visionary thinker, the daring questioner'.[12] The other voice is that of the prescriptive, politically correct voice – of 'the nag, the dictator, the time and motion expert, the boss, the destroyer'. This voice later becomes

> the ideologist, a part of myself I hide from myself. She is afraid of my own creativity. She asks old questions which exclude the possibility of new insights. She has categorical ideas of thought or expression from which she will not deviate. She dismisses my ideas with labels, epithets, catch phrases. She purposely misinterprets me and seizes on small mistakes to humiliate me.

> And she is a martinet.

> (p. 166)

This 'martinet' looks for a totalising world view, insists on the purity and the authority of *feminist* theory, 'she is not interested in unanswered questions, in uncertainties, intuitions, barely grasped insights, hunches' (p. 167). Working towards a new frame, a 'paradigm of diversity', the poet creates a frame that evinces both a desire 'to know' *and* involves taking in 'the unknown' as – 'a way of loving' (pp. 177, 180). The self-divided poet/feminist theorist deplores the human necessity to make another the other: she asks herself whether here must be 'an "I" and a "you", the "you" corresponding to the inevitable "other": the enemy' (p. 161).

This necessary and profound essay recognises the tendency of (even the feminist) superior and righteous to project the denied self onto the 'evil' other, and recognises *within herself* the ideologist who 'creates a "you" ', who is 'politically correct', who is 'moral', whose 'ears are pitched for heresy', who is the (feminist) authority who censors, judges and disapproves of – her poetic self (p. 162). Her poetic feeling self disrupts her rational materialist political theorist or feminist analyst self by acting as questioner, as the one who dreams and seeks and hopes for a new way forward. The ideological frames of feminism itself have given rise to a new splitting, a new censor that wishes to silence the emerging, unsettling *poetic* voice. In daring to question rational premises, the poetic voice encounters an internal censor that resists and fears and wishes to crush the poet's creativity – those bodied forth words that threaten the logical, normative, stability of consciousness. The voice of the body, which reaches back to the mother, cuts across this illusory stability, only lent by the framings of ideology, in its focusing of the attention. This transgressive voice undermines the apparent identity of meaning, destabilises the – not complacent, but rather, theoretically disciplined – feminist consciousness. The poet in her seeks to destabilise her other-self: a rigid and correct feminist consciousness, which rests too secure in its justified patterns of belief. The ordered ideological codes which define the authoritative, the correct, *feminist* critical practice, the correct interpretation – or deconstruction – of the work become themselves held in question.

In the dialectic (or dialogue) between the controlling consciousness and the unconscious mind, theory and poetry, politics and psychology, there open up contradiction, diversity and difference. Her poetic involves facing what is feared: the shameful, unacceptable loves, angers, desires that, denied, would make even the feminist other into an enemy:

> What is really feared is an open door into a consciousness which leads us back to the old, ancient, infant and mother knowledge of the body, in whose depths lies another form of culture not opposed to nature but instead expressing the full power of nature and of our natures. This fear of the knowledge of the body has created a dualism between culture and nature, intellect and emotion, spirit and matter. And the same fear has made of women – as it has of peoples of color and of Jews – symbols of feeling, carnality, nature,

all that is in civilisation's 'unconscious' and that it would deny.

(p. 165)

It is this awesome and terrifying 'open door' to the denied unconscious, that contradictory space in which fear, denied anger, the incorrect and therefore suppressed or silenced wishes reside, that is accessed so often in the poetry of Sylvia Plath.

As a poet, Sylvia Plath became more and more involved with bringing to consciousness her shameful, unacceptable loves and hates. She became very much concerned with exploring the 'full power' of her anger, listening to her 'ugly and hairy' self and facing up to the denied knowledge buried in her body.[13] Her self-divided poetry holds in tension a controlling consciousness and those fearful, upsurging unconscious fantasies whose contradictory meanings were to undermine the stability of her 'I', and leave her utterly vulnerable. Her struggles as a poet were bound up with finding words that could represent the contradictory part of her self, to give words to the unspoken, denied dimensions of subversive female 'knowing' – in order to re-member her self.

It is a traditional part of the poet's role to work in language, to mediate fresh understandings, to strive for effective transmission of awareness, and to construct new possibilities for the production of meaning. Mary Daly comments that this is a process undertaken by 'Journeyers' in order to re-member their 'Selves' and other women:

> Thus Journeyers are developing ways of moving into different cognitive space, even when we are caught in male-controlled physical space. We are finding ways of 'breaking set' – of focusing upon different patterns of meaning than those explicitly expressed and accepted by the cognitive majority.[14]

The motivated woman poet may use all the resources of language to resist and to restructure prevailing values, to remodel the myths, the symbols, the codes, the expectations, the associations and allusions of her poetry – in order to deflect 'semantic danger' to women and 'dis-spell the power of the prevailing myths and symbols'.

The questions I will be asking in the following sections on

44

Sylvia Plath, and overall, centre on the particular mediations made possible in poetic representation, and the production of alternative patterns of meaning that break the patriarchal 'set'. How far, for instance, does the creativity of poetry lend itself to feminist projects of re-vision, particularly those concerning resistance to patriarchal colonisation? How does the woman poet encode a considered refusal to submit to the imposition of patriarchal constructions of reality? How does she articulate her dissent from and denunciation of the orderings and categories, the 'mythic models' of sexist (racist, classist, homophobic) patriarchal ideology which act on us all so powerfully? What poetic strategies do poets actually use as they attempt the various projects of re-visionary mythmaking? How does the woman poet begin to undo, overturn, reveal, expose the myths that act on her so destructively?

The first task, which Plath undertook so courageously, is that of recognising them, thus revealing and exposing them to scrutiny. Plath's work points the way towards a feminist under-standing of how destructive patriarchal *mythic messages* which pattern our language present themselves as the universal order, as the natural way to conceptualise reality. How our inherited, habitual, ritual patterns of representation – the apparently fixed images, attitudes, gestures, symbols, sequences, the social scripts, the systems, the rules, the codes – impose the knowledges, the conventional wisdoms that structure reality. How a multiplicity of social narratives and codes of representational practice func-tion to reinforce patriarchal boundaries and limits, lore and laws. Sylvia Plath's work reminds us that it is dangerous, but not impossible to escape these imposed boundaries to thought and action.

Part II

CONSTRUCTING MYTHS OF THE SELF

4

IDENTITY AND CRISIS
Sylvia Plath's quest for integrity

We also know of cases . . . in which hysterics do not give expression to their phantasies in the form of symptoms but as conscious realisations, and in that way devise and stage assaults, attacks or acts of sexual aggression.

Sigmund Freud, *On Psychopathology*[1]

I felt I couldn't write because she would appropriate it. Is that all? I felt if I didn't write nobody would accept me as a human being. Writing, then, was a substitute for myself: if you don't love me, love my writing and love me for my writing. It is also much more: a way of ordering and reordering the chaos of experience.

The Journals of Sylvia Plath[2]

Through the mouth that I fill with words instead of my mother whom I miss from now on more than ever, I elaborate that want, and the aggressivity that accompanies it, by *saying*.

Julia Kristeva, *Powers of Horror*[3]

Sylvia Plath is an important precursor for contemporary women poets. Her work on femininity has yet to be fully understood, but as the poetry was conceived in the years immediately preceding the resurgence of feminism, when the cult of the feminine was at its height and the pressure of the excluded and suppressed was extreme, it is valuable to explore her work in some detail. An exploration of the intertextual resonances between her poetry and her personal Journal reveals much about how these denied aspects of her self became integrated into her poetry. The Journal constitutes a privileged narrative in which Plath attempted to construct a myth of herself for herself which was to include rather than exclude her disruptive and uncomfortable 'ugly and hairy' voice. I see her as using the Journal as a place of identification where she gives herself a fictional history, where she draws her memories of experience into a writing which continually weighs and assesses the fragmented field of her subjectivity.

The Journal is an important intertext for reading Plath's poetry because both Journal and poetry give voice to her fears and uncertainties. Both articulate in different ways the 'chain of fear-logic' (p. 270) which plunges her repeatedly into crisis – towards the place where meaning collapses, towards what would disturb or collapse identity, towards that which is opposed to her I, which crushes her, makes her suffer. My task is to explore the fears and uncertainties as well as the affirmations, anger or difficulty of these different places or fields of identification.

I see Sylvia Plath as an important re-visionary poet in that she was ready to enter into the fields of 'semantic danger' of her own rage, anguish and desire, ready to question the ideological assumptions of her contemporaries, ready to examine the patterns of value and choice that determine the hierarchies of the heterosexual social script – and to do all this with a full consciousness of living in a female body. I ask of her poems: what strategies does she devise to overwrite damaging internalisations, to 'dis-spell' the power of prevailing (patriarchal) myths and symbols? How does she 'break set'? How does she focus on different patterns of meaning than those accepted by her contemporaries?

It is not my intention here to detail the controversies, crises and confusions engendered by the poetry, nor the too frequently patronising reception of her work. I would suggest, however, that her poetry is a poetry of transgression as well as a poetry of passionate excess. It is this characteristic of her poetry that has provoked much of the hostile criticism she has received. As Alicia Ostriker has pointed out, 'the articulation of female anger, like female body language, is culturally taboo, and a woman who breaks this taboo does so at her own peril'.[4]

Her subversive dedication to the repressed past – her project of reminiscence and retrieval of female rage, the fury of her female rebellion and the eventual articulation within the poems of bitter female despair – all fiercely transgress traditional decorums of the 'feminine' woman poet. Her illicit poetic repeatedly brings to consciousness what fifties' and sixties' respectability would have wished silenced, excluded and suppressed. We find in this poetry the compulsive intensities, the fragmentations and splits, the insistent aggressions, the hatred and complaint of the woman who radically refuses to hold back on her grievances. She refuses to be the silenced hysteric – to be the woman having nothing to say, the woman whose suffering never reaches language. In Irigaray's words, the hysteric is the woman who does not know herself because:

> What she 'suffers,' what she 'lusts for,' even what she 'takes pleasure in,' all take place upon another stage, in relation to already codified representations.[5]

In this poetic of reminiscence, the poet struggles to bring to language, to the stage of representation, the suffering, frightened, despairing, desiring, lustful, raging, *vengeful* woman. The highly condensed, disruptive metaphors, the hieroglyphs and symbolic forms of Freud's 'dark continent', the unconscious, erupt volcanically into her writing. 'Knowing herself' meant, for Plath, writing a highly figurative poetry having its own associative imagistic logic and utilising an elliptic, highly compressed syntax. Retaining a narrative structure, her poetry is none the less open to an endless proliferation of mythic interpretations. It is a writing which allows the often terrifying memories, dreams, fantasies, and condensed, highly symbolic images of the unconscious mind to 'break through' to consciousness. I see her therefore as taking the risk of rendering herself open to all the negativities, divisions, fragmentations of the field of subjectivity.

A restless rage at, and desire to break through, both imposed boundaries and inner censorship, to break out of the codes and conventions of the feminine certainly charge many passages from Plath's Journal. As I have suggested, the Journal can be seen as a form of her writing which draws her memories of experience into speech, as 'ordering and re-ordering the chaos of experience' – and as a writing which continually assesses and analyses the field of subjectivity. Her writing – both in the Journal and in the poetry – continually works towards constructing a polyvalent identity, one which the poet herself knew to be radically traversed, multiform and fragmented.

Plath, speaking in her Journal about her work as a poet, clearly recognises the dynamic interrelation between the construction of a *self that can be loved* and the work of writing.

51

'Writing, then, was a substitute for myself: if you don't love me, love my writing and love me for my writing.' The writing of her poetry, as with the writing of her Journal, may be seen as an attempt to give the self a narrative, to create a sense of self, an identity – and to give it a (fictional) history. As Linda Anderson reminds us, 'inevitably autobiography as the attempt to write the self, or give the self a narrative, is deeply bound up with these questions or questionings of identity'. She suggests that this 'myth of the self' exists as *a place of identification* which will obviously be 'informed by a dynamics of self-becoming'. She suggests that 'it would be as wrong to see the production of autobiographical narratives as having no ideological significance – no basis within nor reference to history or culture – as it would psychoanalysis itself.'[6] The Journal in effect introduces to the reader another of Plath's many voices, and allows her to explore the gaps and connections between texts, to note continuities and disconti-nuities, to evaluate the fears and uncertainties as well as the affirmations of these different places or fields of identification.

This Journal entry, dated Boston 1958–59, records a period when Plath was able to explore her chain of 'fear-logic' with the insightful therapist Ruth Beuscher. The passage examines the fundamental anxiety of attempting to earn a living by writing. Rage against 'mothers', desire to be other than what society wants of women, and a refusal to accept the conventional codes surface strongly:

> *Who am I angry at?* Myself. No, not yourself. Who is it? It is (omission) . . . all the mothers I have known who have wanted me to be what I have not felt like really being from my heart and at the society which seems to want us to be what we do not want to be from our hearts. I am angry at these people and these images.
>
> I do not seem able to live up to them. Because I don't want to.
>
> What do they seem to want? Concern with a steady job that earns money, cars, good schools, TV, iceboxes and dish-washers and security First.
>
> (*J* p. 271)

The poet's resentment and critique is directed as much towards 'all the mothers I have known' as towards the cultural codes informing the 'commercial American superego' (*J* p. 323). Plath inveighs against the competitive consumerisms of her culture which so coercively define the parameters for female success and which play a vital part in constructing the mother's desires for the daughter.

As an unrecognised poet, the daughter, aware of her own desperate need for financial security, is also fully aware of her need for the mother's approval. She needs the 'reward of love' of the mother as much as she needs the approval of the conventional (male-dominated) publishing world, a world which, as yet, does not recognise the necessity for and value of her work. Plath is clear that her identity as a poet becomes negated through publishers' repeated refusals to accept her work: 'Isn't this the world's telling us we shouldn't bother to be writers?' (*J* p. 270). The words of the poet are rejected, yet the writing is, at the same time 'still used as a proof of my identity' (*J* p. 289).

The links between creativity, poetry, identity, mothers, and the desire to win love and approval through writing are complicated but worth exploring as they throw much light on the recurring patterns of imagery to be found in the poetry. I want to focus particularly here on the many compulsive images of the hag's head – an image which is associated with 'mothers', and which seemed to carry an enormous burden of significance for Plath.

In this entry in her Journal, dated 10 February 1957, Plath works out why it was that 'The Earthenware Head was the right title, the only title' for her book of poems. This symbolic 'head' is seen ambivalently as carrying both numinous quality and terror, yet its 'wisdom' is not only symbolised as crucial to her creativity, it also plays an important part in representation as a 'terrible and holy token of identity':

> It is derived, organically, from the title and subject of my poem 'The Lady and the Earthenware Head', and takes on for me the compelling mystic aura of a sacred object, a terrible and holy token of identity sucking unto itself magnetwise the farflung words which link and fuse to make up my own queer & grotesque world out of earth, clay, matter; the head shapes its poems and prophecies, as the earth-flesh wears in time, the head swells ponderous with gathered wisdoms.
>
> (*J* p. 193)

This 'outrageous' earthenware head, dedicated to Ted Hughes, Plath writes musingly, is like an African mask, 'rough terra-cotta colour, stamped with jagged black and white designs, signifying earth, and the words which shape it' (*J* p. 194). This symbolic 'gatherer of wisdoms' – as magnetic sucker-in of words which 'link and fuse' – as word-shaper, prophetic speaker, and 'token of identity' – functions complexly as a place of signification for the poet's material word-world. Crucially, Plath represents this 'grisly' hag-head muse as a necessary and terrifying prophet/poet/sacred object/*hieroglyph* where (already existing) words are shaped into freshly ordered configurations of meaning, to set 'against the whole falling apart, away' (*J* p. 165).

I see Plath as deliberately (and courageously) calling up these malignant, baleful images of the hag's head in her poetry. She gives them their heads (whether or not they have faces/voices) – however grotesque, however devastating. It is a risk. This is a work of reminiscence, in which the poet explores her chain of 'fear-logic' – where condensed figurations loaded with anxiety, are brought to the stage of representation. These configurations are a vital aspect of the poet's quest to symbolise a valid pattern of identity as a woman, as a daughter (later as a mother herself) – who is also a writer.

These images haunted her when, phobic and paralysed by the demons of her fear of writing, she determinedly struggled to write prose: this in the face of repeated rejections from (male-dominated) publishers. These painful rejections she later links to her fear of rejection by the mother, the fear of the mother's withdrawal of affection – 'for not succeeding' (*J* p. 279). It is an equation which goes something like this: necessity for mother's/publisher's approval: desire for love and recognition through the writing = because thereby I am a poet and therefore I am. This is opposed by the frustrated rage and grievance at non-recognition, at the apparent withdrawals of love, at rejection slips from publishers = because therefore I am not a poet, I am nothing, I might as well be dead. As images, then, these hags' heads are emblematic hieroglyphs encoding not only the terror and power of the mother (or the publisher!) to give or withhold love *as approval*, but also the terror and power of writing – or not writing – a 'narrative' in which she could identify her self. Caught up in this destructive dynamic, Plath determinedly made herself face the images that condensed this complex nexus of feeling – the rising, self-destructive terror, hatred and panic that accompanied the wish to write, to be successful *for her mother*.

A reference to Kristeva's work is useful here, to clarify the psychoanalytic logic that underlies my analysis. Following Freud and Lacan, Kristeva suggests that when the good maternal object is found wanting and where it fails to support the subject in its identifications, *symbolic activity itself* takes the place of the mother. She suggests that:

> A representative of the paternal function takes the place of the good maternal object that is wanting. There is language instead of the good breast. Discourse is being substituted for maternal care. . . .[7]

The fear and fascination bound up in this hieroglyphic object, the Earthenware Head, seems to me to partake in what Kristeva calls the *abject*. She defines the abject as opposite to a hysteria which when

> overtaxed by a 'bad object,' turns away from it, cleanses itself of it, and vomits it. In abjection, revolt is completely within being. Within the being of language. Contrary to hysteria, which brings about, ignores or seduces the symbolic but does not produce it, the subject of abjection is eminently productive of culture. Its symptom is the rejection and reconstruction of languages.

The place of abjection is sited at an ambiguous border: in an interspace between *psychosis* in which the drive is unleashed 'without object, threatening all identity, including that of the subject itself' – and *the abject* in which the drive finds a certain object, a heterogeneous metaphor (or hallucination) that is related to orality and is capable of breaking through the 'barricaded discourses' of hysteria. In the context of Kristeva's work, this fearful aggressive image of the hag's head can be seen as a complex drive-governed, heterogeneous metaphor – a 'projected metaphor' which can be represented within language, within 'the strongly structuring power of symbolicity'. It appears not as wordless hysterical *symptom*, but as this different 'symptom' of reconstructed language. Thus the means to break out of the 'walled-in' state of the hysteric is through the production of appropriate metaphors. Plath, as poet, struggles to find metaphors that will negotiate this ambiguous interspace; to find a language that encodes the voice of aggressive *complaint*; and to find a language that 'repudiates the common code'.

In turning to the poetry, we find that an annihilating, devouring mother-figure, the mother of death/dark mother emerges in many of Plath's earlier poems. She appears as a poisonous unwished-for intrusion. In 'Moonrise', she appears as 'Lucina, bony mother, laboring/ Among the socketed white stars, your face/ Of candour pares white flesh to the white bone' (*Collected Poems* p. 98). In 'Frog Autumn', the 'cold-blooded mother' of the waning summer, withdraws her generosity and is blamed for the failure and sickening of the fens, for the 'scant, skinny' insects, for the sun brightening 'tardily' (*CP* p. 99). Meanwhile, off-stage, the masculine gendered 'genius of plenitude/ Houses himself elsewhere. Our folk thin/ Lamentably.' In 'I Want, I Want', another poem from 1958, the baby god of the poem, finding little to satisfy hunger, 'Cried out for the mother's dug./ The dry volcanoes cracked and spit,/ Sand abraded the milkless lip' (*CP* p. 106).

Thwarted desire, loss, grief, failure to nourish, failure to sustain marks 'Point Shirley' also (*CP* p. 110). This time the loved dead grandmother is unavailable to the granddaughter who searches for her, longs for her: 'I would get from these dry-papped stones/ The milk your love instilled in them'. In disappointment, the grieving persona of this poem recognises that, despite her contrivances, the 'stones are nothing of home'.

These poems constitute a litany of pain, of lack, in which the negative imagery of a devouring mother is invoked time and again. In 'All the Dead Dears', Plath images mother on mother as malevolent, evil. Here, the 'long gone darlings' emerge into thought – again as hags, to reach terrifyingly through the poisonous mirror:

As I think now of her head,

From the mercury-backed glass
Mother, grandmother, greatgrandmother
Reach hag hands to haul me in.   (*CP* p. 70)

And when the sinister 'dismal-headed/ Godmothers', with 'heads like darning-eggs' appear in 'The Disquieting Muses', the ineffectual mother of the poem is held to question 'I wonder/ Whether you saw them, whether you said/ Words to rid me of those three ladies/ Nodding by night around my bed,/ Mouthless, eyeless, with stitched bald head' (*CP* p. 74). Mother, being merely human, fails to protect the daughter from the hurricane. She is helpless to prevent the little girl's failure to measure up to the necessity to be feminine – to pirouette and be pretty: 'I could/ Not lift a foot in the twinkle-dress.' The small child's fears – despite all the mother's words, stories, distractions, comforting – remain unassuaged. The child is inconsolable: 'those ladies broke the panes'. The poem touches the daughter's deep anger at the mother for bearing her into this fearful 'kingdom', and, as all mothers do, for imposing her will on the child. But the pride and will of the daughter forbid her to reveal these depths of *anger* and *fear*. She will not betray her 'travelling companions' – she will keep silent, will 'hold her self together'. The poet, at this stage, depicts the daughter as sustaining her sense of a controlled identity through denial of her feelings of terror. Indeed, the structure of the poem itself evidences a self-conscious, deliberate, formality.

The voice, urgent with its passionate, repetitive address to the mother (the word mother is repeated nine times overall) and its many insistent rhythmic phrases ('I learned, I learned, I learned elsewhere'), is tightly bound by the formal discipline of a controlled syllable count (mostly eight per line). The controlled and careful use of echoing patterns of internal rhyme as well as those at the end of the line – stone, gown, born, sun, down, frown, mine – mark this poetry as rigorously ordered and disciplined:

> Day now, night now, at head, side, feet,
> They stand their vigil in gowns of stone,
> Faces blank as the day I was born,
> Their shadows long in the setting sun
> That never brightens or goes down.
> And this is the kingdom you bore me to,
> Mother, mother. But no frown of mine
> Will betray the company I keep.

Although the patterns are not regular, this is none the less highly crafted, *controlled* work. Yet these insistent rhythms and sound patterns paradoxically build to heighten and compound the effect of passionate excess, of serious, intense grievance. However, the terrifying hag-head images, weighty with emotional import are, despite this pressure, held within a tight, logically controlled, linear narrative logic.

In the Journal, the connection of the hag-head image to the difficulties of producing writing becomes overt: 'The ghost of the unborn novel is a Medusa-head' (*J* p. 245). In the poem 'Medusa', Plath transfigures the image of the head of the Medusa to a 'fat and red' placenta 'Paralysing the kicking lovers'. This connection adds weight to the link I am making between the poet's creativity, the mother, and the anxiety-induced paralysis of not being able to write. It also points to the attempt Plath is making to detach and separate herself from the damaging pattern of her emotional dependence on the mother: 'Off, off, eely tentacle!/ There is nothing between us' (*CP* p. 226).[8] The mother/daughter connection must be severed. Again, it would seem that Plath needed to fuel this struggle with anger, with what her unsympathetic biographer Anne Stevenson has called 'unrelieved venom', in order to break free of this complex chain of 'fear-logic'.[9] Perhaps knowing that her mother was always there, ready and wanting to help, ready with succour, aid, faith, hope and promise was not the most helpful thought to someone desperately struggling to establish her independence, her competence, her identity as a writer in her own right. Plath may well have felt compelled to refuse the comfort and forgiveness of the 'Communion wafer' and resolve to 'take no bite of your body', for she must do it by herself – this despite the reproach of (her mother's?) wishes which 'Hiss at my sins'.

The unsuccessful poet – as herself a failed mother who 'miscarries' the words, the poems – is frequently found wanting. The writing – seen as a symbolic act which takes the place of the mother and becomes a symbolic 'substitute for maternal care' – fails to provide a language in which she can identify herself. The threat of being silenced or even of psychosis, looms large for a poet who wishes to identify herself, live and survive economically – in and through her writing. The figure of the dead/unborn poem or novel obsessively haunts the poetry that gets written – images of stillbirth or miscarriage, of barrenness and baldness, of sickness, injury, and 'Death, that bald-head buzzard' recur with compulsive regularity, particularly in the early work (*CP* p. 120).

Good writing became Plath's metaphoric equivalent to good

health. As she put it: 'Writing is my health' (*J* p. 325); 'My health is making stories, poems, novels . . .' (*J* p. 165). When writing failed her, or when publishers rejected her work, images of sickness, barrenness, disintegration, death, threaten: 'Feel oddly barren. My sickness is when words draw in their horns and the physical world refuses to be ordered, recreated, arranged, selected' (*J* p. 319). Thus this frightening metaphor of barrenness, the loss of the ability to speak, to write – carries with it a sense of sick disintegration, of loss of control, of loss of an integrated, ordered subjectivity. Indeed, *the subject is engaged in a desperate struggle to produce itself across the field of identification.*

These images mark *the tendency towards the collapse of her identity as a woman poet.* Having no audience, the poet's words become empty, inert, sterile, infertile (or virginal – as in the 'blank page' experience), or they 'miscarry': they fail to give birth to the poem/poet/mother. In 'Barren Woman', the failure of the public to recognise her work results in the re-absorption of her creativity. The mother/poet here, sardonically imagines her great public, as 'white Nike' and several Apollos. Nike was the victorious Athena, born parthenogenetically from Zeus, and is thus a patriarchal figuration – here symbolised negatively as 'white'. Apollo, also a patriarchal son, is similarly figured – negatively, as 'bald-eyed'. Plath is bitterly deconstructing the usual valorised mythic patterns for these figures. 'Without statues' – that is, without works of art, without poems, *without babies*, which 'desire' attention, which need to be seen to exist, to be recognised and to have people to applaud and love them – the poems are dead, the poet becomes sick and nothing can happen:

Empty, I echo to the least footfall,
Museum without statues, grand with pillars, porticoes,
    rotundas.
In my courtyard a fountain leaps and sinks back into itself,
Nun-hearted and blind to the world. Marble lilies
Exhale their pallor like scent.

I imagine myself with a great public,
Mother of a white Nike and several bald-eyed Apollos.
Instead, the dead injure me with attentions, and nothing
    can happen.
The moon lays a hand on my forehead,
Blank-faced and mum as a nurse.   (*CP* p. 157)

Images of miscarriage, of stillbirth, also populate the numb, diminished void of 'A Life'. The theme of this poem is the failure of life to achieve itself in all its potential dimensions. Again, we encounter images relating to the failure of symbolisation. This poem's dominant image, the embryo in a glass jar, may be related to embryonic poem/corpses which paradoxically 'speak' of the silence, the quietness of creativity/generation cancelled out. The identityless woman who has 'no attachments'; the 'sheet of blank paper'; the 'foetus in a bottle'; the 'sea, flattened to a picture' constitute a metaphoric chain which may be linked to success or failure as a poet:

> A woman is dragging her shadow in a circle
> About a bald, hospital saucer.
> It resembles the moon, or a sheet of blank paper
> And appears to have suffered a sort of private blitzkrieg.
> She lives quietly
>
> With no attachments, like a foetus in a bottle
>
> (*CP* p. 150)

Significantly, this detached, clinical voice, neutralised of feeling or compassion – arrives in a place where 'Grief and anger, exorcized/ Leave her alone now.' This is close to the position of the hysteric, yet not quite, since the poet's words and images are there on the page, symbolised, written. Even if ambiguous, borderline – even if they are not accepted – they have still been brought to the stage of representation. They do signify.

In 'Stillborn' (*CP* p. 142), this interconnecting chain of metaphors: baby/poem; poet/mother; health/sickness; order/disorder; speech/silence; life/death is made explicit:

> These poems do not live: it's a sad diagnosis.
> They grew their toes and fingers well enough,
> Their little foreheads bulged with concentration.
> If they missed out on walking about like people
> It wasn't for any lack of mother-love.

Just as the mother within the poem finds it impossible to revive her child/poems, so the poet is unable to give them an identity, a life in the world – though 'They are proper in shape and number and every part'. She cannot breathe life and feeling into them:

'the lungs won't fill and the heart won't start'. Suspended in time and space in 'pickling fluid' and unable to walk about 'like people' in the public realm, the poems are not, cannot be recognised for what they are, only for what they are not:

> They are not pigs, they are not even fish,
> Though they have a piggy and a fishy air –
> It would be better if they were alive, and that's what they
>   were.
> But they are dead, and their mother near dead with distrac-
>   tion,
> And they stupidly stare, and do not speak of her.

The 'I' voice of the poem is not represented as being in a position of mastery – and only appears once to make a despairing exclamation, almost a cry: 'I cannot understand what happened to them!' The 'I'/mother implicit in the first two verses collapses by the third: the products of her labour, the poems, are dead, and she is 'near dead' – and not spoken of.

In representing her sickness, distraction, melancholy, depression – in words signifying absence, emptiness, flatness, silence; in the fading of voice, the effacement of identity to a mere shadow, a ghostly echo – the poet gradually fades into insignificance. However, in *writing* of the collapse of maternal fecundity, in which the poet signals or symbolises her desperation, she has also created the possibility to lift herself out of it.

This writing marks Plath's struggle to transform her suffering. Describing it, thematising it, identifying it to herself also allows for the possibility of re-symbolisation, in words. The poet may de-form, decompose the psychic patterns that have informed the writing. She may overwrite time, the past – 'the years draining into my pillow'. She may cleanse it, vomit it away: 'The nauseous vault/ Boomed with bad dreams and the Jovian voices of surgeons/ Then mother swam up, holding a tin basin./ O I was sick' (*CP* p. 156). She may also *kill off* her figural representation of fear, 'the dewlapped lady', and become, instead, the 'good mother' to herself. She may mythically generate a transformed identity as innocent *neonate*:

> Now she's done for, the dewlapped lady
> I watched settle, line by line, in my mirror –

Old sock-face, sagged on a darning egg.
They've trapped her in some laboratory jar.
Let her die there, or wither incessantly for the next fifty
    years,
Nodding and rocking and fingering her thin hair.
Mother to myself, I wake swaddled in gauze,
Pink and smooth as a baby.

This aggressive rejection of the loathed but fascinating 'dewlapped lady' shows the poet finding and articulating the angry voice of the destructive avenger. The fury attached to the image finds itself symbolised in vicious, uncompromising language: 'Let her die there, or wither incessantly'. This marks a violent turning against the threatening, repugnant, abject images. The feeling intensity and rage of this writing suddenly bursts through the barricades – and the 'current flows' into symbolicity. As Kristeva says:

> A language now manifests itself whose *complaint* repudiates the common code, then builds itself into an *ideolect*, and finally resolves itself through the sudden irruption of *affect*.[10]

I do see Plath as recognising the potential for the poetic language of metaphor and hieroglyph to reorganise the constructs of identity. That she desired to reach other women through the writing also seems important. This was clearly her concern in this statement, dated 15 September 1959: 'I must move myself first, before I move others – [be] a woman famous among women' (*J* p. 259). She turns away from the inscriptions, identities, systems, and orderings that had kept her so bound up in suffering, and moves towards the construction of a new field of identification, one where she could mark out a new myth of/for herself and also, hopefully, for other people, for other women. For her to commit herself to be a writer constituted an act of faith in the writing – that it could change our view of things and people:

> Writing is a religious act: it is an ordering, a reforming, a relearning and reloving of people and the world as they are and as they might be. A shaping which does not pass away like a day of typing or a day of teaching. The writing lasts: it goes about on its own in the world. People read it: react to

it as to a person, a philosophy, a religion, a flower: they like it, or do not. It helps them, or it does not.

(J p. 271)

The writing, in Plath's terms, takes on a material presence in the world – as person, philosophy, religion, flower – which people 'react' to. It allows Plath to operate as confident 'I', as woman, as poet, as writer – but only if the poetry finds public acceptance. The 'I' as subject becomes 'i', a ghost of itself, in the absence of such approval.

Mythically replacing the 'lost' m/Other, the daughter's writing, and its success (or lack of it) becomes all-important as sustainer of the fictional integrity of the desired *identity as writer*.[11] When editors/publishers approve (confirm) or disapprove (disintegrate) the position taken up by the poet in her struggle for recognition of her identity as a writer, they apparently displace the anxiety relating to the mother. Indeed, in Plath's terms, they seem to take the place of the mother as a necessary source of approval and judgement – and the absence of their approval is just as devastating:

> Mother didn't matter – she is all for me, but I have dissipated her image and she becomes all editors and publishers and critics and the World, and I want acceptance there, and to feel my work good and well-taken. Which ironically freezes me at my work, corrupts my nunnish labour of work-for-itself-as-its-own-reward.

(J p. 303)

Publishers, critics, editors, the public, the world – all participate in and are necessarily constitutive of her poetic identity: the poet is formed (constructed) *in relation to* her public. To make of the woman a subject, as producer of poetry, a contributor to culture – as an apparently unified agential self – requires the Other to materially re-present the ideal, loving m/Other, that is, to provide the dynamics of accepting relationship; to uphold the woman poet by affirming her value and existence-as-poet, whose work is valued and respected *within the cultural symbolic order*. All this is necessary to constitute her securely as a poet who is a woman in the eyes of the world.

Thus indeed the mirroring response of mothers as m/Others does matter, and deeply, for, anchored in the language of the

63

m/Other is the existence of the self *as subject*. Aurelia Plath clearly recognised this: 'They say she wrote the letters to keep me happy, to hide the darker side. Sylvia? Putting herself out day after day? The reason she wrote those letters was to get a reply, and she always did.'[12] She needed her mother to confirm her in her self – especially since publishers had failed to recognise her through the *ten years* of 'hopeful wishful waits (and subsequent rejections)', which preceded the publication of 'Mussel Hunter at Rock Harbour'. (So runs Plath's Journal entry for 25 June 1958. (*J* p. 242).)

In this further fragment from Sylvia Plath's Journal (3 January 1959), we find this struggle, this quest for understanding: to make sense of her desire for confirmation from her mother:

> What do I expect or want from Mother? Hugging, mother's milk? But that is impossible to all of us now. Why should I want it still? What can I do with this want? How can I transfer it to something I can have?
>
> (*J* p. 285)

Plath's mythmaking strategy required her to explore the contradictory dynamics of the relation between mother and daughter, to examine the forms of its organisation and to make overt the pain and suffering bound up in her 'chain of fear-logic'. This led to the self-conscious collapse of her defensive idealisation – of the good and beautiful relation, clung to in so many of her *Letters Home*. Plath deliberately risks the pain of decomposition of identity, the emptiness of separation: the 'plunge to the bottom of nonexistence, of absolute fear, before I can rise again' (*J* p. 250).

In Plath's particular situation, it does seem simply too naive to blame either Plath or her mother. I hope I have shown that Plath's self-conscious and deliberate poetic strategies necessarily led her to explore the idea of the mother in both positive and negative terms. The conviction grows for me that Plath's real flesh and blood mother, in her cultural situation and moment, could have done little to alter the tragic course of events of her daughter's life.

I am moved at this point to comment that beneath the strongest anger, hostility, hatred, lies concealed an equal measure of love (indifference would tell another story); that the psycho-dramas which inhabit the poems probably drew both their awesome power and their hostile energy from this love, the love of the daughter for the mother.

The developmental necessity for Plath as daughter – to become separate, to create her own identity independent of her mother – may have compelled her to try to cut herself off from such an intensity of love. The desires fuelling the compulsive primal need – 'to be what the mother desires' – may well be terrifying, threatening to any sense of separate integrity for many women.[13] For to re-open the pathways to primal, pre-Oedipal *overwhelming* desire is always dangerous. To write poetry, to be a poet, means to take that risk.

5

'WHAT GIRL EVER FLOURISHED IN SUCH COMPANY?'[1]

A number of Journal entries made from 1958 onwards make it clear that Plath made a self-conscious decision to study women. Her critique of the ideology of the feminine; her critical consciousness of women's emotional, erotic and economic loyalty and their subservience to men can be shown as developing continuously from this time. The Journal informs us of the distance Plath begins to feel between herself and men – 'How odd, men don't interest me at all now, only women and women talk' (*J* p. 293). She struggles to break out of her dependence on male approval, eventually telling herself 'write and show him nothing: novel, stories and poems' (*J* p. 259); 'DO NOT SHOW ANY TO TED' (*J* p. 294).

Intensely competitive, she measures herself against all the major women poets and cherishes ambitions to be 'The Poetess of America (as Ted will be The Poet of England and her dominions)':

> Who rivals? Well, in history, Sappho, Elizabeth Barrett Browning, Christina Rossetti, Amy Lowell, Emily Dickinson, Edna St. Vincent Millay – all dead. Now: Edith Sitwell and Marianne Moore, the aging giantesses, and poetic godmother Phyllis McGinley is out – light verse: she's sold herself. Rather: May Swenson, Isabella Gardner, and most close, Adrienne Cecile Rich – who will soon be eclipsed by these eight poems.
>
> (*J* p. 211)

Through these years, she gradually commits herself to 'work on femininity', declaring that she wants to be 'a woman famous among women'. Hatred against men begins to fuel the vitriolic stance of many poems. As the Journal notes:

> I have hated men because I felt them physically necessary;
> hated them because they would degrade me, by their
> attitude: women shouldn't think, shouldn't be unfaithful
> (but their husbands may be), must stay home, cook, wash.
> Many men need a woman to be like this.
>
> (*J* p. 290)

To be able to write out of her frustration, rage and desperation at
her own position as a woman did not come at all easily. Here she
speaks of the frustration and conflict of *wanting both/and* – both
baby and career, an inadmissible project for the feminine female
of the fifties:

> I, sitting here as if brainless wanting both a baby and a
> career but god knows what if it isn't writing. What inner
> decision, what inner murder or prison break must I commit
> if I want to speak from my true deep voice in writing . . .
> and not feel this jam-up of feeling behind a glass-dam
> fancy-facade of numb dumb wordage.
>
> (*J* p. 295)

There is a strong sense in this passage of having to deal with
something inside herself – to decide about it, to destroy it or break
through or out of, its limitations. There is also a fierce, intense
pressure behind what Plath images as a 'glass-dam fancy-facade
of numb dumb wordage' and behind which her 'true deep voice'
and her feeling seem trapped. How is she imprisoned? – by
words? by dumb words? How can you have words which do not
speak – which are emotionally numb? – or that can form an
impenetrable barrier to feeling?

'Poems, Potatoes', was written late in 1958, not long before this
Journal entry was made (*CP* p. 106). This very formal philoso-
phical poem with its tightly controlled stanzas, linear develop-
ment of theme and somewhat strained syntax hardly allows the
feelings and rhythms of the spoken voice to break through and be
heard. This is very much written language, highly self-conscious,
reticent, detached, ironic. The poem's disciplined logic works to
hold in check the anger which charges individual words: 'muz-
zles', 'murderous', 'shortchange', 'dissatisfy'.

> The word, defining, muzzles; the drawn line
> Ousts mistier peers and thrives, murderous,
> In establishments which imagined lines

Can only haunt. Sturdy as potatoes,
Stones, without conscience, word and line endure,
Given an inch.

The murder and muzzling that these enduring stones/words/
lines are guilty of, even if they have no conscience about it, is of
the unwritten story, the unheard inner voice, the unpictured
poem – symbolised in the poem as the 'unpoemed' brown potato.
('The brownness is my dead self' – 'Three Women', *CP* p. 179).
The 'mistier peers' and 'imagined lines' cannot break through
the rigid formal discipline that holds both the words and the
raging emotion firmly in place – imprisoned, as it were, in a
syntactical cage.

By the time she wrote 'Magi' (1960) Plath recognised that the
defining words of the Fathers of Platonism, as of Christianity,
had imposed the 'deathly' logic of their philosophy on the vital
and life-enhancing female (*CP* p. 148). She introduces the poem
in the following terms: 'Abstractions, by definition, are with-
drawn from life and formulated in despite of life's minute and
vital complexities. In this poem, "Magi", I imagine the great
absolutes of the philosophers gathered around the crib of a
newborn baby girl who is nothing *but* life' (*CP* pp. 289–290). The
poem attacks the faceless, bodiless, 'dull', lifeless principles of the
patriarchal logos:

Their whiteness bears no relation to laundry,
Snow, chalk or suchlike. They're
The real thing, all right: the Good, the True –

Salutary and pure as boiled water,
Loveless as the multiplication table.
While the child smiles into thin air.

These abstractions are encoded as negative attributes in the
poem: they are weightless, pure, loveless, spiritual, blank and
white. The embodied baby girl, the female child – in the world
and of it – cannot escape their culturally transmitted ideas, the
weighty definitions which surround her from infancy: their
'heavy notion' of woman, defined as Evil, attends her even from
the nursery. Plath's question 'What girl ever flourished in such
company?' shows her as self-consciously valorising the female
against logocentric conceptions of what constitutes the Good and

the True. The poem also makes a (limited) attempt to transform the cultural ordering of value: the insubstantial abstracts, products of their theorising, are negatively evaluated. Only maternal love, imaged as 'Love the mother of milk' is valued positively: it takes on material, physical form for the girl child – and is no theoretical concept.

Many of these patterns are repeated in Plath's poem 'Tulips' (*CP* p. 160). This poem explores the feminine task of learning submissiveness, of accepting the passivity of femininity and allowing herself to be mastered. Plath deliberately immerses the woman/patient into the wintery whiteness and sterile orderings of the patriarchal logos, into an order which is disturbed only by the distraction of the tulips:

> The tulips are too excitable, it is winter here.
> Look how white everything is, how quiet, how snowed-in.
> I am learning peacefulness, lying by myself quietly
> As the light lies on these white walls, this bed, these hands.
> I am nobody; I have nothing to do with explosions.
> I have given my name and my day-clothes up to the nurses
> And my history to the anesthetist and my body to surgeons.

Having given up her name, her clothes, her body, her history, her self, and her active agency to the hospital hierarchy, the woman assumes the position of meek self-effacement, of utter subjection: 'I have lost myself.' The place of identity becomes an emptied void: numbed, anaesthetised, acted on – the woman wants nothing and nothingness, wants only the peace which is death. It is a form of happiness to be withdrawn from active life: it is pleasurable to be tended, to become helpless, to become numb, oblivious to the world and its demands. The virginal purity, the chastity of the body, the humility and holiness of the spirit, the perfect goodness of the nun are invoked as the symbolic essence of this model of female self-denying masochism: 'I am a nun now, I have never been so pure.'

Plath is here presenting woman as transcending the world of the material, of necessity, of the body – through casting away the physical necessities that bind her to the earth. She yields up control over her body, her personality, her worldly goods, her sexual life (in relation to husband and children) – all of the 'baggage' of physical existence. Shedding the exuberance of life and of the sexual/maternal body she becomes the abstract

epitome of the feminine: the idealised, sexless bodiless woman –
spiritualised, quiet, inert, utterly subjected – of conventional
forms of Christian patriarchy. This identityless woman-as-
martyr (or as victim) takes up a consolatory position that is
peaceful and painless: it is a welcomed death/sleep which she
accepts gratefully.

There is a problem though. The tulips upset things. The
woman resents the 'too-red' 'excitable' tulips which hurt her:

> The tulips should be behind bars like dangerous animals;
> They are opening like the mouth of some great African cat,
> And I am aware of my heart: it opens and closes
> Its bowl of red blooms out of sheer love of me.
> The water I taste is warm and salt, like the sea,
> And comes from a country far away as health.

These tulips can breathe, they can see, they are active, they are
excitable, they draw attention to themselves, they are noisy, they
open their mouths, they have a 'dangerous' animal vitality – and
they are a challenging manifestation of the life force, of *love*,
calling the woman to an awareness of herself as she has become.[2]
This ironic poem recognises the pleasure a woman gets in being
mastered, in yielding her power to others, thus transcending the
necessity to act for herself. Plath sardonically derides this empty
collusive transcendence, the subjected flattened presence of this
'I' voice is absurd: 'I see myself, flat, ridiculous, a cut-paper
shadow/ Between the eye of the sun and the eyes of the tulips,/
And I have no face, I have wanted to efface myself.' But the
passionate tulips recall her to life: to her body, to her heart, to her
senses – she can now know colour, danger, movement, warmth,
taste. She is restored to a consciousness of the sea, the earth –
aspects of the materiality of healthy existence *in the world of the
body*. This is a very self-conscious and aware critique of myths of
femininity.

Plath was clearly aware of the repressiveness of myths of
femininity as of language, just as she recognised that her own
'true deep voice' of (angry) feeling was not being allowed to come
to the fore in the poems. The internal battle for Plath was to
learn to respect rather than to silence this unpleasant, rebellious,
sometimes violent voice that struggled for utterance. Her poem,
'In Plaster', dramatises this struggle between the 'two of me' (*CP*
p. 158).

George Stade tells us that this poem was written whilst Plath was in hospital recovering from an appendectomy and 'alludes to the condition of a woman in a bed near Plath's own'.[3] Quoting from a comment of Ted Hughes, Stade reads this poem as an exploration of the 'defensive forces of containment'. He suggests that this poem 'takes the form of a monologue by the imminent volcano on the subject of its relations to the prickly defense-relations that have become close, explicit, murderous'. His reading sees the 'white person' as 'character armour' in murder-ous conflict with a 'yellow' 'repressed self'. Given Plath's focus on the problems of femininity, however, a feminist reading can throw further light on this accomplished poem.

The internalised 'white person' is as pure, saintly, superior, cold, dead, immortal, immaterial – as the abstractions of 'Magi'. The conventional, tidy, patient, passive, virtuous, calm, beautiful, grateful, uncomplaining (resentful) qualities of this feminine self mask the angry yellow *unpleasant* self. In this poem, the poet images the conventional feminine cast or mould, myth or model – as a plaster case which reflects the 'sun' (the male principle?). This case is presented as critical of the nasty old yellow self – of the aggressive inner voice that 'she' hopes will die of its own accord. The white plaster 'torso' – headless? armless? legless? wants to leave the nasty yellow one, and looks after her badly –

And secretly she began to hope I'd die.
Then she could cover my mouth and eyes, cover me entirely,
And wear my painted face the way a mummy-case
Wears the face of a pharaoh, though it's made of mud and
    water.

The terrifying prospect of the white person killing off the yellow inner voice is contemplated here. Plath presents her reader with an image of the silenced, blinded, mummy – brown, bandaged, long dead – as stiflingly masked with the brightly painted face of femininity.

Knowing that she is in no position 'to get rid of her', the 'ugly and hairy' yellow self despises the white feminine persona as 'stupid'. This manifestation of the feminine ideal in herself is hated – because this self lacks power, lacks identity, lacks any sure sense of 'I'. She has no voice, has 'no personality', has a 'slave mentality', is subservient. These opposing, contradictory and utterly divided aspects of the self - the yellow self and the white self, held close to each other, depending on each other as if in 'a kind of marriage' - seem to enact the patriarchal sado-masochistic scenario. The avenging, powerful and dominating voice of the 'yellow' self blames, patronises, hits the 'white person' who holds still 'like a true pacifist'. In concluding the poem, the poet anticipates that one day the conflict will be resolved in favour of the strong, active, passionate self: she dreams of a day when the ugliness and hairiness of this powerful self 'doesn't matter a bit'.

> I used to think we might make a go of it together -
> After all, it was a kind of marriage, being so close.
> Now I see it must be one or the other of us.
> She may be a saint, and I may be ugly and hairy,
> But she'll soon find out that that doesn't matter a bit.
> I'm collecting my strength; one day I shall manage without her,
> And she'll perish with emptiness then, and begin to miss me.

The poet allows the power to speak to remain with the strong self of the woman: it is this self that will sustain. The superior but stupid self will have to go.

This poem can thus be read as a critical examination of the cultural myths and models of femininity imposed by a (Christian) patriarchal society. Plath assesses the agenda for 'correct' behaviour and finds it unacceptable. She refuses as far as possible the mask of the feminine woman, at the same time recognising that the women of her time were not yet 'in any position to get rid of her'.

Plath's self-consciously critical revaluation of oppressive cultural constructs - *as the product of men* - as supported by the feminine woman and as sustained in and through language, reaches a new sophistication in 'Three Women' (*CP* p. 176). This is an important poetic dramatisation of what seemed to be 'the options' for women in the early sixties. I show how each voice represents a mode of coping, a particular strategy for survival - in a world dominated and defined by men.

Sandra Gilbert has spoken of the voice of the 'First Woman, the healthily golden and achieving mother' as 'obviously the poet's own, or at least the voice for which the poet strives'.[4] But

this gloss which optimistically looks for some redeeming whole-
ness – 'a liberating sense of oneness', a transcendence – fails to
recognise the ambivalence that runs through this woman's story.
It is important for the reader to follow the narrative through for
each of the voices, for then a very different picture is built up.
Pamela J. Annas, rather more convincingly, tells us that ' "Three
Women" is about what stands in the way of creativity – biologi-
cal and aesthetic . . . in a capitalist society that alienates the
producer from what is produced, including babies, and com-
moditizes most products including poems.'[5] Annas notes that the
play is based on one of Ingmar Bergman's films, *Nära Livet (The
Brink of Life* or *So Close to Life)*, a film which also centres on
three women in a maternity hospital. But the play is significantly
different. Structurally, it comprises three intercut monologues in
which the women 'do not hear and consequently cannot respond
to each other' (pp. 75–76). This structure produces an effect of
extreme alienation:

> in Plath's play no other characters speak: only the three
> women – the Wife, the Secretary, the Girl – each locked into
> her own experience. Failure to communicate and the lack of
> potential for change through some relation to others is,
> then, not only a theme but a formal element in the play.

The women are isolated within their own experience 'and, more
crucially, inside the social definitions of the experience'. Thus it
is important to examine each narrative in turn.

The first mother is represented as a 'shell' who finds herself
used, like Mary submitting to the visitation. She is without
thought, is slow, patient, fertile, calm, waiting – *ready* – a
woman who is unwillingly, inescapably taken over, over-
whelmed, engulfed – then prepared, cleansed, sacrificed to the
'cruel' miracle of childbirth: 'I am the center of an atrocity.' Her
life must be given over, she must service and protect the
'innocent' boy child. This unrealistic, highly romantic mother,
associated with the bright reassuring colours, the simplicities of
the nursery, copes by living in an imaginary world which holds
at a distance the 'terrible' deformed children (of Hiroshima? of
thalidomide?) – 'Who injure my sleep with their white eyes, their
fingerless hands'. Her chosen task is to nurture, console and
protect this vulnerable 'pink and perfect' Christ-like boy child, to
'Be a bandage to his hurt' – she will not let him go, this child

with 'no guile or warp in him. May he keep so.' The child 'does not walk', 'does not speak a word' – is still 'swaddled in white bands'. He cannot therefore act, move or speak as a male, the woman acts and does for him, has created his environment for him: 'I have papered his room with big roses,/ I have painted little hearts on everything.' She wills him to fulfil her desires of him: to be common, 'To love me as I love him', not to be 'exceptional' – certainly not to be as Christ upon the cross, for 'It is the exception that climbs the sorrowful hill'. This male child is represented by the poet as being defended by the mother/woman from the world (of men) – and he may be identified as being constructed within the field of female desire. It is, however, an imaginary field, a vision impossible to sustain – except in meditative states in which desire will not meet the rebuff of reality.

Plath's poetic project undoubtedly did involve her in going beyond the bounds of censorship to find the repressed of patriarchal culture, seeking the 'inner voice' that resists both the damaging cultural edict and the acts of domination. The third voice of 'Three Women' strongly resists: she is not ready. She points to the 'doves and words' of patriarchal Christianity which are recognised as dangerous to the woman, as are the 'conceptions' and acts men have engendered in and through language: 'Every little word hooked to every little word, and act to act.' The attentions and 'terrible look' of the 'great swan' are fearful and unwanted. Devastatingly, the penile intrusions of the Ledian rapist/swan/God 'coming at' the frightened woman 'like a castle' – overpower and terrify. The world 'small, mean and black' that she sees forming in his eye, as well as his progeny shaping itself within her 'as if I was ready' – are all shown as *other* to the woman, as an alien and threatening force that will colonise her (*CP* p. 178):

And all I could see was dangers: doves and words,
Stars and showers of gold – conceptions, conceptions!
I remember a white, cold wing

And the great swan, with its terrible look,
Coming at me, like a castle, from the top of the river.
There is a snake in swans.
He glided by; his eye had a black meaning.
I saw the world in it – small, mean and black,
Every little word hooked to every little word, and act to act.

Man's 'conception' is the world, his creation which he rapes and dominates. The woman is taken over by this conception which grows in spite of her refusals, her denials and her lack of reverence towards it. When she has reached 'readiness' she too will be compelled to enter the unhappy 'place of shrieks' – to enter his world of shiny instruments, the 'white clean chamber'. This mother is self-consciously aware of the cost: 'I should have murdered this, that murders me.'

Her furious girl child, unhappily separated from her mother, continues the pattern, the passivised cycle of deprivation: the image of the child's 'mouth wide open' resonates with the 'O gape' face of the moon mother of 'The Moon and the Yew Tree'. Adrienne Rich was later to observe this pattern:

> Many daughters live in rage at their mothers for having accepted, too readily and passively, 'whatever comes'. A mother's victimisation does not merely humiliate her, it mutilates the daughter who watches her for clues as to what it means to be a woman.[6]

This father's daughter will be abandoned by the mother: 'I leave someone/ Who would adhere to me: I undo her fingers like bandages: I go.' This mother, a self-conscious, liberated mother, breaks out of the circularity of patriarchal oppression, is bound for college, the sunny meadows, the single life – having left the rapist swan's conceptual burden and his girl child behind her. She glories in her freedom but is regretfully nostalgic for what has been lost: 'What is it I miss?' This is hardly a viable solution in Plath's eyes. This woman's story does represent one of the options open to the mother of the sixties – to separate from her child and leave her to someone else's care in order to do her own thing. Doing both, being a mother and going to college, did not then seem all that possible.

The story of the second woman takes up the question of the feminine woman held in thrall to the 'ideas, destructions' of the flat men 'in the office'. These 'flat' men are the direct descendants of the malevolent angelic abstracts of 'Magi':

> I watched the men walk about me in the office. They were so flat!
> There was something about them like cardboard, and now I had caught it,

That flat, flat, flatness from which ideas, destructions,
Bulldozers, guillotines, white chambers of shrieks proceed,
Endlessly proceed – and the cold angels, the abstractions.
I sat at my desk in my stockings, my high heels.

These 'cold angels, the abstractions' are still the deathly harbin-
gers of destruction and endless 'shrieks'. Facing the cold angel,
the deprivations, lost dimensions and lack, the second woman
asks 'Is this my lover then? This death, this death?' Are logocen-
tric abstractions both lover and death for the woman? Do they sap
her of life energy? Do they leave her desires unsatisfied? Do they
condemn her for her imperfection, her inability to carry his
conceptions, his progeny, his philosophical 'baby', his *poetics*,
his *world*? For this woman it is clear: she miscarries and knows 'I
am found wanting' in his terms. She knows she can never deliver
his idea of perfection, his ideas of goodness and of truth: she
cannot look at 'The face of the unborn one that loved its
perfections,/ The face of the dead one that could only be perfect/
In its easy peace, could only keep holy so.' Logocentric ideas of
holiness, goodness, perfection, peace, passivity, of the world of
men in this poetic revaluation, signify flatness, destruction and
death.

Subordinate to him and bound up with his demands of her, the
second woman sits at her desk – dutifully feminine in her high
heels; working for him, mindlessly, mechanically – 'my
alphabetical fingers, ordering parts/ Parts, bits, cogs, the shining
multiples.' This is the world of men which the woman can
'catch' like a disease, a world dominated by the powerful
hierarchies of 'The faceless faces of important men' – a world
ordered not only by 'Governments, parliaments, societies', but
also by the starchy ideologies of the patriarchal God, the Father
and His Son:

It is these men I mind:
They are so jealous of anything that is not flat! They are
    jealous gods
That would have the whole world flat because they are.
I see the Father conversing with the Son.
Such flatness cannot but be holy.
'Let us make a heaven,' they say.
'Let us flatten and launder the grossness from these souls.'

(*CP* p. 179)

This woman's lot is to be 'accused', to 'hate herself', to 'create corpses' (poems that do not live?), to 'lose life after life', and to prophesy the outcome: 'Old winter-face, old barren one, old time bomb./ Men have used her meanly. She will eat them./ Eat them, eat them, eat them in the end.' As a 'failed' mother (in patriarchal terms) she is immersed in anguish, in the faceless, featureless, whiteness and fragility of the uncertain, threatened, hardly constituted identity of the passivised woman who tries 'not to think too hard', who tries 'to be natural', 'to be blind in love, like other women'. She does not even seek to be identified: she is 'Not looking, through the thick dark, for the face of another.' Unhappily, the frail, insignificant mother of 'Stillborn' haunts these lines: there is no assurance of fecundity: symbolic restoration is 'not yet' to be. The condensed abject metaphors of the world of dreams, of the unconscious mind then take over. Agony, suffering, self-hatred, fear, guilt, evil, vampires, bloody massacres – the poet, here, represents a 'feminine' field of disorder and irrationality where death is loved, corpses are created, and the earthly vitality of conception is indistinguishable from the sick cessation of life. This is an ambiguous, abject place, this garden, where sin, darkness, death and femininity are to be identified:

> I am accused. I dream of massacres.
> I am a garden of black and red agonies. I drink them,
> Hating myself, hating and fearing. And now the world
>   conceives
> Its end and runs toward it, arms held out in love.
> It is a love of death that sickens everything.
> A dead sun stains the newsprint. It is red.
> I lose life after life. The dark earth drinks them.
>
> (CP p. 180)

The movement 'north' into winter, into emptiness, cessation, blackness, shadowy genderlessness, lack – the abyss – continues. The 'restless and useless' moon mother makes yet another appearance. The abyss of feminine guilt is weakly avoided. Ultimately, this bespoken woman decides to accept her marginality: she will be 'heroine of the peripheral'. She will darn his socks, sew his buttons on, be ordered by his clock, and she will not be found wanting – 'The clock shall not find me wanting, nor these stars/ That rivet in place abyss after abyss.'

On leaving the 'maternity' ward, this second woman puts back on her old mask of femininity, her former, feminine identity: 'I draw on the old mouth./ The red mouth I put by with my identity/ A day ago, two days, three days ago.' This damaged, partially sighted, lame, silenced creature pathetically but bravely hopes to replace what she lacks:

> And so I stand, a little sightless. So I walk
> Away on wheels, instead of legs, they serve as well.
> And learn to speak with fingers, not a tongue.
> The body is resourceful.
> The body of a starfish can grow back its arms
> And newts are prodigal in legs. And may I be
> As prodigal in what lacks me.

> (*CP* p.184)

Returned home, she takes up the old life as wife gathered in to domesticity, and takes a muted, gentle pleasure in what she has to do: wait for health to return, mend, stitch lace, be at home with a husband who 'Can turn and turn the pages of a book'. This constitutes a collusive, humiliated consent to be the debilitated patriarchal feminine, to try to be contented, to find some limited hope in the spring, the light, the little grasses, in life – but immateriality, insubstantiality, lack remain a constant threat to the integrity of her identity as a woman. It is a compromised position, to stay as wife bathed in this field of domestic tenderness, in order 'To find myself again'. Her wounds ache. There is more waiting to be done before a healing restoration can occur.

Overall, I see Plath as moving towards a concept of patriarchy in which she recognises and acts on the recognition that there is poetic work to be done on the male-defined woman as well as on male-defined language. As Hélène Cixous puts it: 'There's work to be done against . . . the pervasive masculine urge to judge, diagnose, digest, name . . . not so much in the sense of the loving precision of poetic naming as in that of the repressive censorship of philosophical nomination/conceptualisation.'[7] Plath was also, with difficulty, struggling to explore 'the identifications of an ego no longer given over to an image defined by the masculine'.

These were the fields of identification for Plath herself, as a woman poet. She set herself the task of inventing a poetic that could explore the oppressive ideologies of the feminine woman of her time, and she sought to make overt her growing suspicion of the codes, categories, conceptualisations of a world dominated by men.

6

SEDUCTIVE SCENARIOS:
Fighting back

I shall unloose –
From the small jeweled
Doll he guards like a heart –

The lioness,
The shriek in the bath,
The cloak of holes

'Purdah' (CP p. 244)

A myth always implies a subject who projects his hopes and his fears towards a sky of transcendence. Women do not set themselves up as Subject and hence have erected no virile myth in which their projects are reflected; they have no religion or poetry of their own: they still dream through the dreams of men. Gods made by males are the gods they worship. Men have shaped for their own exaltation great virile figures: Hercules, Prometheus, Parsifal; woman has only a secondary part to play in the destiny of these heroes.

Representation of the world, like the world itself, is the work of men; they describe it from their own point of view, which they confuse with absolute truth.

Simone de Beauvoir, *The Second Sex*[1]

For women to transform the cultural ordering of 'fact', for them to change ideas, for them to participate in the power of naming in order to transform culture, women must write their own 'stories', must become producers of 'history' from their own standpoint. They must be the mediators rather than the mediated within language. Catherine Clément and Hélène Cixous stress that 'If women begin to want their turn at telling this history, if they take the relay from men by putting myths into words (since that is how historical and cultural evolution will take place) . . . it will necessarily be from other points of view. It will be a history read differently.'[2] The history written by women will not be a 'true' history but will be reconstituted, re-membered out of the exclusions and negations of patriarchy, and will be written by those who play out their lives 'between symbolic systems, in the interstices, offside'. Thus, the history produced by women, in Clément's and Cixous' terms,

> is a history, taken from what is lost within us of oral tradition, of legends and myths – a history arranged the way tale-telling women tell it. And from the standpoint of conveying the mythic models that powerfully structure the Imaginary (masculine and feminine, complex and varied), this history will be true. On the level of fantasy, it will be fantastically true. It is still acting on us. In telling it, in developing it, even in plotting it, I seek to undo it, to overturn it, to reveal it, to *expose* it.
>
> (p. 6)

Far from the universalising and ahistorical versions of myth produced within a religious or Jungian perspective, this mythology of reminiscence emerges from a specific cultural and historical context, and articulates an individual, culture-bound mode of relating to the symbolic system.

In the frame adopted by Catherine Clément, the hysteric and the sorceress as producers of incommunicable, individual symbolism are particularly named as in danger from, and dangerous to, the symbolic order. They are seen as anomalous figures, but ones who are ultimately conservative in that they are incapable of disturbing the social formation. None the less, in pointing to the woman on the periphery who is situated at the margins of the symbolic system as especially placed to dramatise the repressed of culture, this post-Freudian, post-Lacanian perspective proves extraordinarily fertile to the analysis of women's poetry.

Plath's later work, above all, presents us with the spectacle of femininity in crisis. It symbolises the aggressive return of the repressed through a dramatic poetry of mythic formulas, plots and patterns – in which the stage is set for the poet/woman to introduce her shrieks, her suffering, her anguish, her murderous fury, her disruptive *disorder* into the well-regulated, gendered codes of conventional patriarchy. Through creating a language for her poetry in which the dramatic inner world of fantasy is consciously realised in words, images and symbols, Plath contrives to set the stage for a dangerous exorcism of the mythic patterns that have for centuries held women in thrall to men.

Susan Bassnett has spoken of 'a recurrence of a sinister dominant male figure' within the poems – figures which she associates with 'the male principle', 'patriarchy and the worship of things male'.[3] If the earlier images (of 'The Colossus' and 'Full Fathom Five') were marked by wit and irony, the later images 'add up to a collective image of males as figures of power that block and obstruct'.[4] Plath's female personae dramatise their hatred of these male figures. Enacting their scenes of victimisation, of punishment, of refusal, of grief, they subversively fascinate, disturb, challenge, destroy the bridegrooms, the voyeurs, the doctors, the surgeons, the jailers, the Nazis, the fascists, the men who have imposed their will on the woman.

There are many poems which explore devastating experiences of suffering and loss – of voice, of identity, of agency – which are experienced as a torture, and as being inflicted by those having authority and power over the woman. Here, in 'Elm', we find the shattered voice of complaint which dissolves to a shriek:

> I have suffered the atrocity of sunsets.
> Scorched to the root
> My red filaments burn and stand, a hand of wires.
>
> Now I break up in pieces that fly about like clubs.
> A wind of such violence
> Will tolerate no bystanding: I must shriek.
>
> (*CP* p. 192)

Acted on so brutally, the identity must split, fragment, fly apart, disintegrate. Plath used many images to signify the splits, emptinesses, absences, immolations and annihilations of this loss of an 'identity' at the mutilated extremity of subjection and despair. Thankfully, these images are, in Plath's later work, displaced, at least for a time. Another voice, a powerful, angry voice charged with a sense of outrage begins to be heard. Here, in 'Stings', a valiant attempt is made to recover the self, the 'I' of the woman/queen/bee, who might be dead or merely 'asleep':

They thought death was worth it, but I
Have a self to recover, a queen.
Is she dead, is she sleeping?
Where has she been,
With her lion-red body, her wings of glass?

Now she is flying
More terrible than she ever was, red
Scar in the sky, red comet
Over the engine that killed her –
The mausoleum, the wax house.

(CP p. 215)

I read this as an attempt to construct a place of identification
outside the seductive scenes of femininity. The flying, terrible
woman/red comet seeks vengeance, fights back. Fighting back
involves the poet in the task of constructing a dynamic of 'self-
becoming' within the poems, one in which the 'sunk relics of my
lost selves' are rewoven 'wordwise' into the fabric of language (*J*
p. 196). This unloosing or release into flight - of the bee queen/
lioness 'self' in 'Wintering' marks a tentative but hopeful resti-
tution through an aggressive rejection of things male –

The bees are all women,
Maids and the long royal lady.
They have got rid of the men,

The blunt, clumsy stumblers, the boors
Winter is for women

(CP p. 218)

– as well as a somewhat frightened affirmation of things female!
Though women, these bees can be militaristic, and can have
phallic 'Stings big as drawing pins'. They are scary. As Plath
represents them, they have a 'black intractable mind'; they are
dangerous, 'all prickles', mini-soldiers brandishing swords,
imperious Napoleons whose forceful macho-masculine power is
very questionable. As a symbolic place of identification, these
images ambiguously represent female power and strength in a
form too close to the macho-masculine pack mentality; they are
too mindless, too dumb. They are also all too easily drawn back
into captivity - into 'the mausoleum', the bee-hive. And,
ultimately, they are too dangerous, even lethal: 'They would have
killed *me*' (*CP* p. 217).

Great fear and extreme loathing of the macho-powers of the Jovian male 'In whose shadow I have eaten my ghost ration' – is found inscribed in many poems (*CP* p. 227). However, in 'Daddy', Plath's aggressive 'ugly and hairy' voice re-emerges bitterly triumphant – as a powerful transgressor of the gendered hierarchies of patriarchy (*CP* p. 222). In this poem, the poet gathers together many fear-inducing images (all images which she associated with the forceful Power of the Father and, obliquely, the husband) – of war, of fascism, of concentration camps, swastikas, torture. The Jew/woman declares: 'I have always been scared of *you*'. Plath also gathers together all the namings, voices, sounds of Nazi Germany – of the German tongue, of the engines 'Chuffing me off like a Jew', of all the 'gobbledygoo' – which have reduced her woman's voice and presence to a mere stammer, *in an other-tongue* alien to her:

I never could talk to you.
The tongue stuck in my jaw.

It stuck in a barb wire snare.
Ich, ich, ich, ich,
I could hardly speak.

Plath then constructs a ritualistic, incantatory *witchy* scenario in which a mythic exorcism of these malevolent images and words can take place: they are banished, murdered, expunged from consciousness.

I made a model of you,
A man in black with a Meinkampf look

And a love of the rack and the screw.
And I said I do, I do.
So daddy, I'm finally through.
The black telephone's off at the root,
The voices just can't worm through.

The voodoo 'stake' in the fat, black heart of 'Daddy'; the rhythmic dancing and stamping rituals of the 'villagers' (echoed in the rhythmic sounds and syntactic stresses of the poem itself); the tearing out of the telephone wires that bring to her the voices of the fathers, mythically restores the sorceress/woman to an emphatic if magical sense of her own integrated presence, her own voice and her power of agency: 'And I said I do, I do.'

In effect, Plath strives to break into the circular game of victims and torturers, master and slave, by tracing or inscribing a new ritual. She writes a spell, creates a ceremonial rite in which the woman destroys the voice of the Father, his Law, and his power over her. This symbolic enactment, in which the murder and silencing of 'Fathers' is dramatised, constructs a scenario in which the loser can be enabled to win. The poet can thus 'break set' and work to 'dis-spell the power of prevailing myths and symbols'.[5]

A rather different mythic 'set' is broken in the slightly later poem: 'Lady Lazarus'. The persona of Plath's 'Lady Lazarus' can be seen as a feminine hysteric/exhibitionist/sorceress who, in choosing to suffer spectacularly before her voyeuristic audience, stages for the reader a dramatic transformatory passage – from colonised female victim to phoenix-like avenger (*CP* p. 244). Following Freud and Michelet, Cixous suggests that 'the repressed past survives in woman; woman, more than anyone else is dedicated to reminiscence' – that the hysteric is one 'whose body is transformed into a theatre for forgotten scenes, relives the past, bearing witness to a lost childhood that survives in suffering'.[6] Undoubtedly, in writing this poem, Plath drew obsessively on her own long-standing inner suffering, her own attempts to commit suicide and her own murderous anger against her 'oppressors'. But the poem becomes more than an individual statement, for it, in Cixous' and Clément's words, 'resumes and assumes the memories of the others' who have suffered. In targeting the fascistic and authoritarian aspects of patriarchy for critique, Plath also holds up to ridicule the mythic patterns of fascism, with its many forms of fetishistic ritual.

'Lady Lazarus' is presented as a 'sort of walking miracle' – to the horrified gaze of the reader. This hysteric persona makes public her confessions and reminiscences, and engages in gruesome self-display for the benefit of her audience. As the fascinating, feminine woman, she entices them into a series of pathological, repugnant, and pornographically captivating scenarios only to turn on them vengefully. This subversive feminine position is not that of passivity but rather that of actively entering into her role as dispossessed other. She deliberately and purposefully abases herself, enters into these compulsive perverse rituals in order *to cash in*. The woman, dispossessed, possessed, enters fully into the position created for her – as macho-male-defined woman/fascist-defined Jewess.

Symbolically this demonic seductress, this sardonically 'smiling woman', becomes the horrific, destroyed and self-destructive other, the ultimate victim – who provocatively confronts her 'enemy'. Here, she reveals the appalling outcome of fascism, of its obscene, sadistic acts:

A sort of walking miracle, my skin
Bright as a Nazi lampshade,
My right foot

A paperweight,
My face a featureless, fine
Jew linen.

Peel off the napkin
O my enemy.
Do I terrify? –

This revelation, this 'theatrical' demonstration – her dying, her miraculous 'Comeback in broad day' – are ostensibly for the benefit of 'The peanut crunching crowd', but the real targets of her hatred who must 'Beware', are symbolic figures, male representatives of medical, militaristic, heavenly or diabolical patriarchal power: Herr Doctor, Herr Enemy, Herr God, Herr Lucifer.

A prostitute ready to flaunt herself, this persona would make them pay – a lot – to indulge their fetishistic attachments to women as part-objects. To gaze upon the woman or to hear her, to touch her fragmented body, smear her blood or feel her hair or her clothes –

There is a charge

For the eyeing of my scars, there is a charge
For the hearing of my heart –
It really goes.

And there is a charge, a very large charge
For a word or a touch
Or a bit of blood

Or a piece of my hair or my clothes.

She would display herself provocatively to her procurer as his 'valuable', his 'opus'. She would pretend to belong to him, to be his great work, his possession, only to teasingly withhold what he wants of her – 'you can't have it'. In this passage Lady Lazarus spectacularly immolates her old self: the used and abused woman/the despised, violated and massacred Jewess (whom Sartre recognised as having 'a very special sexual signification' in the literature of pornography).[7] She transfigures herself to ashes:

So, so, Herr Doktor.
So, Herr Enemy.

I am your opus,
I am your valuable,
The pure gold baby

That melts to a shriek.
I turn and burn
Do not think I underestimate your great concern.

This menacing, sardonic ritual of self-immolation, as an exhibition carried out before her enemies' eyes, allows the woman, even as she poses before them, to escape their look of possession, to slip away from the gaze which had seized her, had regulated her, held her. She is no longer willing to fulfil their desires of her: she has left the ritual exchanges of macho-fascist patriarchy. She has absented herself:

Ash, ash —
You poke and stir.
Flesh, bone, there is nothing there —

A cake of soap,
A wedding ring,
A gold filling.

From that stage to another stage: from the looked-at, exploited and degraded woman, circumscribed by male economic or fascist military power, Plath imagines a liberating transfiguration to an engulfing furious female. Out of this transfiguring fire, a new woman is created out of the old, a woman capable of repudiating the dysfunctional patterns of hysterical femininity. Lady Lazarus, as vindictive sorceress, seizes the stage, transgresses the codes that have enslaved her. Phoenix-like, Plath's emerging, avenging woman tells her readers: 'Out of the ash/ I rise with my red hair/ And I eat men like air.'

It is a symbolically effective metamorphosis – a magical transcendence is achieved. It is fictive rather than real, but it brings to articulation a fiendish force-field of dissident, if not paranoid, female hatred and anger. Ultimately, it is not a convincing restitution: Hélène Cixous and Catherine Clément suggest that –

> This feminine role, the role of sorceress, of hysteric, is ambiguous, antiestablishment, and conservative at the same time. Antiestablishment because the symptoms – the attacks – revolt and shake up the public, the group, the men, the others to whom they are exhibited . . . . The hysteric unties familiar bonds, introduces disorder into the well-regulated unfolding of everyday life, gives rise to magic in ostensible reason. These roles are *conservative* because every sorceress ends up being destroyed, and nothing is registered of her but mythical traces.[8]

As I read this poem, these roles – of hysteric and sorceress – Plath both enjoyed and pressed to their limits. As Cixous and Clément go on: 'both sorceress and hysteric, in their way, mark the end of a type – how far a split can go'. Perhaps Plath knew that too. But, in opening up the field of subjectivity to furious female anger, with its potential for transforming social relations between oppressor and victim, Plath was a poet before her time.

Plath's later work thus calls into question very different aspects of the patriarchal feminine. Women of the fifties and sixties, accepting the cultural myths and models of the time, found themselves living out their lives within constructs which held them in subjection to other's desires of them. However, the struggle to escape such entrapment was beginning. Luce Irigaray's Alice symbolises for us the feminine woman trapped 'behind the screen of representation', who struggles to escape 'the limits of properties', that is, those organising categories that differentiate *'what was looked on with approval from what wasn't. Made it possible to appreciate, to recognize the value of everything. To fit in with it, as needed.'*[8] Alice's identity as a woman is deeply divided by the demands made of her by others (and not always male others): a frozen Alice asks her other self:

> *How can I be distinguished from her? Only if I keep on pushing through to the other side, if I'm always beyond, because on this side of the screen of their projections, on this plane of their representations, I can't live. I'm stuck,*

paralysed by all those images, words, fantasies. Frozen.
Transfixed, including by their admiration, their praises,
what they call their 'love.' Listen to them all talking about
Alice: my mother, Eugene, Lucien, Gladys . . . . You've
heard them dividing me up, in their own best interests. So
either I don't have any 'self,' or else I have a multitude of
'selves' appropriated by them, for them, according to their
needs or desires.[9]

In trying to fulfil others' *'best interests'*, and always *'busy conforming to their wishes'*, many women find themselves positioned to receive very little nurturance themselves, becoming faced instead with a blank mirror, one that fails to reflect or is cracked. This blank mirror fails to provide the nurturing or chastising verbal, visual or tactile inter-personal response that would recognise her and validate her in her chosen identity. The paternal symbolic ordering of language may similarly fail to offer any recognition, any mooring, any anchoring representation to secure her identity from the irruption of meaninglessness. Is it possible to forget Plath's pain-laden words in her poem 'Contusion', written eight days before her suicide, alone before the symbolic 'sheeted mirror' that, in failing to confirm her in any position of value, signified not only imminent psychic death but also her imminent actual, physical death by her own hand?

Color floods to the spot, dull purple.
The rest of the body is all washed out,
The color of pearl.

In a pit of rock
The sea sucks obsessively,
One hollow the whole sea's pivot.

The size of a fly,
The doom mark
Crawls down the wall.

The heart shuts,
The sea slides back,
The mirrors are sheeted.

(*CP* p. 271)

The integrity of identity, as well as the wholeness of the body, is threatened by the hollow void, the pit, the abyss of non-entity.

The body loses colour, solidity, integrity, substance in this hopeless, irresistible movement towards the dissolution of her subjectivity, towards ending her life. No generous nurturing image is granted to her in this moment of psychic extremity. In the terrifying metaphors – which depict the obsessive movement of overwhelming fluid form around the hollow void – we are motioned towards the pre-Oedipal chaos of undifferentiation, of hollowness, of unsatisfied yearningful sucking. This a moment when 'the mother' *as mirror* is missing, when there is no one, no word, to validate her. The assumed social identity is not merely threatened by her loss, the loss of the m/Other, but has become passively and hopelessly resigned to the immediate inevitability of dissolution of identity, to psychic and physical death. For real.

It is tragic that Sylvia Plath did not find any material or symbolic restitution to counter the situation she found herself in. Neither did she, finally, find a sufficient mythic mode of displacing the feminine model, that is, the male projection, the patriarchal scene/screen of representation. There was no sufficient field of identification for her as a desperate, hard-up single parent/woman poet in the sixties. There was too little recognition/response to help her anchor her identity. There was apparently nothing that could shore her up against the crises of meaninglessness she faced. In no sense did she find any kind of 'sky of transcendence', though her poetic efforts did lead her some way towards reactively constructing a 'virile myth' and 'great virile figures' having a primary role in her own scene or stage of representation.

7

RE-CREATING 'MY OWN LEGEND'
H.D.'s *Helen in Egypt*

The importance to poetry of Freud's theories of dreamwork and the unconscious has been repeatedly noted, not least by Susan Friedman, who, in her fine study of the poetry of H.D., links the epic form of *Helen in Egypt* to the epic quest of psycho-analysis. Its project is to reconcile and reintegrate fragments of a disintegrated personality through techniques of free association, recovery of painful memories, dreamwork, and meditative inter-pretation. Pointing out H.D.'s use of Greek masks, to give form to and to speak out of her own experience, Friedman suggests that Theseus, the healing therapist, represents Freud, and the multiple mythic personalities of Helen, the distressed H.D. herself. It is always a risk to attach the mythemes of poetry to real persons and situations: a new myth is inevitably created. None the less, I want to explore how H.D. reframes and mythicises an experience from her life: the experience of being an analysand on the couch and analysed by Sigmund Freud. In the process of re-writing, H.D. re-creates her own story/history/myth: 'For me . . . it was so important, my own LEGEND. Yes, my own LEGEND. Then, to get well and re-create it.'[1]

Helen in Egypt is a long, book-length poem which cannot be treated fully here, but certain passages are relevant to themes I am developing: specifically, the exploration of personal suffering and the attempt through reminiscence to recall past experience. Such reminiscence constitutes a struggle to reach further into the unconscious mind – to delve deeper into the forgetfulness of things repressed in order to find a new place of identification, a new position for the subject. For a writer, it involves the reinscription of old stories, scripts, narratives. *Helen in Egypt* explores the various dimensions of different versions of the myth of Helen. The poet re-creates the legend – just as H.D. worked with Freud in re-creating her memories. In 'putting together the shards of her own history' she works to find a more helpful ordering of the chaotic palimpsest of her own experience.[2] Her attempt to re-create 'my own LEGEND' – to re-create and integrate a mythic identity – is a heroic task undertaken in order to help her to face another war.

The epic quest or spiritual journey of Helen is paralleled in the psychoanalysis by the continuous process of 'emergence' into the present of past 'lost' or repressed inscriptions or interpretations. H.D.'s *Tribute to Freud* is an important intertext in this respect in that it can be seen as offering a subtly coded version of H.D.'s own journey through psychoanalysis with 'the Professor'. H.D.'s comments in *Advent* seem relevant: 'I must find new words as the Professor found or coined new words to explain certain as yet unrecorded states of mind or being' (*TF* p. 145).

In this passage from Leuké, Book V, section 5 *Helen in Egypt*, Helen must find her 'way through despair', helped by the thoughtful Theseus who listens attentively. He takes care of her: '*She is safe, she need not be afraid "to recall the shock of the iron-Ram, the break in the Wall", or, equally, she is free to forget everything*':

Rest here; shall I draw out
the low couch, nearer the brazier,
or will you lie there,

against the folds of purple
by the wall? you tremble,
can you stand? walk then,

O, sleep-walker; is this fleece
too heavy? here is soft woven wool;
wrapped in this shawl, my butterfly,

my Psyche, disappear into the web,
the shell, re-integrate,
nor fear to recall

the shock of the iron-Ram,
the break in the Wall,
the flaming Towers,

shouting and desecration
of the altars; you are safe here;
remember if you wish to remember,

or forget . . . 'never, never,'
you breathe, half in a trance . . .
'Achilles.'[3]

The journey of the 'sleep-walker' – not wrapped in the 'fleece'
which is too heavy, but in the 'soft woven wool' shawl – takes on
the symbolic value of Jason's quest for the Golden Fleece. This
quest, though, takes a somewhat more refined and feminine
form! Helen is depicted as protected and safe. She may venture to
explore the different mythic versions of Helen's story. These
dangerous adventures/voyages/journeys of Helen as represented
by H.D., however, are grounded in very different ethics and
values to the epic stories/spiritual journeys of Greek myth.

In this passage, H.D. symbolises the complex metamorphic
process of psychoanalysis, of quest – iconographically. The
butterfly/psyche of Helen/H.D. may 'disappear into the web,/
the shell, re-integrate'. The Greek 'Psyche' is identified by Susan
Friedman as a mythical persona chosen by H.D. 'to stimulate the
unfolding reflections of memory and myth'.[4] Psyche is 'the
mortal woman whose search for Eros has frequently been inter-
preted as the soul's quest for divine immortality. The name
"Psyche" comes from the Greek word for "soul", often portrayed
in Greek art as a butterfly that leaves the body at death'.

As an image of transformation, the cocoon/butterfly/psyche
represents a continual movement through different stages of
development, different changes of state. The shawl/shell/
'cocoon', like the privacy of the ante-room of Freud's study,
shelters and keeps 'safe' the vulnerable psyche as it re-experiences
painful traumas of the past – in the present moment. The couch
and the brazier, which can be drawn closer together, or not, take
on parallel symbolic value as locations where such transforma-
tion 'happens'. The couch 'supports' the transmutation of con-
sciousness as it reintegrates repressed material – just as the brazier
is the alchemic container where fire transmutes all things.
Theseus' gentle encouragement enables Helen to recall 'the
flaming towers', 'the iron-Ram'. These Trojan/Greek metaphors
may be seen as mythic displacements, symbolising H.D.'s dis-
tressing experiences during both World War I and the German
blitz of World War II. H.D., though, tells us that she was actually
unable to speak to Freud about her fears: 'I cannot talk about the
thing that actually concerns me, I cannot talk to Sigmund Freud

in Vienna, 1933, about Jewish atrocities in Berlin' (*TF* p. 135) – or attempt to 'bring my actual terror of the lurking Nazi menace into the open' (*TF* p. 139).

Theseus' confirming *maternal* presence permits Helen to remember the shock, the 'shouting and desecration/ of the altars' of her traumatic experiences. As in the psychoanalytic situation with Sigmund Freud, she may remember or she may forget, just as she wishes. The displaced personal and psychoanalytic quest, in its mythic dimensions, takes the form of the reconciliation of the fragmented selves of the mythic Helen, preoccupied as she is with the web, the weaving of her memories. Helen/Helena must move among and between the different mythic versions of Helen's story, imprinted on the palimpsest of memory/myth. It is the recall of intensely heightened epiphanic moments, or 'hieroglyphic tableaux', as Susan Friedman calls them, rather than any linear narrative, that structures the action of H.D's female epic:

> Helen's identity and the meaning of war are contained enigmatically in heightened moments or tableaux. The action of the epic is the 'reading' of those moments, just as the 'action' of psychoanalysis is the interpretation of the unconscious. The corresponding type of plot is meditative, not active; it moves through reflection and association, not through external circumstances or logic.[5]

This pivotal *tableau*, profound in its unconscious resonances, depicts Theseus and Helen, 'seated before the glowing coals'. This heavily symbolic scenario is central to H.D.'s poetic strategy of displacement and condensation whereby she is concerned to make new pathways through what had been loaded with difficulty – both in the culture and in her own life. The epiphanic moment of re-interpretation of these 'glowing coals' or resonant symbolic tableaux of the epic journey is crucial for both writer and reader. Both are engaged in the quest for elusive meaning, which is the illusive scenario of the quest for identity. And for H.D., the memory as *mother* plays a crucial role in creating a mythic transcendence of the 'I'. This moment of re-construal of her past experiences establishes a sustained moment of equilibrium, of balance, of clearly focused vision. This is only possible, according to H.D., within what she called the 'procreative' consciousness: 'memory is the mother, begetter of all drama, idea, music, science or song'.[6] In this sense, all art, all identity, all meaning becomes mythic. Meaning is held in timeless suspension, but only until the next re-interpretation of author or reader.

The process of reading and reconstrual of the dense symbolic web of H.D.'s tableaux is complex. Perhaps the early H.D. of 1919 would have been happy for the reader to use the hypnotic effects of 'certain words and lines' in the tableaux as 'signposts', as 'straight clear entrances . . . to over-world consciousness' (p. 24). She certainly pondered deeply about an 'over-mind' in her writings (p. 23). Whatever we make of this, it is evident that the reader is all-important. She too must meditate upon the symbolic tableaux presented by the poet – deliberately 'seeded' with visual, sensory, tactile, auditory, bodily-aware symbols – in order to receive them fully. Only then will the reader recognise and confirm the poet: 'There is no trouble about the art, it is the appreciators we want . . . .We want receiving centres for dots and dashes' (p. 26).

By the time she wrote *Helen in Egypt*, H.D., like Yeats, had developed a complex symbol system out of her synthesis of ancient religious traditions. This synthesis has been extensively explored by Susan Friedman in *Psyche Reborn*. The mythological frame of H.D.'s later poems permitted her to re-present ancient religious symbols, which become transformed in the new context of her re-visionary poetry. These then add another layer to the palimpsests of myth and memory. These symbols first found their conventional meanings in ancient times, in cultures now utterly 'other' to contemporary western materialist society. H.D.'s symbols are drawn from Hermeticism, Greek and Egyptian mythology, Esoteric and Occult traditions; but they are given fresh significance in her poetry.

In effect, these symbolic references condense and freeze those epiphanic moments into new patterns. H.D. endeavours to create reconciling configurations. The poet/reader is engaged in the attempt to construct a unifying gestalt out of difficult, fragmenting experience. To move through analysis, clearly examining every separate detail, discovering interrelationships, establishing patterns of connection and significance becomes a process of re-membering and re-inscribing the narrative script of her story as a meaningful whole. This is an *artistic* experience, a creative

95

experience similar to that of H.D.'s painter 'who concentrated on one tuft of pine branch with its brown cone until every needle was a separate entity to him and every pine needle bore to every other one, a clear relationship' (pp. 42–43). Perhaps this is a cue to the desired exceptional reader/appreciator to bring a meditative intensity and concentration to the fine detail and complex interrelationships of the poetry – to the cultural critique offered, as well as to her new syntheses. H.D.'s work, indeed, demands such attention.

In his work on dreams, Freud stressed repeatedly that 'psychical energy' held under restraint and inhibited by the censor, could be released by means of the symbolising potential of the psyche – and that this was, in itself, 'reviving and healing'.[7] A poetic that wished to enhance this potential for release of energy – of desire, aspiration, motivation – would need to employ *significant* symbols, especially ones that found their pathway through those laid down in primal attachments. I would suggest that H.D.'s idea of 'magical potency' had much to do with the activating of primal drive pathways, and with the release of the energy of (erotic) desire by means of the epiphanic, illuminatory, 'glowing' symbol. Often in H.D.'s work, these coded representations gesture towards the deepest (earliest) levels of the psyche, beyond the symbolic Father of Law to the pre-Oedipal mother/child nexus.

Examining the personal and mythic tableaux of Book I of *Helen in Egypt*, an important pattern emerges. A complex web of images repeatedly invokes the omnipresent mother. She, though absent physically, is everywhere symbolically. She is behind the text – remembered as a 'presence', an 'I' full of agency, an 'I' that is longed for. The desire for this powerful (phallic) mother is set alongside a desire that her power and influence will compel the male to resist the heroic call to arms. To show these patterns it is necessary to offer a fairly detailed reading of selected passages.

The first book of *Helen in Egypt*, introduces the familiar 'Helena, Helen hated of all Greece' of our inheritance (*HE* p. 2). She is a 'phantom' who has been 'substituted for the real Helen'. She is 'Daemon', devil, or daimon (from the Greek: the soul or spirit). Jane Harrison speaks of the daimon as 'the reflection, the collective emphasis, of a social emotion' or 'a collective representation expressing not a personality so much as a function'.[8] This daemonic Helen I see as just such a cultural reflection –

functioning as the mythic representation of the patriarchal seductress. Her legendary figure becomes a collective projection of the beautiful woman – as both product of male desire and as object of barter and military negotiation. This substituted (false, or illusory) *ghost* of Helen, is transposed and transformed as H.D.'s epic proceeds. She becomes the reinstated 'Helen of Egypt' of Euripides' play, *Helen*, which itself overwrites the centuries earlier 'Pallinode' of Stesichorus. This Helen gathers to her self a significant degree of integrity in becoming 'both phantom and reality' as a partly constituted subject (*HE* p. 3). The Helen of the following passage is 'stricken, forsaken', yet may speak – at least to the dead! She may address the gathered spirits of the lost Greek legions and correct their historic and collective, oral or inscribed, patriarchal vision (or version):

> Alas, my brothers,
> Helen did not walk
> upon the ramparts,
>
> she whom you cursed
> was but the phantom and the shadow thrown
> of a reflection
>
> (*HE* p. 5)

In telling us that *this* Helen never 'knew' Achilles (sexually?), in telling us that she 'is not to be recognised by earthly splendour nor this Achilles by accoutrements of valour' (p.7), H.D. deconstructs the cursed patriarchal iconograph of both Helen and Achilles. In doing so, she further restores them both to the mundane world of mortality, to the solidity of bodily integrity (p.6):

> but we were not, we are not shadows;
> as we walk, heel and sole
> leave our sandal-prints in the sand,
>
> though the wounded heel treads lightly
> and more lightly follow,
> the purple sandals.

Though this lightweight, yet royal and embodied self of Helen acquires a minimum of corporeality, she must still 'follow'. There is yet much to be done to overwrite the old patriarchal script. The hero-god Achilles, in a transvaluational shift, is reduced in status to mere mortal man by 'Love's arrow', the arrow of the bi-sexual god Eros, son of Aphrodite. His body armour (his excess of material substance and power?), his immortality, and his heroic glory, is shed:

> it was God's plan
> to melt the icy fortress of the soul,
> and free the man;
>
> God's plan is other than the priests disclose;
> I did not know why
> (in dream or in trance)
>
> God had summoned me hither
> until I saw the dim outline
> grown clearer,
>
> as the new Mortal
> shedding his glory,
> limped slowly across the sand.
>
> (*HE* p. 10)

This is a different rite of passage to that envisaged by Freud, who saw the hero as 'someone who has had the courage to rebel against his father and has in the end victoriously overcome him'.[9] Achilles' encounter with Aphroditian Love alters his course as a son of the fathers, and the story proposes that the male yields to Love rather than War.

Important in this quest to transform patterns of significance in the epic, is the recovery or recall of the memory trace – 'the graven line . . . graven in memory' – along with its forgetting, or its wiping out or its overwriting. Helen, the woman, does not want to forget this Achilles, the transformed son. He is the mortal Achilles, whose wounded heel makes him the common 'man among the millions', that is, the man freed from the icy fortress or the iron casement of his warrior self. However, Helen may not yet place trust in him, for he still remembers his anger.

In Book I, Helen sets out, very much in danger of losing what integrity she has as subject. She is under threat from the violent Achilles, from 'his autocracy', as a man who 'knew not yet' the true *identity* of Helen. She conceals her own identity, and (with some mockery) colludes with his projection. She ironically accepts his image of her: 'I am a woman of pleasure.' Here, Achilles names her as the evil witch 'Hecate', and taunts her:

are you Hecate? are you a witch?

a vulture, a hieroglyph,
the sign or the name of a goddess?
what sort of goddess is this?

where are we? who are you?
where is this desolate coast?
who am I? am I a ghost?

(*HE* p. 16)

Whilst she is patriarchally named as evil, she dare not do other than collude. She must perforce accept his definition of her as sexual object. Depending on him to protect her, she remains fearful for her safety. As the reconstruction proceeds, the identity of each becomes increasingly unstable. Identity, location, substance, are repeatedly called into question: what is this Helen? where are we? who are you? who am I? am I a ghost?

Helen's prayer to the controlling male god Amen, whose dream created the 'phantasmagoria of Troy' (*HE* p. 17), is that he will wipe out the memory of the heroic past, and the traumas of the carnage of battle. This is to allow Achilles to be set free of its masculist imperatives: *'let him forget,/ Amen, All-father,/ let him forget'* (*HE* p. 12). But Amen is silent, is aloof, a little too far away, does not respond. This silence is critical, for the enormously exalted father/god fails to fulfil his role as provider and protector and, instead, issues decrees, makes laws, and dreams of strife: the woman, Helen, cannot rely on him either.

It is the mother goddess, rather than the father god who responds to her prayers. The mother sends the symbol or the 'letter', the hieroglyph of the night-bird/vulture. This is a symbol of rebirth in Egyptian mythology, whose sacred script invokes Isis/Thetis, the sea-mother. H.D., who knows 'the script', knew from her study of Egyptology that vultures were seen as female angels of death who carry the dead piecemeal to heaven. She would have known also that the hieroglyph of the vulture in Egyptian script and iconography was the sign for the mother/Mut/Nekbet/Isis. In H.D.'s religious poetic of quest, the prayer to the mother is an essential element of the spiritual path H.D. maps out. Helen's voice may challenge Achilles, she may justify her innocence, and claim her position as woman/subject against his constructions but only by invoking the mother.

99

She prays to his mother that she will be able to love Achilles despite his inability to recognise her. It is a prayerful moment of reminiscence –

'Isis,' he said, 'or Thetis,' I said,
recalling, remembering, invoking
his sea-mother;

flame, I prayed, *flame forget*
forgive and forget the other,
let my heart be filled with peace,

let me love him, as Thetis, his mother,
for I knew him, I saw in his eyes
the sea-enchantment, but he

knew not yet, Helen of Sparta,
knew not Helen of Troy,
knew not Helena, hated of Greece.

(*HE* p. 14)

In response, the mother sends the night-bird, the vulture – as letter, as sign, as hieroglyph. This hieroglyph, H.D. tells us, 'represents or recalls the protective mother-goddess. This is no death-symbol but a life-symbol' (*HE* p. 13). She prays *'let me love him, as Thetis, his mother'* (*HE* p. 14). Helen, *as* the mother, 'is nearer, his own mother' (*HE* p. 15). It is the goddess whose sign appears, who is Helen, who is the mother, who is Hecate; who, in the multilayered identity of Helen, *is* the mother-goddess herself: 'She herself is the writing' (*HE* p. 22). The woman must become a transcendent identified subject – whether as *the writing*, or as 'knower' of the script. She can be mother to herself through the mother – who must be invoked, represented, recalled *through* the hieroglyph. Helen *'achieves the difficult task of translating a symbol in time'* by displacing the symbolic values still held by the patriarchal Achilles through the 'magic', that is, the transcendent power of *naming*:

she invokes (as the perceptive visitor to Egypt must always
do) the symbol or the 'letter' that represents or recalls the
protective mother-goddess. This is no death-symbol but a
life-symbol, it is Isis or her Greek counterpart, Thetis, the
mother of Achilles.

(*HE* p. 13)

The patriarchal signification of the 'night-bird', hieroglyph, symbolic sign – as deathly *'carrion-creature'*, 'Isis', 'vulture' – is challenged by the narrator. The hieroglyph must be 'translated' (transvalued?) into the life-enhancing hieroglyph/'letter'/life symbol of Thetis – the sea-mother of Achilles. Seen as a symbolic *'sign-post'*, the sign of the hieroglyph, the symbol of the vulture/mother also invokes the pre-Oedipal drive pathways, fuelled by the flame (spark? glow?) of incestuous desire.[10] In H.D.'s terms, it will invoke the universal mother, as *'divine origin'* (*HE* p. 15).

The process of reinscription – that is, of critique, deletion and reconstitution – in *Helen in Egypt*, shows a movement from patriarchal into matriarchal forms. Helen works to re-member herself. But Achilles also has to do this work, he too must learn to re-member himself. He must learn to affirm Helen, just as he has to learn to *forgive* Thetis, his mother. In this heterosexual script, he must forgive her so that he will forget his hatred of women. He must forget the memory of heroic valour in order to be set free from his patriarchal past. He must forget his image of death as female, as scavenger, as vulture, as *'carrion-creature'*, consumer of blood and flesh. He must become able to recognise the validity and integrity of Helen's self-identification and, finally, he must acknowledge the 'mystery' of the hieroglyph.

In writing the hieroglyph, Helen writes herself, creates the script in which she can identify herself. But, in writing 'I do not care for separate/ might and grandeur,/ I do not want to hear of Agamemnon/ and the Trojan Walls,/ I do not want to recall/ shield, helmet, greaves,/ though he wore them', she writes a woman's condemnation of the masculine imperatives of war-making (*HE* p. 18). Diana Collecott has noted H.D.'s use of Greek myth 'to confront feminine experience, and to express it in direct opposition to the predominant masculine ideology – an ideology that oppressed women and promoted war'.[11] Collecott suggests that in her project of re-membering and reinterpretation, H.D. sought 'the reconciliation of "masculine" and "feminine" principles'. This work involved 'recovering the positive values of love and creativity that H.D. identified with female divinities, to offset the negative values of hatred and aggression that dominate heroic legend'. This feminist and pacifist work of re-vision is a crucial aspect of *Helen in Egypt*.

Unless Achilles *forgets* the brutal male world of 'Typhon the

Destroyer', the imperatives of command, of control, the father/
son hierarchies of power, the masculine iron-Ring of war-
making, Helen will get nowhere. She meditates on this:

> Will he forever weigh
> Helen against the lost,
> a feather's weight with a feather?
>
> does he dare remember
> the unreality of war,
> in this enchanted place?
>
> his fortress and his tower
> and his throne
> were built for man, alone;
>
> no echo or soft whisper
> in those halls,
> no iridescent sheen,
>
> no iris-flower,
> no sweep of strings,
> no answering laughter,
>
> but the trumpet's call . . .   (*HE* p. 30)

The male identity/world is defined here by repeated negatives, it
lacks and lacks – laughter, music, sensuality. It lacks the iris
flower, which is the Greek mother of Love, the rainbow of the
goddess. It lacks lustrous vision, the soft whisper of womanly
speech. Instead the imperative call of the trumpet, voice of war-
making. His lonely fortress, tower, throne, characterises the
isolation and alienation of the masculine as a boundaried and
heavily defended world – both in terms of identity, and in the
forms of culture that have been shaped by his egocentric warrior
mentality, his relentless aggrandisement of power.

In finally pointing the finger of blame at Amen, the male
patriarchal god, she ascribes *to him* responsibility and *guilt* for
the war. At the same time, she refuses to believe his story of the
battles as true *history*, it is his dream:

> 'Zeus be my witness,' I said,
> 'it was he, Amen dreamed of all this
> phantasmagoria of Troy,
>
> it was dream and a phantasy'   (*HE* p. 17)

In thus speaking out, Helen must face the murderous anger of
Achilles: for her trouble she is 'throttled': *O Thetis, O sea-
mother,/ I prayed, as he clutched my throat/ with his fingers'
remorseless steel,/ let me go out, let me forget,/ let me be lost* (*HE*
p. 17). She may not yet take up a position of authority within
discourse for she still does not possess intellectual *knowledge*.
She does not know the why, when, where, how of Achilles' anger,
and there are many as yet unanswered questions.

I seemed to know the writing,

as if God made the picture
and matched it
with a living hieroglyph;

how did I know the vulture?
why did I invoke the mother?
why was he seized with terror?

in the dark, I must have looked
an inked-in shadow; but with his anger
that ember, I became

what his accusations made me

(*HE* p. 23)

Despite her verbal assertiveness, she is overpowered by his
accusing words as well as his violent response. The violence
inflicted on her *throat* means her voice may not yet take up any
confirmed position as subject, or speak with integrity from her
own identity. Helen is not yet in possession of her being; nor can
she yet speak her own story. Thus, in the dénouement of Book I,
Helen faces her crucial test: can she sufficiently assert *her* version
of truth? Can she be the subject of her own discourse, rather than
object of his? The moment of greatest danger comes when Helen
must revoke Achilles' accusation and strongly assert her identity
in order to claim her full presence as female subject – as someone
who is able to define her own field of identification.

The new (old) patterns of significance that I am discerning in
this text so far are very much to do with the *forgetting* of
patriarchal heroics, and the *re-membering* of the maternal (or
matriarchal) pathway. 'Only let Thetis, the goddess hold me for a

while/ in this her island, her egg-shell' (*HE* p. 197). These patterns of significance show H.D. as making a re-visionary attempt to 'reconcile Trojan and Greek'; matriarch and patriarch; Eros and Thanatos; love and death. H.D. also offers a counterproposal to Freudian mythologies of woman's desire, dethroning his overvaluation of the role of the father and showing the importance of the mother's role in shaping infantile sexuality. The maternal pathway of love for the mother, according to Freud, should have been relinquished at the resolution of the little girl's Oedipal crisis. 'But the Professor was not always right' (*TF* p. 98):

> The Professor speaks of the mother-layer of fixation being the same in girls and boys, but the girl usually transfers her affection or (if it happens) her fixation to her father. Not always.
>
> (*TF* p. 175.)

Desire in *Helen in Egypt* takes several pathways – the most important of which lead to the mother. This is also true of *Tribute to Freud*, in its explorations of the scientific Freud's 'diagnosis' of H.D.'s *problem*. 'The Professor', so H.D. tells us, 'had said in the very beginning that I had come to Vienna hoping to find my mother. Mother? Mamma. But my mother was dead. I was dead; that is, the child in me that had called her mamma was dead' (*TF* p. 17). She records her longing as a child, to get near her mother: 'But one can never get near enough . . . . *If* one could stay near her always, there would be no break in consciousness' (p. 33). It is perhaps also significant that she relates to Freud 'as mother' in the transference. On a personal level, H.D.'s primal attachment to the mother takes on great importance in the autobiographical account of her analysis with Freud. On a mythic level, H.D.'s hallucinatory experience of the 'Writing on the Wall', which Freud interpreted as 'a desire for union with my mother', points to another dimension of desire – the religious desire for an alternative to god-father religion: the deity imaged as female, as goddess (p. 44).

For H.D.'s work cannot be read one-dimensionally. Is this 'pathway' to the mother personal or mythic, psychoanalytic or religious? Is 'this "symptom" or [is] this inspiration' (p. 47)? H.D., the mystic, suggests that the scientific Professor 'was not always right'. Can we see this book as an inspirational narrative that is motivated towards the religious quest for psychic 'whole-ness', or as one devoted to exploring the psychoanalytic dimensions relating to the integrity (or lack of integrity) of identity? If not, what other readings are possible?

In this mythic reconstruction of the field of identification of Helen, H.D. somewhat unpredictably moves between the differ-ent myths and mythic personae of both Helen and Achilles. She disturbs the reader's sense of space and time, and employs great technical skill in creating shifting points of view, varied angles of vision, voices, echoes, reverberations. She sets the voice of interior monologue against that of omniscient authorial pronounce-ments. Her voices shift between she, he, I, we, in rapid dialogic interplay. All this may perplex the reader, but ultimately her skill contributes not to a sense of fragmentation but rather to a sense of holistic transcendence of the limited, individual subjectivities of her personae. The multiple personae/identities of H.D., Helen, Helena, Thetis, Isis, Hecate; Achilles, Apollo, Typhon, Osiris, Orpheus, Phaethon – not only collapse into each other, they also expand into universal mythic figures, representatives of their sex.

Yet, despite this universalising tendency, this careful, detailed re-vision of myth, religion, epic, science, and the heroic aspects of patriarchal ideology, in no way is H.D. setting up a new set of universals, whether of science or of theology, that would dogmatically claim the authority and transcendent unity of overarching truth. Helen '*flings Knowledge away*' in this fight for identity, claiming that '*The pattern itself is sufficient*' (*HE* p. 32). What I have done is to pick out a few of the patterns that resonate significantly, that 'glow' for me, that are visible to myself as a woman reader. I have tried to show how, in her re-visionary strategy, H.D. is very concerned to transform the patterned narrative sequences of action and response typical of heroic quest literature into a pattern of quest centred around desire. The desire for the mother is crucial to both male and female protagonists. Interwoven in her text and questioning and displacing patriarchal forms are patterns of emotional attach-ment and of distress that are both matrifocal and patrifocal. The narrative explores the crises of love and war, of attraction or hostility, of desire and its thwarting. This alternative pattern, of the *emotional* and *relational* process of quest, examines male and female hierarchies of value. These are shown as in opposition to each other: the dualist opposition of Love and Death, incarnate in man and woman – in Helen and Achilles.

Deciphering such complex symbolic systems demands the utmost commitment of intelligence. The reader cannot be the remote and disinterested spectator, she must think/experience the writing, make what creative appropriation she needs, out of the gift of the writing. Needless to say, she dare not fall into the dogmatism of fixing meaning, of erecting a rationalist master code for interpretation, which would inevitably be reductive. For, always, there remain unanswered questions: does the symbol of the sacred parallel the dream symbol? Is the religious impulse derived from 'the feeling of infantile helplessness' as Freud would have it? [12] And does the symbolic representation of the woman, sacred or secular, draw its energy from repression, invoking not the desire for the father's protection but the desire for the care and protection of the phallic mother? Does this poetry, in invoking the repressed pre-Oedipal attachment to the mother, energise the 'magical', 'glowing' potency of the maternal pathway? Does H.D., in effect, reinscribe or reactivate needs sacrificed or renounced by the girl child in her necessity to survive in patriarchal civilisation? In what sense do we see H.D.'s question, 'Do I wish myself, in the deepest unconscious or subconscious layers of my being, to be the founder of a new religion? ' (TF p. 37). Should this perhaps be read as – do I wish to be the founder of a new consciousness for women? One or other – or both/and?

I must leave H.D. at this point, having indicated a few of the complexities of this major modernist poet. I have risked imposing a reductive linearity quite alien to the indirectional strategies of H.D.'s work, and have merely touched upon the profound, meditative questions pondered and posed disturbingly throughout: 'how did I know the vulture?/ why did I invoke the mother?/ why was he seized with terror?' (HE p. 23). The questions might perhaps lead us to the answers to the problem of male violence – but not before society has struggled with further, even more difficult questions: 'O child, must it be forever/ that your father destroys you,/ that you may find your father?', 'O child, must you seek your mother/ while your father forever/ attacks her in jealousy?' (HE p. 28).

I am left thinking, with H.D.: 'why do I lie here and wonder,/

and try to unravel the tangle/ that no man can ever un-knot?' (*HE* p. 298). It is not so simple.

Part III

WRITING THE BODY: DESIRE AND THE M/OTHER-TEXT

8

ON THE NEED TO GO TO
THE SOURCES

Re-visionary mythmaking often attempts to shift the coherences
of patriarchal language, not into incoherence but rather into
something more, breaking against and exceeding the symbolisa-
tions of patriarchal discourse. The difficult process of re-making
meaning involves the questioning and undoing of patriarchal
propositions, codes, and positions. It calls for a poetics of
suspicion when exploring traditional symbolic values and codes
relating to women, and, most particularly, to the mother. It
involves a critical reorientation that must become conscious of
the play of difference, displacement and opposition which orga-
nises the terms that constitute a woman's *meanings* and her
supposed identity.

According to Juliet Mitchell's Lacanian account of feminine
sexuality, the mythic identity of the split subject is 'a mirage
arising when the subject forms an image of itself by identifying
with others' perception of it'.[1] The human subject can only
conceptualise itself 'when it is mirrored back to itself from the
position of another's desire'. Subjectivity, then, is formed, both
initially and subsequently, in and through the process of looking
for the 'lost object', the mother, in an other who can be the mirror
in which she can recognise her self. The presence and look of the
mother 'who grants an image *to* the child', plays a part in the
formation of the ego of the child. Jacqueline Rose quotes Lacan:

> the idea of the mirror should be understood as an object
> which reflects – not just the visible, but also what is heard,
> touched and willed by the child.[2]

The construction of identity which occurs within the (a)symme-
try of relationship, cannot be conceived in static terms: person-
ality/ego formation cannot simply occur at a particular frozen

moment in infancy, never to be repeated. Identity formation has to be a dynamic continuing process, occurring through time. In that relational *process*, each individual (woman or man) experiences her/himself in relation to others as a *social* being. The constructs that institute our identity, that render our perceived reality coherent and our lives comprehensible, we build out of intersubjective *and intertextual* relationships.[3]

That this is a deeply political process crucial to feminist theorising, to poetic strategy and to political/critical practice, has been apparent ever since the first consciousness-raising groups began in the early seventies. The intersubjective and intertextual process which rigorously interrogates the established social order and perpetually analyses its premises, its presuppositions, also enlarges the signifiable. It expands the forms of knowledge permitted within social praxis and produces a continual re-visionary, open-ended, relativising movement. I see this movement as capable of modifying and shifting the grounding concepts within language that inform and *mediate* the interpretation of experience. These in turn play a crucial part in the constitutive process integral to identity formation, that is, to forming the operational constructs of the ego.

So, too, poetry, as m/Other, as mythic mirror, as 'mirage', can participate in the process of bringing words out of experience in a movement towards significance, towards a sense of coherence, of presence, of integration. Poetry may work to produce that fictional wholeness, that illusory sense of presence, that 'organic' unity sought by all who ever loved/hated their mothers. In the glow of her praiseful recognition, in her love, even in her *negative* condemnation, the child, like the reader, can conceptualise her self, always in relation to an Other, in relation to the *m/Other/text*. Women's poetry can hardly avoid being caught up in the fundamental human necessity of identity formation. Poetry can form a vital and necessary part of the human search for wholeness, for the integrity of identity, for the presence of the m/Other. It can become an important dimension of the dialectics of desire and be bound up with that passionate extremity of 'idealisation, ambivalence, fear and, above all, desire for the beloved total *presence*'.[4]

Historically, however, this idealising desire has been manifested in literature written by men, as an annihilating demand for the total possession and appropriation of the lover.

As many powerless women know to their cost, this power-to-demand of the male is often gained at women's expense. Women have too often denied themselves to act as 'mirror' to 'reflect' and magnify the male ego. The written (and spoken) 'I' of the woman-as-subject in conventional modes of representation may thus be rendered mute, silenced, absent. In this way, women in more oppressive forms of patriarchy become vulnerable to being used as a screen for the projections and fantasies of men, many finding themselves squirming and often powerless beneath the constructions, both material (economic) and psychic, imposed on them. Luce Irigaray suggests that this places woman in a position where she can experience her own multiple desires only in fragmented forms. In her essay 'This Sex Which Is Not One', she comments:

> The rejection, the exclusion of a female imaginary certainly puts woman in the position of experiencing herself only fragmentarily, in the little-structured margins of a dominant ideology, as waste, or excess, what is left of a mirror invested by the (masculine) 'subject' to reflect himself, to copy himself.[5]

This happens as if inevitably in cultures economically resourced, shaped and sustained in relation to masculine 'economies' of desire – where compulsory heterosexuality is the norm and where girls are encouraged from infancy to fulfil specific cultural expectations of the 'feminine'. Familiarly, for white European and North American women at least, those norms which function to sustain the myths of femininity and which assert the premise that woman should be passively feminine, by their sustained insistence within cultural forms, too often convince the woman that she should accept her designated role as beautiful sexual object of male desire. In the psychoanalytic frame I have been exploring, this dominance of the masculine economy can be seen as instituting a repression of the specificity of woman's desire that has, since Plato at least, been accompanied by a relentless condemnation of woman's dreadful difference from logocentric thinking.[6] Elaine Marks, in her review essay, 'Women and Literature in France', suggests that

> Logocentrism is . . . a sign of nostalgia, of longing for a coherent centre. In order to satisfy this longing absence,

113

difference and death are repressed; presence, identity, and life are given a privileged role. For Luce Irigaray and Hélène Cixous it signifies that women have always been on the side of the term that has been repressed. Women are the absent, the unacknowledged different, and the dead (the buried, the decapitated, the alienated).[7]

This theoretical 'absence', alienation, even *death* of women excluded from a repressive phallogocentric discursive practice has been a constant provocation to theorists on both sides of the Atlantic. It has given rise to attempts to write 'woman' back into language, to restore her to presence, life, voice – in her own terms. *Ecriture féminine* may be seen as the inscription of the specificity of the female body and female difference – in language and in texts written by women, for women. Is such a sexually specific feminine writing, an *écriture féminine*, possible? Or even desirable?

Arguments, often heated and acrimonious, have seemed to pivot on the issue of whether an *écriture féminine* can actually 'serve as a springboard for subversive thought, the precursory movement of a transformation of social and cultural structures',[8] or whether, instead, it should be viewed as an unhelpful and reactionary practice which looks back to essentialist notions of 'Woman as Nature' – towards images more characteristic of apocalyptic nineteenth-century feminism. Teresa Brennan here offers a useful resumé of this mainly Marxist critique of essentialism: 'essentialist theories are those that believe in some essential aspect of "human nature"; in something pre-given, innate, natural, biological; in something which cannot be changed . . . essentialist theories are those which appeal to sexual biology.'[9] If woman's nature is fixed, then what chance for social change? But Lacan's theories, Brennan argues, were taken up precisely because they 'theorised femininity as a non-biological construction', making available an unfixed 'feminine position' to both males and (in a qualified way) to females. She points to the difficulties of Lacan's position: 'as numerous critics have said, this account of femininity still implicates biology: femininity, as the negative term in sexual difference is constructed in relation to the phallus; and the thoroughly natural, essentialist penis lends itself to the representation of the phallus. The symbolic depends on this construction, and the symbolic is a universal structural event.'[10] Is 'non-essentialism', then, such a virtue? Brennan suggests that it is 'a kind of sclerosis in the system of feminist enquiry' in that it 'smooths over' conflict and tension between psychical and social realities. Neither position fully answers the problems posed in juxtaposing the Anglo-American socio-cultural perspectives and French feminists in their reliance on Lacanian theory – even when they are engaged in theorising difference and producing *écriture féminine*.

Questions as to whether or not 'feminine writing' characteristically refers to an innate femininity of an ahistorical nature, and whether or not this line of approach constructs a reductionist essentialism that plays right into the hands of men by limiting the woman to her biological role, are still thrown back and forth in the dialectic of argument, mostly from entrenched positions. For me, as for Arleen Dallery, there is a degree of paranoia in these charges of essentialism.[11] I prefer to see the erotic textual body of *écriture féminine* as, in fact, a mediated sign, as being as open to analysis as phallocentric writing. It is equally accessible to modes of analysis which reveal how the meanings it carries are produced and organised in language. *Ecriture féminine* is fundamentally 'open' to the continuing re-visionary strategies of writers and critics, and is therefore vital to the re-constitution of the 'I' of writing, especially when it focuses on the retrieval or recovery of the unidentified 'I' 'behind the mirror' of representation. This recovery or retrieval of the *suppressed* (and we may well ask how much of the 'repressed' is actually suppression, denial, censorship) I see as happening already as a result of poetic/political strategies employed by women writers, poets and critics.

Hélène Cixous makes a significant though hotly contested contribution to these poetic strategies of representation. Her particular practice of writing, which I find so im/pertinent, so exuberant, strives for the 'multiplication of the effects of the inscription of desire, over all parts of my body and the other body', through a bi-sexuality that 'doesn't annul differences, but stirs them up, pursues them, increases their number'. [12] Cixous exhorts woman (and, indirectly, man) to write her (his) body, so that s/he may 'invent the impregnable language that will wreck partitions, classes and rhetorics, regulations and codes' of the phallic organisation of language (p. 256). Where Kristeva sees the pre-Oedipal modality, for man or woman, as unrepresentable in language, as inherent only in the semiotic dimensions of language, Hélène Cixous insists not only that it is possible, but that a specifically female, libidinal economy of writing is essential for the liberation of women. In her deconstruction of patriarchal language, the woman is not mute, her voice may speak the body, she may ecstatically 'undo' repression to allow her desires a freer expression. Forbidden incestuous yearnings for the mother are crucial to Cixous' apparent and contradictory valorisation of the biological (hence material, physical), *real-life* female. As when Rich recalls 'a woman's voice singing a child/ against her heart' in 'Transcendental Etude', Cixous tells us –

> In women's speech, as in their writing, that element which never stops resonating, which, once we've been permeated by it, profoundly and imperceptibly touched by it, retains the power of moving us – that element is the song: first music from the first voice of love which is alive in every woman.
>
> ('*Medusa*', p. 251)

The parallels between Cixous and Rich are striking. The woman's voice becomes the 'echo' (the sound sent back) and is the 'incarnation' of the voice of the mother that 'springs from' the 'nameless' pre-Oedipal depths (incarnate: to embody in flesh; give human form to; to personify; to manifest; to heal). This maternal body (the libidinal voice of the drives, which echoes the first voice of love) in each woman, Cixous tells us, is suffused with an eroticism that knows no limits: 'her libido is cosmic, just as her unconscious is worldwide' ('Medusa', p. 259).

As in Rich's work, the image of the mother emerges as both a sublime metaphor *and* as partaking of the real, the concrete, the material, the physical *bloody* milky rawness of the body. As readers we are plunged into the primal drive pathways of desire and its frustration. Again, the dualistic division that marks one as transcendent and the other immanent no longer operates in her non-dualistic representation. The mother continues her 'song' within and through and across the body of the daughter in an apparently unproblematic fusion of subject and object: '*In* her, matrix, cradler; herself giver as her mother and child; she is her own sister-daughter' ('Medusa', p. 252).

To speak the body, then, in Cixous' poetic, is to seek

liberation of libidinal desire for the mother rather than to appeal directly to a biologistic, anatomically determined *essential* female body as origin *as such*. She stresses the *intersubjective* continuities between mother and daughter, and the physical exchanges that predicate desire *in relation* to m/Others. Desire manifests itself as a 'force': 'that force which produces/is produced by the other – in particular, the other woman' ('Medusa', p. 252).

This is to see writing the body, not as a retrieval of any kind of eternal truth, as a source of long-lost transcendent power, or as an idea 'dominated by a conception of unities'. Rather, the body may be seen as 'an element in a particular construction' produced within and through the dialectical exchanges and organisation of social relations.[13]

How can this maternal bio-physical pretext for the symbolic inspire cultural change? Cixous suggests that its dangerous ambiguous power in and through language lies in its potential to disrupt the historical unconscious, the inscribed maternal nexus, or complex – of both women and men. 'She doesn't deny her drives the intractable and impassioned part they have in speaking' as well as in writing, writing that 'retains the power of moving us' (p. 251). More than that, in accepting Lacan's suggestion that the place of the feminine in language is one of refusal of the '*discourse of the master*', the refusal of 'the tyranny of the all-knowing', she refuses any knowledge that is gained at the cost of excluding fantasy, subjectivity, and feeling. In Lacan's terms, she refuses the '*discourse of the university*' and resists its mode of producing knowledge itself as the ultimate object of desire.[14]

Instead, her writing sets heterogeneity and transformation against knowledge. Her language continuously moves away from positions of coherence, and she resists any attempt to position or to secure subjectivity. These shifts in language provoke *thought*[15] as *jouissance*, through a movement

> dynamised by an incessant process of exchange from one subject to another. A process of different subjects knowing one another and beginning one another anew only from the living boundaries of the other: a multiple and inexhaustible course with millions of encounters and transformations of the same into the other and into the in-between, from which

woman takes her forms (and man, in his turn; but that's his other history).

('Medusa', p. 254)

In the search for liberation from phallocentrism, Cixous situates writing in the *in-between* of intersubjectivity, seeing it as an inexhaustible, generative process of exchange and transformation of 'the same into the other'. In wishing to 'bring about a mutation in human relations', Cixous finds it necessary to deconstruct the language that works to perpetuate the psychic economy typical of patriarchal culture: in this process, her words throw the potential field of meaning wide open.

Toril Moi chastises Cixous for her 'lyrical, euphoric evocation of the essential bond between feminine writing and the mother as source and origin of the voice' – she scolds her for producing 'the very metaphysics of presence she claims she is out to unmask'.[16] It therefore seems necessary to look very closely at these lyrical transcendent moments produced in/for the Imaginary – where passion, desire for the mother, *jouissance*, are regenerated in Cixous' work.

In a sense, Cixous' writing is of the essence of contradiction: all polarities are represented, including the mystic. Certainly Moi is right to point out that Cixous transgresses the structuralist (and feminist) codes which prescribe against essentialism, against ideologies that posit notions of origin, of presence. Whether Moi is also right to condemn this facet of the holistic multiplicity of Cixous' work is at least debatable.

Cixous' deconstruction of the discourses of knowledge, ultimately, is about mechanisms of power, control and authority – and the mechanisms of its deposition. It is about the drives, about motivation, direction, about personal/political action in the real. About how the energies of libidinal desire may be realised in/through the symbolic, about how it may be mobilised towards a specific mode of gendered relation. Not the power-over of knowledge, but the *generosity* of diversity, of bi-sexuality, of knowing as a process. How this can happen: this is what concerns me. How are energy and desire to act in particular ways to be mobilised? I want to suggest that it can be through the agency of the symbol of the mother.

In this passage from *Vivre l'orange*, Hélène Cixous refuses to allow her symbolic invocation of the mother to be read as backward looking nostalgia for a past golden age of ideal moments. She insists that the orange – which can be read as a suggestive, juicy metaphor for the maternal breast – is symbolised as an inspirational 'globe of light' that reaches forward *into the future* – is 'present here and tomorrow'. Women's yearnings for peace and plenitude, their desires for 'the lost orange' here reach forward out of the present and are oriented towards the future. Cixous points to a process of search – a search motivated by the desire for the lost object, the maternal source, which is symbolically returned 'into the deserted hands of my writing':

> The orange is the nearest star. With all of my life I thought it, with all of my thought I went toward it, I had the peace in my hands. I saw that the world that held the answer to the questions of my being was gold-red, a globe of light present here and tomorrow, red day descended from green night.
>
> I asked: *'What have I in common with women?'* From Brazil a voice came to return the lost orange to me. *'The need to go to the sources. The easiness of forgetting the source. The possibility of being saved by a humid voice that has gone to the sources. The need to go further into the birth-voice.'*[17]

The roundness of this glowing, gold-red symbol suggests not only the orange but also, multivalently, the sun/world/breast/peace. Again the breast is symbolised in its 'good aspect' as 'foundation' for 'hope, trust and belief in goodness'.[18] Cixous searches for the humid *'birth-voice'* of the mother, a voice that is shared 'in common' with other women; a voice that serves as an expansive metaphor for female authenticity and truth – and as a woman's voice that can possibly 'save' woman and the world. Her desire, her feminine libidinal economy centres around this symbolic reminiscence, which is present now and gives hope for the future. Her thought inscribes the mythic return of 'the lost orange' – the return or awakening of the mythic or real world which holds 'the answer to the questions of my being'.

Cixous' text, despite its emphasis on going to the maternal sources, 'the birth-voice', is not involved in a nostalgic and regressive demand for the comforting securities of meaning. Nor does it claim to find in the metaphor of the mother any original, unitary source of truth. The maternal 'sources' cannot be originary in the Romantic sense of being a transcendent ego-centre of subjectivity, the sole genius–creator of original thoughts and insights, bearer of Universal Truth, of the Word. Her search is rather to find out what she has *in common* with other women: she will listen for the words of another woman. For the words of Clarice – who puts 'the word in my ear' and who returns to her the symbolic orange/sun of energy/love/breast/globe of light that nourishes 'all of the thoughts that a woman can nourish'.[19] The term 'mother' loses its patriarchal connotations. The mother is no longer 'the accomplice of reproduction: capitalist, familialist, phallocentrist reproduction'[20] – but is now to be defined in woman-identified terms as 'nonname', 'matrix', 'cradler . . . she is her own sister-daughter' ('Medusa', p. 252). For Cixous, the term 'mother', as I have suggested, is a metaphor for the healing gift of love of women between women: recall the lines, 'The mother, too, is a metaphor. It is necessary and sufficient that the best of herself be given to woman by another woman for her to be able to love herself and return in love the body that was "born" to her.' Cixous herself, in effect, passes on the orange to the reader as a hand gives a gift, the gift of the writing, which is that of a manifold, generous woman's voice, present now in the culture, as another point of departure for her.

Starting out from this 'given' orange – and claiming that 'a feminine text starts on all sides at once' – Cixous pursues a logic of reciprocal interconnection, and posits 'an abundance of non-egos' who freely take up a multiplicity of subject positions ('Castration', p. 53). These poetic strategies refuse transcendence, ego-centrism, individualism, originary presence, and attempt, rather, to connect subject and object, inner and outer, woman and world in a mystic (and hence transcendent) *immanence* that claims One is All, All is One: 'I am myself the earth, everything that happens on it, all the lives that live me there in my different forms.'[21] The pre-Oedipal space, in this poetic, is not a primary organiser of the structure of subjectivity. It does not produce a transcendent 'I' and neither can it produce an essence of femininity for if there is no division, there can be no other, no negative term to define what is femininity. The word 'feminine' is itself interrogated and comes to acquire a new meaning as that which refuses such essentialist categorisation. In this process of return

120

to bisexual undifferentiation, the logic of the organisation of phallogocentric language is overthrown.

Cixous thus inscribes this 'return' as a moving away from the positions of coherence for subjectivity that language constructs. She projects the maternal pathways of desire, of search, as endlessly thrown forward into the future – knowing is endlessly deferred, forgetting is always easy. She repeatedly precipitates fresh beginnings, offers always renewed perspectives. This perpetual renewal of knowing, patterns the drives, draws her towards its promise of 'knowing more', 'understanding more', feeling more, becoming more erotic, more sexual, living more fully, more abundantly: 'there is a nonclosure that is not submission but confidence and comprehension; that is not an opportunity for destruction but for wonderful expansion'.[22] *As the desire for a source, the desire for the mother can only ever be an empowering, drive-sustained source of motivation.* As the desiring reader engages in this search, she immerses herself in the proliferating processes of identifying in the text further elaborations of relevance that are important to her. S/he finds herself perpetually in the process of quest, looking to the future, exploring the text's polyvalent, multilayered complexity. Thus, though the 'humid voice that has gone to the sources' speaks as the voice of the maternal saviour, this maternal 'source' only promises endlessly deferred identity. Meaning, wholeness, is only promised in some indeterminate, unknowable future time – out of time, in eternity or never. The reader finds herself engaged in 'self-constituting a subjectivity that splits apart without regret':

> Unleashed and raging, she belongs to the race of waves. She arises, she approaches, she lifts up, she reaches, covers over, washes a shore, flows embracing the cliff's least undulation, already she is another, arising again, throwing the fringed vastness of her body up high, follows herself, and covers over, uncovers, polishes, makes the stone body shine with the gentle undeserting ebbs, which return to the shoreless nonorigin, as if she recalled herself in order to come again as never before . . . .

> She has never 'held still'; explosion, diffusion, effervescence, abundance, she takes pleasure in being boundless, outside self, outside same, far from a 'centre' . . . .[23]

The endlessly deferred identity, meaning, wholeness of the maternal voice of *écriture féminine* seems to me comparable to the patriarchal religious promise of heaven in the hereafter! Cixous' text, however, will never offer such heavenly satisfactions as truth, resolution, closure, ending, certainty, death. Language is, rather, destined to suffer endless rebirths into numinous, proliferating, cyclical, labyrinthine, metamorphic - Life.

The vital, desiring process of search is all important, yet at the same time it produces a circular movement marked by metamorphic shifts that posit 'invisible links . . . between all of the thoughts that a woman can nourish' ('Castration', p. 39). Metaphors of voice, hand, meeting, attraction, direction, words and things; all circulate in the following extract - meaning cannot be firmly grasped. In interpreting this poetic passage written in such a densely symbolic mode, the reader makes multiple connections through and across the text. She must again resist division: that is, the separation, or polarisation into binary contrasts. This language 'includes all' rather than atomistically categorises, partitions, classifies. A reader remains in relative uncertainty in the presence of meaning, not yet holding it firmly in place: attentive to it, yet not possessing it absolutely - *just as a good mother would.*

> And to all of the women whose hands are like voices that go to meet the things in the dark, and that hold words out in the direction of things like infinitely attentive fingers, that don't catch, that attract and let come, I dedicate the orange's existence, as it has been given to me by a woman, according to the entire and infinite bringing-together of the thing, including all that is kin of the air and the earth.[24]

The problem of interpretation, of recomposing or producing significance out of this web of unlimited semiosis requires the reader to appreciate the expansive symbol's indeterminacy of allusion. Umberto Eco's account of the radical openness of symbols incidentally throws light on Cixous' strategy here: readers have to come to terms with 'their vagueness, their openness, their fruitful ineffectiveness to express a "final" meaning. [For] . . . with symbols and by symbols one indicates what is always *beyond* one's reach.'[25] Yet significance is hardly absent: it is simply not in order, not under control, not disciplined. Cixous' symbolic mode is thus interpretable but not anchored:

the reader can conceive and reproduce meaning but is always and everlastingly pregnant with further meanings which can be developed progressively. Meaning is thus simultaneously present and everlastingly deferred in that Cixous' symbols continue to suggest further dimensions of significance. Her use of what Eco calls the symbolic 'content nebula' generates an unlimited, intertextual plenitude of meaning, which can never be fixed or brought into other than temporary stasis.[26] The reader is only limited in her creative effort by her level of competence in invention, or her capacity to draw upon preceding traditional cultural usage. That is, her width of experience of French feminist theory, of psychoanalytic practice, of mysticism – or, her depth of comprehension of women's poetry, of the literary culture or of the frames of her own life experience. As Umberto Eco suggests, contextual pressures or inferences of ideological and historical significance will alert her as to 'which semes to bring into focus and which to drop' in the active process of re-creating the 'universe of content' of the text – *in her own terms.*[27]

The bountiful generosity of this living body of textual signifi-cance is analogous to the nurturant body or breast of the mother who, 'outside her role functions' flows with 'at least a little of that good mother's milk. She writes in white ink.'[28] As a woman her sexuality, her imaginary and her drives, like the writing, are 'inexhaustible'.[29] She is frequently represented in Cixous' work in terms of cosmic or oceanic imagery: luminous torrents, streams, waves, floods, outbursts. The metaphor of the ocean, familiar to us from biblical sources, can be seen as alluding to untamed, unreduced, chaos. Out of such formlessness comes the primary impulse to create: out of wells, springs, lakes or seas come new forms of life. Water can be seen as an ancient fecund *maternal* metaphor, then, for the *process* and creativity of the life force (God) – and for Love itself – without which the material world would become an arid desert, as in Eliot's *The Waste Land.*[30]

Those involved in the formation of the biblical canon were very aware of a related problem, of the difficulties they exper-ienced in interpreting the utterly mobile symbols and metaphors of the scriptures. They knew about writings which say every-thing, which potentially will yield every possible meaning, which say 'too much'. Cixous' evocation of the maternal pre-Oedipal text – which symbolises that space before the Law of the

Father intervenes to define, order and control language, before binary division, before oppositional systems of presence and absence inscribe difference, before separation into self and other, masculine and feminine – is comparable to that 'space' before the process of forming the biblical canon occurred, before the canonical texts of the bible were agreed as the authoritative voice of the church, systematising and fixing the 'right' interpretation, cutting the 'key' to the symbolic gate of biblical rhetoric. When the church fathers had ratified what was the 'true meaning' of the Words of the Christ, of the Logos, and determined what interpretations were permissible, they were able to determine what they thought to be the 'true' Word. According to Eco – 'the gate-keepers of the orthodoxy were the winners (in terms of political and cultural power) of the struggle to impose their own interpretation'. They were the ones who controlled and ordered the canonically 'correct' and legitimated way of interpreting the Word.[31]

Toril Moi's suggestion that Cixous' 'investment' in the world of myth, fairy-tale, religion, necessarily leads her towards a meaningful, ideal world of closure and unity, in which 'all difference, struggle and discord can in the end be satisfactorily resolved', needs careful rethinking.[32] Moi's argument seems to try to limit the meaning of the symbol of 'the mother' – to an ideal, essential, closed, womb-like security of meaning that no *symbol* or *metaphor* can possibly possess. Perhaps (valid) feminist ideological pressures to eschew essentialisms of any sort have led her to bring into focus only certain semes as having significance. The wayward symbol or, as Eco terms it, the content nebula, can in this way be reduced to a static, fixed term. The mother and the myth can then become viewed as a sanctuary or refuge, closed off from the world. Not only is the metamorphic anarchy of Cixous' text controlled and fixed by this movement – but also the transvaluations of the world of mysticism and myth can be limited to certain legitimated meanings. It seems that in any form of critical practice, the contribution of the interpreting reader must be taken into account when engaging with any form of cultural representation.

Cixous' deliberate textual strategy encourages illimitable readings: she shifts meaning, context, frame continually. The language of patriarchy, in an equally deliberate strategy of containment, strives to define and fix in place, to control, to master. As when the mystic transmutes the meaning of the religious symbol, and thereby throws established theological wisdom into discomfiture and disarray, so the language that acts as a matrix or cradle to continually generate change and transformation promises to 'bring about a mutation – in human relations, in thought, in all praxis'.[33] Thus, the metaphoric return to the womb, seen by Toril Moi as a place of closure, I envisage as a place of generativity and cyclical openness – a product of the women's *movement* of struggle and labour to create anew, to go beyond, to exceed the boundaries of patriarchal definition. Revitalising the m/Other, which includes transforming the power relations between class and class, oppressor and oppressed, white and black, man and woman, is not an individualist project limited only to the lesbian community, or even to the wider women's liberation movement. Nor is the liberation of language and the vision of loving intersubjectivity between women and women, women and men, men and men – and all that is on the earth – envisaged by Cixous, devoid of significance in real, material, social and cultural terms. The power to define what is true, what is right, what goes and what does not must lie at the very centre of any nexus of power relations.

9

MOTHER, DAUGHTER, SISTER, LOVER
Adrienne Rich's dream of a whole new poetry

> Mothers and daughters have always exchanged with each other - beyond the verbally transmitted lore of female survival - a knowledge that is subliminal, subversive, preverbal.
>
> Adrienne Rich, *Of Woman Born*[1]

> Text: my body - shot through with streams of song; I don't mean the overbearing, clutchy 'mother' but, rather, what touches you, the equivoice that affects you, fills your breast with an urge to come to language and launches your force; the rhythm that laughs you; the intimate recipient who makes all metaphors possible and desirable; body (body? bodies?), no more describable than god, the soul, or the Other; that part of you that leaves a space between yourself and urges you to inscribe in language your woman's style. In women there is always more or less of the mother who makes everything all right, who nourishes, and who stands up against separation: a force that will not be cut off but will knock the wind out of the codes. We will rethink womankind beginning with every form and every period of her body.
>
> Hélène Cixous, 'The Laugh of the Medusa'[2]

Luce Irigaray pays particular attention to the relation between mother and daughter, a relation inadequately theorised either in Freud or Lacan. She draws attention to the fact that, within western patriarchal cultures, women's relationships with their mothers, and with other women, are devalued. She argues that the little girl suffers 'narcissistic distress' because this primary 'carnal' relation to her mother is so censored, her own body is underestimated, even 'reviled', like her mother's, as castrated (in Freudian and Lacanian psychoanalytic terms). She argues that 'a woman, if she cannot in one way or another, recuperate her first object (that is, make real the possibility of keeping her first earliest libidinal attachments by displacing them onto an/ Other), is always exiled from herself'.[3]

How does she return from exile? How does a woman reclaim her 'self' and (as Irigaray puts it) re-mark, in language, her different economy of representation? Can she articulate an economy of desire that is not based on an assumption of the anatomical inferiority of the female and that will not concede anything to the hierarchy of values ordained within heterosexual phallocentric ideology? In particular, how does the lesbian poet put her relation to other women into words and inscribe the specificity of her desire within the symbolic? Is it possible to reconstitute herself as subject through the body, touch, words and gaze of the lesbian Other – within, and in despite of, the debilitating and destructive systems of patriarchy? Adrienne Rich, in her poem 'Origins and History of Consciousness', explores this struggle:

> It was simple to meet you, simple to take your eyes
> into mine, saying: these are eyes I have known
> from the first . . . It was simple to touch you
> against the hacked background, the grain of what we
> had been, the choices, years . . . It was even simple
> to take each other's lives in our hands, as bodies.
>
> What is not simple: to wake from drowning
> from where the ocean beat inside us like an afterbirth
> into this common, acute particularity
> these two selves who walked half a lifetime untouching –
> to wake to something deceptively simple: a glass
> sweated with dew, a ring of the telephone, a scream
> of someone beaten up far down in the street
> causing each of us to listen to her own inward scream
>
> knowing the mind of mugger and the mugged
> as any woman must who stands to survive this city,
> this century, this life . . .[4]

Rich does not here imagine an ideal separatist world in which women may freely and ecstatically rejoice in their discovery of one another.[5] Rather, the poet shows these lesbian women as actively struggling for survival, working together as lovers who trust each other. Lowered down this rope, they explore new ways of being in relationship. The metaphors of darkness and light point to a relationship in which contradictions and negativity are fully searched out and revealed. The women recognise each other, identify each other in the metaphoric darkness of the womb, and this new 'conception' is for them an *illumination*. They are 'drenched in light' within the darkness. Their coming together is marked by a joyful ecstasy – sexual, spiritual, mystic – as each identifies the other in the non-dualist patterns of language Rich has taken so much care to construct:

> Trusting, untrusting,
> we lowered ourselves into this, let ourselves
> downward hand over hand as on a rope that quivered
> over the unsearched . . . We did this. Conceived
> of each other, conceived each other in a darkness
> which I remember as drenched in light.
>
> (p. 9)

Each woman is desired by and desires both the m/Other, and her woman lover as Other. Each woman participates in the symbolic 'conception' of the other: they are 'mothers' *birthing* each other into language *through trust*. In Irigaray's words: 'We find ourselves as we entrust ourselves to each other.'[6] Yet, at the same time, both live in a world of darkness, crisis and painful contradictions, a world where the 'inward scream' is matched by the scream of 'someone beaten up far down in the street'.

In using her metaphors of conception, Rich draws on the watery, oceanic (heart) beating imagery of the womb/mother. The metaphors of conception, darkness and drowning – the suffocating panic of the birth trauma – interconnect with metaphors of illumination, of awakening, of being 'drenched in light'. The women accept the mutual affirmation of the maternal gaze – and the associated pattern that inevitably accompanies this relation: the 'trusting, untrusting' that none the less enables the women to 'take each other's lives in our hands, as bodies'. The poet's use of 'us' indicates that both women simultaneously experience this return to the maternal oceanic space of womb/water as well as experiencing the exit from that space, the waking moment of rebirth. Their return is not, therefore, to some idyllic place of *origin* to re-establish contact and continuity with the mother but is, rather, conceived as a painful rebirth or spiritual awakening – into a fuller understanding of the situation of women in patriarchy.

The poem itself is deceptively simple. Paradoxically, the mutually returned gaze between herself and her lover, of 'eyes I have known/ from the first', may again be interpreted as signalling the women's recuperation of the gaze exchanged between infant and mother. This symbolic desiring connection to the mother is recalled as difficult and dangerous. Yet the women 'conceive' of each other, recover each other from exile. This 'return' enables the women to become 'two selves' in relation. The lives of the women, together '*as bodies*' are present to each other, just as they are able to revalue each other. The women are no longer represented as *object* to the male gaze, but as equally participating in a mirroring interrelationship:

> We did this. Conceived
> of each other, conceived each other in a darkness
> which I remember as drenched in light

The all-important adjunct 'of' differentiates active from passive mode, actor from acted upon, but the phrase 'each other' will not permit the patriarchal dualistic and hierarchical division into acting subject and acted-on object: each *conceives* the other, each is mother and daughter interchangeably, is both subject and object, is dark 'drenched' in light, reciprocally. As Irigaray puts it: 'Night and day are mingled in our gazes, our gestures, our bodies.'[7]

The mutuality and equality of this womanly mode of relating seem to be crucial to constructing an ideal, one which serves the utopian goal of building a 'gender/class/race-free' community for the social support and sexual and emotional enrichment of lesbian lives. At the same time and paradoxically, this seductive and inspiring utopian vision tends to deny, or seems to transcend, differences in economic power, class status and the experience of racial discrimination, not only within society, but also between one lesbian woman and another. It is necessary to be aware of the inbuilt contradictions of this position. It is also necessary to recognise that this effacement of the differences of race and class is a mid-seventies phenomenon which responded to the political urgencies of the time, those of forging an initial sense of solidarity between all women to set against the devastating fragmentation between women created by patriarchal social structures.

Today feminists face a somewhat different task, that of claiming and naming – sometimes celebrating, sometimes mourning – diversity and difference between women. Yet, the necessity for making this commitment to mutuality and equality – and creating a political and cultural context in which such a relation may have a chance of being realised – remains important. We still have a political need to sustain and celebrate the woman–woman bond as between one subject and another subject, rather than conceding anything to the subject/object model typical of heterosexual patriarchy – spelt out for us by Simone de Beauvoir, so long ago.

The 'I'–'I' of subject and subject in equal relationship, may be seen as a radical calling into question of the hierarchical structures of the nuclear family – or of any extended patriarchal family situation where institutionalised and conventional heterosexual modes of relating still prevail. This challenge to the hierarchies of patriarchy underlies Rich's poetic (as it does that of Irigaray). But the ideal language that restores the object to speech and, in a sense, banishes the transcendent patriarchal 'I' to silence, is the language of desire: that is, a language that escapes from repression, that emerges from the desire-laden unconscious, from the world of the dream. A dream from which, while patriarchy still exists, the women must wake – to the reality of 'a scream/of someone beaten up', that chilling sound that echoes her 'own inward scream' (p. 8).

Adrienne Rich has courageously explored these boundaries between the mother and the daughter. In many of her poems she makes a powerful attempt to dissolve the boundaries between subject and object, as well as those between women – between mother and child and between lover and lover. Her passionate desire to disrupt the patriarchal symbolic through a poetic reclamation of the maternal body involves a brave acceptance of the pain of dismemberment. She takes the risk of losing her bearings, her anchorage in conventional social meanings and finds her way through to a new stability, a new integrity grounded in her lesbian identity.

This movement is most evident in 'Transcendental Etude', one of the finest poems of *The Dream of a Common Language*. In this poem, Rich reminds us of the primal bodily connection to the mother that gives rise to the infant's first sensational experiences of *jouissance*, a term I take to mean the totality of enjoyment – sexual, spiritual, or physical – a total joy or ecstasy in the presence of the mother:

> that acute joy at the shadow her head and arms
> cast on a wall, her heavy or slender
> thighs on which we lay, flesh against flesh,
> eyes steady on the face of love; smell of her milk, her sweat,
> terror of her disappearance, all fused in this hunger[8]

In this poem, Rich returns us to those first communications between child and mother which are traced in the memory as an experience of bodily contact, of mutuality of the gaze, of security in being held; the memory of being offered the breast, warmth, nourishment, tenderness. The 'knowledge' Rich speaks of is this preverbal knowledge of the body, acquired prior to the entry into language, acquired by the infant in its relation to the mother. Rich invests this relation with the mystery of sameness, with the *jouissance* of two alike bodies, not yet caught up in the gendered codes that will eventually detach a girl child from her mother and win her allegiance to the father, to the heterosexual contract. It is within the maternal relation between mother and child, in the 'flowing between' body and body, that the child will receive the subversive imprinting of the pre-Oedipal phase.

Again and again, Rich returns to that space before language begins to assign experience according to the gendered codes of the Law of the Father. She mobilises desire for the mother, returning to that archaic ground-note of the psyche, the sound of the mother's heartbeat, a sound that carries both the *jouissance* of the mother's presence – the feelings of enwrapment, tenderness, love, security, mutuality – and the anguish of her loss, her absence, the aching lost emptiness of separation, of abandonment:

> At most we're allowed a few months
> of simply listening to the simple line
> of a woman's voice singing a child
> against her heart. Everything else is too soon,
> too sudden, the wrenching-apart, that woman's heartbeat
> heard ever after from a distance

She reminds us of the primary maternal imprint, the sensual experiences of the infant body, the first tracings of this life laid down in the unconscious mind. The touch, taste, smell, facial expression, gesture of the mother in relation to the child – as the child's first vital communication with another person – are represented by the poet. At this stage the infant hardly experiences herself as separate from her mother. Through her choice of sensory images, Rich reaches into this past, enables the recall or remembrance of the sensual experiences of the infant body. For the reader, the poem may re-awaken and re-inscribe these early tracings of the mother/daughter connection. The 'limitless' desire, the 'hunger', the 'homesickness' – the yearning, the joy, the eroticism, the *jouissance* of the mother's nearness, her presence – are invoked by these words, these rhythms, these syllables. The powerful longings, hungers, desires for the mother which are inseparable from the 'terror of her disappearance', take on a primal intensity. The poem, then, plays erotically across what Dorothy Dinnerstein has called 'the massive orienting passions that first take shape in pre-verbal, pre-rational human infancy'.[9] These are the precursors of those passions that continue to resonate through and across the forms and patterns of adult sexuality. I want to suggest that Rich's poetic strategy in *The Dream*, constitutes an attempt to release from repression (or undo the forgetting) around this primal, bodily based desire for the mother, seeing this as a move not without significance in a lesbian poetic committed to disrupting the heterosexual contract encoded in patriarchal language.

On another level, this desire for transcendent return to the mother is the impossible desire to recover pre-natal wholeness, the desire for unity with the mother, for *identity* with an other, or failing that, then at least for access to a source of bountiful maternal nurturance. This desire may well underlie and perhaps even inspires the ideal of woman/woman connection whether it is between mother and daughter, between the lesbian and her lover, or between feminists united in sisterhood. This fantasied return is clearly articulated in 'Transcendental Etude'. Here, Rich creates a vision of the desired and desiring mother that is

> all fused in this hunger
> for the element they have called most dangerous, to be
> lifted breathtaken on her breast, to rock within her
> – even if beaten back, stranded again

132

As Rich invokes this primary maternal imprinting, she also recalls the moment of birth, which, according to Julia Kristeva, assumes great importance as the moment when a daughter herself becomes a mother. Kristeva comments:

> Such an excursion to the limits of primal regression can be phantasmatically experienced as the reunion of a woman–mother with the body of *her* mother . . . .

> By giving birth, the woman enters into contact with her mother; she becomes, she is her own mother; they are the same continuity differentiating itself. She thus actualises the homosexual facet of motherhood, through which a woman is simultaneously closer to her instinctual memory, more open to her own psychosis, and consequently, more negatory of the social, symbolic bond.[10]

If this is so, then reconnection to those early months before entry into language acquires a particular urgency for a lesbian poetic committed to the necessity of negating the heterosexual social contract. Regression to the time before symbolic coherence is established, to a time–space even before the differentiation of the 'me' from the 'not-me' (the other) – is a regression to the biological-corporeal grounding of the psyche. According to Kristeva, in this space, fragments, echoes, rhythms, flashes – the precursors of language – musically 'whirl'. This state of primal bodily and sensational flux is prior to the naming processes that programme and constitute, classify and encode experience in constraining logical syntax. It is thus prior to the processes which place the child according to their sex into gendered categories and regulates and orders the identity of meaning and truth within the sentence.[11]

Kristeva alerts us to both the danger and the potential for change of this space of the semiotic: the danger is that woman can be rendered 'more open to her own psychosis'. The lure and the promise is that the patriarchal social symbolic bond, that is, the patriarchal cultural codes that organise our language, can possibly be negated through this return. It seems that to revive this instinctual memory, this loving connection to the mother, or to relate to an Other woman as lover may precipitate a crisis of identity through the disruption of heterosexual systems of meaning. Patriarchal systems, conventions, words, codes can no longer make sense. A woman may panic as she loses her bearings, common-sense understanding may lose its coherence, reference may slip its anchor in solid facts, for facts themselves may become suspect. There may be a sense of isolation, of disorientation, of chaos, of flux. This crisis of meaninglessness can feel like the 'pitch of utter loneliness':

> No one who survives to speak
> new language, has avoided this:
> the cutting-away of an old force that held her
> rooted to an old ground
> the pitch of utter loneliness
> where she herself and all creation
> seem equally dispersed, weightless, her being a cry
> to which no echo comes or can ever come.

The anguish of this time of rift, of 'free fall' that Rich describes as 'rootless', 'dismembered', 'the pitch of utter loneliness' is a crisis of both meaning and identity – for the 'whole new poetry' of woman/woman love cannot be entered without encountering both *jouissance* and the return to formlessness, disintegration, isolation, disconnection, death of the old identity and of reasonable language. Preceding meaning, exceeding it: the maternal imprint, the lesbian trajectory – sensual, intense, passionate – begins to map the terrifying glorious territory of the mother.

Once she has positioned herself outside of patriarchal systems, the lesbian experiences the shattering of patriarchal identity and meaning, the patriarchal 'I' of her old self dissolves, old truths no longer convince. Reduced to a silent cry of distress, the 'I' must break out of the old conceptions, refuse the old constraints, confront the outlived voice of heterosexual conscience. Lesbians find themselves constructing a new coherence in seeking a return to dependable truth. The lesbian must find or invent an alternative system of value and belief in her quest for a reintegration of identity. As Kristeva reminds us –

> the problem is to control this resurgence of phallic presence; to abolish it at first, to pierce through the paternal wall of the superego and afterwards, to reemerge still uneasy, split apart, asymmetrical, overwhelmed with a

desire to know, but a desire to know more and differently than what is encoded-spoken-written.[12]

The cry of distress, of desire, is for a new way of knowing, to seek a lesbian rather than heterosexual path towards symbolic restoration in order to create some degree of personal and group integrity. These restorative codes find themselves set against hostile and condemnatory codes which define the lesbian as sick or sinful. A new web is continually woven, an ever-renewed, always freshly synthesised web of meanings and values. A web is woven directly out of each lesbian woman's experience, perpetually in process of becoming, worked out in and through the love shared by lesbians, in and through and out of each woman's daily life:

> *This is what she was to me, and this*
> *is how I can love myself –*
> *as only a woman can love me.*

This complex recognition of the love between mother and daughter, and between a lesbian and her lover points to a crucial dynamic essential to the processes of identity construction. The loving, the caring, the touching, the looks, the words they share, convey to the Other woman a sense of her own integrity – affirming and validating her as a woman who loves and is loved. This caring connection does much to help women create, for themselves as for the other woman, an identity through which they can respect and be respected, love and be loved.

Implicitly, through the use of the extended musical metaphor, Rich invokes her own mother who was a 'skilled and dedicated' pianist and composer.[13] The poem is thus symbolically grounded in her own experience, the study of her own life, her own struggles:

> No one ever told us we had to study our lives,
> make of our lives a study, as if learning natural history
> or music, that we should begin
> with the simple exercises first
> and slowly go on trying
> the hard ones, practising till strength
> and accuracy became one with the daring
> to leap into transcendence, take the chance
> of breaking down in the wild arpeggio
> or faulting the full sentence of the fugue.

In the first section, the romantic transcendence of the pastoral mode is undercut by the threat of subsequent destruction, the young deer being 'fair game' for 'hit and run hunters'. In the second stanza the lyric sweetness of the green world of Vermont is cut through by 'rotgut violence,/ poverty gnashing its teeth like a blind cat at their lives'. In the third section the 'wild arpeggio' and the 'full sentence of the fugue' break down – for nowhere is perfection to be found, and no sublime transcendence of patriarchal forms is possible. Salvaging the truth 'from the splitting-open of our lives' is a comparable process of struggle towards. The symbolism of music – an art form which can only be fully experienced in its duration, which has to be lived through and listened for, which goes on until it finally stops – is an appropriate metaphor for the work that is involved. But the lesbian woman's music, her 'tale', is mostly as yet unheard, her life has not yet been articulated, her experience is not yet revealed to us:

> The woman who sits watching, listening,
> eyes moving in the darkness
> is rehearsing in her body, hearing-out in her blood
> a score touched off in her perhaps
> by some words, a few chords, from the stage:
> a tale only she can tell.

Disenchanting herself from the 'oratory, formulas, choruses, laments, static/ crowding the wires', giving names to, finding words for her own feelings, perceptions, insights requires a return to silence and a 'severer listening'. She must 'grasp her experience' in words, hopefully in words that will re-envision her experience and affirm her lesbian existence:

> The lesbian/feminist lives in a complex, demanding realm
> of linguistic and relational distinctions. One of the tasks
> ahead of us is to begin trying to define those distinctions
> (and the overlap of female experience that is synch-
> ronymous with them) . . . .

> For us, the process of naming and defining is not an
> intellectual game, but a grasping of our experience and a
> key to action. The word *lesbian* must be affirmed because to
> discard it is to collaborate with silence and lying about our

very existence; with the closet-game, the creation of the *unspeakable*.[14]

Due attention should be given to the words 'overlap' and 'synchronymous' in this passage: Rich is not working here with a naive, untheorised understanding of language as co-terminous with the authenticity of experience. There is some overlap, some co-incidence in time, some simultaneity, but the two spheres are not the same. To 'grasp' experience is to endeavour to seize and hold something which is always slipping away, always elusive. Such a grasping of 'experience' within language is strategic and political, part of the poet's creative use of words within the constructs of poetry.

In the final section to the 'Etude', Rich again depicts a woman who finds herself in quietness, alone after walking away 'from the argument and jargon in a room'. This section has attracted some hostile criticism from feminist critics, which I wish to consider briefly here. Margaret Homans' sharp critique accuses Rich of ending *The Dream* 'with a woman who turns into a rock'![15] She argues somewhat dismissively that Rich's attempt to create a ' "Whole New Poetry" will spring from the identity of self, lover and mother through the enlarging and consoling of the self'; that the 'woman is passive and stereotypically lacking in an identity of her own' (p. 228); and that 'Rich bewilderingly celebrates a number of male visions of femininity that have always restricted women, both humanly and poetically' (p. 227). The final lines of the poem are, in her terms, 'poetically terminal' (p. 229).

In that Homans reads Rich's poems in relation to Romantic theory, I am surprised that her 1980 critique does not recognise that 'Transcendental Etude' is a systematic appropriation and critique of this 'exclusively masculine system of value', that is, of the myths and models of the Romantic tradition (p. 4). In her criticism of this tradition, Homans tells us that 'where the masculine self dominates and internalises otherness, that other is frequently identified as feminine, whether she is nature, the representation of a human woman, or some phantom of desire' (p. 12).

In claiming the right of the woman to test her poetic skills in creating a different kind of transcendence, Rich refuses, in this poem, to master or to make an other of nature, or of woman as feminine. She would, rather, institute an ethic of care for the world. The edict of Genesis 1: 28: 'fill the earth and subdue it; have dominion . . . over the whole earth' – which resourced and so dominated the thought of the nineteenth century – is here re-visioned. Rich refuses to idealise nature as all good, to passivise it or to consider herself outside – above or beyond – its processes. For her, the earth is the material context 'in which she finds herself', she has only 'care for' the earth's many different and other 'unending' forms. Ambiguously, the woman seems both to be part of the earth and to be distinct from the earth, but Rich is hardly creating another fatal or beneficent Mother Nature after the Romantic models created by Wordsworth and others.

I would emphasise that the earth – the 'clear tones of the world/ manifest' – is nowhere named either in the poem or elsewhere in Rich's work, as 'mother'. Such a connection exists only in the mind of the reader. If we make this connection as readers interpreting symbolic resonances, we should recognise our responsibility in doing so. To interpret the image of the rockshelf, as Homans does, as 'the emissary from Mother Nature that prevents her from continuing both her search and her poem' (p. 229) is to contribute to the poem more than what is there.[16]

The symbol of the 'rockshelf' need not be read as 'an image of mother as nature, the cthonic feminine object whose existence as the valorised image of womanhood has impeded and continues to impede the ability of women to choose among many other things, the vocation of poet' (p. 229). Certainly to valorise the patriarchally defined feminine as object has not been helpful to women or to women poets. To valorise a re-visioned female space of subjectivity-in-relation and explore its difference from male definition is not the same thing. The image of the rockshelf can be read otherwise, and with responsibility to the political and theoretical concerns of feminism, as I hope to show through my extended analysis of this important poem.

Inspired by and criticising Romantic thought, Rich, in the final section of the 'Etude', makes an attempt to create another kind of transcendence. She creates a grounded (immanent) transcendence, 'splendid' in its celebration of an ideal utopian world (p. 4).[17] This female space apart, this vision or dream of a non-patriarchal language feelingly desired by the woman, is recollected in meditative tranquillity. The section deals with materials from the common life, treats lowly subjects in common language (a language common to women), and draws on a selection of language really used by women. Like the Romantics, she uses a poetic symbolism in which objects are charged with a significance beyond the present, beyond the merely tangible. Her solitary, unheroic, even humble, woman-in-the-kitchen (as opposed to the man of genius, the great, godlike creator, supreme source of eternal truth) engages in a very altered Romantic quest for new beginnings.

Like the Romantics, Rich does in this poem nurture desires – aspirations beyond the limits of human possibility. The poet's imagination/vision/dream is of a mythic world of rustic simplicity in which the woman exists in a space apart from the hit-and-run motorist, the argument and jargon that signifies the violence, competitiveness and combativeness of macho-modes of relating to the world. In that sense, the poem is decidedly an abstraction from life-as-it-is. The poet, speaking in the prophetic mode of the visionary, transcends time and space without, however, transcending gender, her passionate desires for 'transcendence' of the real being defined in terms of caring for, rather than egocentrically dominating the world. At the same time, she never loses her sense of connection to the world of time, space and materiality. There are few moments of sublime transcendence of the patriarchally given in Rich's work overall: perhaps her 'Floating Poem' is another such moment. And in my view these poems are poetically 'splendid' rather than 'poetically terminal'!

In my reading, Rich is not setting up a feminist poetic manifesto to be judged as such, but is, rather, concerned with a testing out of the possibilities within language of creating a feminist visionary mode that questions many of the terms given both by normative heterosexual social codes and by the Romantic poets. An étude is after all 'a composition intended either to train or to test the player's technical skill'.[18] This section constitutes an illumination of a different and experimental structure of thought, an articulation of a (female) desire for another kind of subjectivity-in-relation, in reaction to the male-defined myths and models of heterosexual high Romanticism. It implicitly criticises the lofty egocentric transcendental formulations of Romanticism through its questioning of the construction of subjectivity.

Refusing the seizing of mastery, the conflicts of power, the overarching spiritual transcendence which assumes mastery and claims the power and authority of truth typical of patriarchal Romantic forms, the woman muses 'one with her body'. She meditates, giving full recognition to her sensual bodily experience of loving relation, of connection to the m/Other, the lesbian lover – in order to pull the 'tenets' of her life together. In order carefully to 'compose' herself:

> Such a composition has nothing to do with eternity,
> the striving for greatness, brilliance –
> only with the musing of a mind
> one with her body, experienced fingers quietly pushing
> dark against bright, silk against roughness,
> pulling the tenets of a life together
> with no mere will to mastery,
> only care for the many-lived, unending
> forms in which she finds herself

The authoritarian urge to seize power, to control and master – which justifies its usurping of authority through reference to Absolute Truth, the Almighty Father God, and the deeply patriarchal, transcendent 'I', which assumes superiority over things, over nature, over woman for all time – is here displaced. It gives way to an 'I' inseparable from 'the many-lived, unending/forms in which she finds herself'. This shift entails a different conception of the 'I', one in which the distinction between the 'me' and the 'not-me' is not made: the subject–object distinction dissolves, becoming instead that of subject to subject. Human subjectivity becomes an integral part or aspect of the environment. Rather than omnisciently lording over it, an onlooker separate from and outside its process, the woman's body and the world share life-energy, are saturated with each other's meanings. The boundaries between self and other, created when the child first recognises that the mother is other to herself, no longer operate. We are the world and share responsibility for it.

This is a feminist ecological/spiritual vision comparable to but not the same as that of Susan Griffin, Rosemary Radford Reuther, and Sallie McFague, which asserts the interrelatedness and interdependence of all life. Christian feminist theologian Sallie McFague, writing much later (in 1987), articulates this vision very clearly:

The ecosystem of which we are part is a whole: the rocks and waters, atmosphere and soil, plants, animals, and human beings interact in dynamic, mutually supportive ways that make all talk of atomistic individualism indefensible. Relationship and interdependence, change and transformation, not substance, changelessness, and perfection, are the categories within which a theology for our day must function.[19]

McFague argues further that individualistic, hierarchical, dualistic, and utilitarian ways of thinking are 'destructive of life at all levels' and must be replaced. She calls for an ethic of 'responsibility and care' grounded in a logic of justice which gives due weight to the 'competing rights of other levels of life'. This ethical model may seem in some lights to be both utopian and essentialist but it has relevance to our global survival in ecological terms. In McFague's thought, this ecological vision is linked to a model of God as mother, lover and friend: her work, unlike Rich's, constitutes an attempt to remythologise the relation between God and the world. In comparison, in Rich's poetry, there is the body and the body's world – but no talk of God as mother:

> The problem is
> to connect, without hysteria, the pain
> of any one's body with the pain of the body's world
> For it is the body's world
> they are trying to destroy forever
> The best world is the body's world
> filled with creatures   filled with dread
> misshapen so   yet the best we have[20]

As the matrix out of which all life evolves, the earth in McFague's terms embodies God, just as the earth may be conceptualised as God's body. As a metaphor, this model of the earth as God's body and as mother/lover/friend, though nurturant and giving, is also to be considered as tough-minded, judging and angry, when 'bedrock justice' is denied, when the world is at risk, when militarism, poverty, and discrimination are allowed to continue. In Rich's 'Etude', this astute, critical, judging aspect seems to me to be symbolised in the image of 'broken glass/slicing light in a corner, dangerous to flesh'. As with the judging and angry 'terrible mothers' of her poem 'Hunger', women's powerful 'love' for the world can be frighteningly destructive:

> We shrink from touching
> our power, we shrink away, we starve ourselves
> and each other, we're scared shitless
> of what it could be to take and use our love,
> hose it on a city, on a world,
> to wield and guide its spray, destroying
> poisons, parasites, rats, viruses –
> like the terrible mothers we long and dread to be.[21]

Cora Kaplan also condemns Rich for what she sees as an essentialist slippage 'from bad culture back to good nature'.[22] In 'Hunger', as in her 'Tracking Poems', the world of nature is depicted as far from benificent, all-providing. A poisoned and polluted nature will result in the famines, drought, parasites, rats, viruses which threaten Chad, Niger, the Upper Volta. A male god 'that acts on us and on our children', and a male state that ignores people's suffering and fails to take 'the decision to feed the world' has to carry the responsibility – responsibility for both inaction and for those acts of exploitation which, in their effects, function to sustain malnutrition and continue to engender the manifold deprivations of poverty. But Rich is also very aware that assimilated women are just as capable of being producers of culture and of acting destructively. Her discussion of the 'first American woman astronaut' in her 'Notes Towards a Politics of Location' stresses that the woman astronaut has 'no questions about the poisoning and impoverishment of women here on earth or of the earth itself. Women, too, may leave the earth behind.'[23] Women are not fundamentally and naturally good nor are they intrinsically morally right in Rich's thought.

Cora Kaplan's critique condemns Rich for what she sees as her biological determinism, and the essentialism of depicting nature in female terms. In Rich's work, according to Kaplan, 'Benign nature is female – affectionate and sensual as well as creative, revolutionary and transcendent. In its political inflection it opposes an innately vicious male nature whose ascendency has produced the bad dream of phallocratic culture.'[24] As we have seen, there are problems with this fundamentally dualist critique: in Rich's work nature is not necessarily benign; both women themselves and women's 'love' can be destructive in different ways. Nor does Kaplan's principled criticism give due weight to Rich's acknowledgement of the debt she owes to male poets, teachers and writers, especially Yeats, Francis Otto Matthiessen, James Baldwin, W. E. Du Bois: all men are not 'innately vicious' because they are biologically male, in the overall trajectory of Rich's thought.

It is important to stress that Rich's writing, developing and exploring in its many inflections over time, cannot and should not be frozen at one specific moment. Self-critical as ever, in 1986, the same year as Kaplan's book was published, Rich uses this quotation from Cynthia Enloe to clarify her position regarding men:

> *An approach which traces militarism back to patriarchy and patriarchy back to the fundamental quality of maleness can be demoralising and even paralyzing . . . . Perhaps it is possible to be less fixed on the discovery of 'original causes'. It might be more useful to ask, How do these values and behaviors get repeated generation after generation?* [25]

Very aware of the dangers of biological determinism, she has also never considered herself to be a separatist:

> At no time have I ever defined myself as, or considered myself, a lesbian separatist. I have worked with self-defined separatists and have recognised the importance of separatism as grounding and strategy. I have opposed it as a pressure to conformity and where it seemed to derive from biological determinism. [26]

To condemn Rich's work on these grounds is also to deny the metaphorical complexity of Rich's holistic textual strategies. It is worth spending some time looking further at interesting experimental passages from the 'Etude' in order to appreciate its linguistic daring. Returning again to the final moments of the poem, we find a complex metaphoric chain which depicts the woman/mother as gradually 'becoming' that which is other to her. She is engaged in a transformational process, continuous, unending – a process that is enacted not only metaphorically, but also through syntactic and verbal structures. Parallel forms, continuous tenses and lengthy, constantly extended sentences all enact that on-going 'becoming' process. This metamorphosis is located temporally as existing in the present time, the 'now' of the immediate moment:

> becoming *now* the sherd of broken glass
> *now* the plentiful, soft leaf
> *now* the stone foundation

Paradoxically, this emphasis on the continuous present conveyed by '*now*', and the repeated use of indicative verbs that carry the momentum of unfinished action (slicing, soothes, finds, becoming, forming) effectively transposes the reader to the mystic time-space of the eternal present. In its verbal structures the poetry joins cause to effect, space with time, materiality and spirituality in a paradoxical whirl of metaphoric possibility:

> becoming now the sherd of broken glass
> slicing light in a corner, dangerous
> to flesh, now the plentiful, soft leaf
> that wrapped round the throbbing finger, soothes the wound

The broken splintered 'woman' is figuratively transformed into an object, 'the sherd of broken glass' – an object which is, in the structures of this poetic language, endowed with the power of action (it/she?/he? aggressively *slices* light). It is actively dangerous to the flesh, the acted-on body (of the passive woman? of the male? of human flesh generally?). This 'flesh' transforms itself again to become the leaf which is 'plentiful, soft' – generous words which resonate with the sensuality of the woman's body, its nurturing, receiving quality. This 'leaf' will heal, will dress the wounds. Rich's dynamic metaphors can be shown as playing ambiguously through and across the terms of dualistic opposition – challenging the constitution, disorganising boundaries, rendering incoherent, chaotic, the ordering of Absolutes under the Law of the Father/God. Nature is no longer opposed to culture, passive to active, inertia to transformation, stasis to flux, rationality to non-sense: each exists simultaneously without negating the terms of its opposition. Rich has clearly engaged very deeply with the question of whether a female poetic language is possible, but should Rich's work be read in relation to French feminist ideas around *écriture féminine*? The parallel effort to write the body into language is clearly evident.

For a woman poet to find her own coherences, of identity as of meaning, she must move 'very close to the voice, very close to the flesh of language'.[27] The rhythmic parallel forms, the networks of alliteration that form the texture of this language, the intonations, the cadences – personal, intense, emotional – all these work across the linearity of these clausal sequences, opening up the possibility of allowing the instinctual body to shortcircuit rational, unemotional objectivity. Judicious use of line-breaks, of dovetailing which allows phrases to agree in different ways, encourages further ambiguity and play. All this surreptitiously undermines the singularity of reasonable meaning. Hélène Cixous suggests that women writers –

> don't rush into meaning, but are straightway at the threshold of feeling. There's *tactility* in the feminine text, there's touch, and this touch passes through the ear. Writing in the feminine is passing on what is cut out by the Symbolic, the voice of the mother, passing on what is most archaic. The most archaic force that touches a body is one that enters by the ear and reaches the most intimate point. This innermost touch always echoes in a woman-text. So the movement, the movement of the text, doesn't trace a straight line. I see it as an outpouring.
>
> (p. 54)

Suffused throughout this section is the quiet joy, the sensuality, the emotional connection to the mother 'singing a child/against her heart'. The poet *becomes* the mother whose musicality, interwoven textures of alliteration, pulsing intonations and 'throbbing' rhythms are closest to the flesh, whose touching tendernesses powerfully release the instinctual body – 'passing on what is most archaic'. The polymorphous multiplicity of the pre-Oedipal returns and returns.

As I have mentioned, the poet chooses to locate the action in traditionally female space, in the only place of power freely given to women that could be shared by the 'spirit sisters' of the past – the kitchen – a place heavy with historical resonances and evoking memories of all our mothers. Here, Rich reminds us that the institutions of motherhood have never been symbolically embodied in architectural form as have the institutions of the patriarchy:

Motherhood calls to mind the home, and we like to believe

145

that the home is a private place. Perhaps we imagine row upon row of backyards, behind suburban or tenement houses, in each of which a woman hangs out the wash, or runs to pick up a tear-streaked two-year-old; or thousands of kitchens, in each of which children are being fed and sent off to school. Or we think of the house of our childhood, the woman who mothered us, or of ourselves.[28]

I have this passage very much in mind as I read for it permits me to comprehend what resonances the idea of the kitchen may have had for Rich – since my own associations lead me to resist such a return! A patriarchal place traditionally assigned to women of almost all classes, races, creeds – and yet also a maternal space where a woman/mother may (rather than engaging in kitchen duties) subversively compose her 'whole new poetry' – where a woman

> sitting down in the kitchen, began turning in her lap
> bits of yarn, calico and velvet scraps,
> laying them out absently on the scrubbed boards
> in the lamplight, with small rainbow-colored shells
> sent in cotton-wool from somewhere far away,
> and skeins of milkweed from the nearest meadow –
> original domestic silk, the finest findings –
> and the darkblue petal of the petunia,
> and the dry darkbrown lace of seaweed;
> not forgotten either, the shed silver
> whisker of the cat

Jan Montefiore draws attention to the resonating echoes of H.D.'s poetry in a similar passage from Rich's poem 'Natural Resources':

> These things by women saved
> are all we have of them
> . . .
>
> these scraps, turned into patchwork,
> doll-gowns, clean white rags
>
> for stanching blood
> the bride's tea-yellow handkerchief [29]

146

She notes that 'this contemplation of apparently valueless objects recalls the visionary beginning of "The Walls Do Not Fall" '.[30] In H.D.'s contemplative vision of houses smashed by the Blitz 'poor utensils show/ like rare objects in a museum' - trivial objects become invested with a significance far beyond their material value.[31] In Montefiore's words: 'What ignorance would dismiss as rubbish, Rich's poem values as precious relics of a female history otherwise obliterated, and "without these . . . no purpose for the future/ no honour to the past".'[32]

Rich too enters the space of the visionary. She depicts a meditative ritual, in which material objects are 'turned' in the woman's 'lap'. They are precious objects, yet are homely domestic items to be felt, touched, gazed at. The charm of their appeal is to the sensual body, to the symbolic realm of the unconscious - to our dream of history, to the archaic memory, to the maternal imprint. This invocation, resonant with historical nuance, acts as a bridge that connects the past to the present experience of women, the mother to the daughter. The yarn, calico, scrubbed boards, lamplight, original domestic silk: items, words, voices from women's past lives here contribute to the textures of today's language. Time-laden words - generating women's timeless activities - are interwoven into the sentence, calling up the past into the 'now' of women's ever-constituting consciousness. The accumulations of this long sentence, having many of its clauses and phrases linked by 'and', are strung together like a list, in non-sequential combination - in a childlike use of syntactical forms. The syntax here functions like a matrix, a safe maternal matrix which allows the play of consciousness to range back and forth, again childlike - conveying a sense of reverence and delight: feel this one, touch that, look at this, and this . . .

Overall, in Rich's invocation of the maternal ground, the tactility of the voice, the melody of speech in the ear, the mother's touch resonating intimately through and across the poem, produces at times a whispering sibilance full of longing. This is echoed by the chiming of suggestively physical alliterative and assonantal rhyme patterns. Potent syllables carry the charge of her body's rhythmic energy: the movement of breath, tongue, lips. These pulsing kinaesthetic patterns form interconnecting pathways of rhythm, rhyme and sound: lap, scraps, scrubbed, skeins, silk, small, shells, sent. Unobtrusive connections as well as more obvious parallel repetitions, disturb the linearity of the syntax:

> and the darkblue petal of the petunia,
> and the dry darkbrown lace of seaweed;

This pattern of plosives p t k b d particularly involves the tongue and lips, damming back the breath, then releasing it, slowing down the movement of sound. There is a rich consonantal texturing that is softened by liquid l's, r's, n's and m's: strength and tenderness, tension and release – creating a mood that is caring, empathic, strongly protective. The attitude, of quiet reverence for creativity and life – conveyed through gentle undulations of pitch and intonation – is introspective, intuitive. Falling slow rhythms, feminine line endings, unemphatic stress-ings, and subtly restrained internal rhymes, the tonally intimate cadences of this lyric voice make this act of naming paradoxically non-assertive. It is the negative to the 'argument' and 'jargon' – the competition, dominance, authority and controlling logical directiveness – of patriarchal discourse. The absence of tonal closure at the ceasing of the list implies that it is unfinished. In this way the sacrifices and exclusions of closure are also resisted.

Things here are given equal importance to the woman through language that is expressive and open – whose focus constantly shifts between far and near, land and sea, nature and culture, wet and dry, animal and plant, bird and insect, past and present. This poetry of meditation, charmingly sung, invokes a limitless polysemic openness that generously exceeds the ratio-nal, categorical and restrictive forms of patriarchal discourse. As a written form, it works to reintegrate the split-off negatives of dualistic thinking, a project that Rich has declared important for feminism:

> Truly to liberate women, then, means to change thinking itself: to reintegrate what has been named the unconscious, the subjective, the emotional with the structural, the ratio-nal, the intellectual; to 'connect the prose and the passion' in E. M. Forster's phrase; and finally to annihilate those dichotomies.[33]

The ordering, judging, rational, logical, prose-bound intellect, the structuring of the narrative, firmly located in time and space – and the mostly linear syntax of this poem overall – are sufficiently assured to maintain the coherence necessary to sustain communication, the social identity, the agency of the 'I'. But everywhere, the transcendence of this 'I' is transgressed by the intuitive, the sensational, the *passionate*. The displacements and condensations of metaphor – of memory and myth, of symbol and image, of dream and fantasy – create an openness, an unsettling, unlimited multifocal polysemy. Open, that is, to the transgressive, passionate forces of desire. The rational self-conscious 'I' is shown as inseparable from the unconscious/ intuitive dimensions of the psyche: the secular and worldly as inseparable from the spiritual and mystic; the subjective as inseparable from the objective world – such boundaries become blurred and the dualistic polarities of the Name of the Father are no longer able to control and order the woman so absolutely, through the dominating logic of the sentence. Phallic presence becomes unsettled, its constraining, legislative, judgmental character is everywhere subverted, rendered non-masterful, non-controlling, and held perpetually in question. Rich's naming becomes a *knowing* rather than a knowledge. Authoritarian, adversarial, hierarchical modes of patriarchal thinking, the striving for detached impersonality, the exclusion of the emotions and the dissociation from the body of the objective, heterosexual, patriarchal point of view, find no place in this passionate, holistic lesbian poetry.

Little trace of the exclusive, male-God-centred presence of phallogocentrism remains. The Apollonian virtues: light, order, balance, harmony, rationality, consciousness, intellect, creativity, goodness, spirit, life – which have been seen as typically male attributes – are here found grounded in the female body, or held in the 'lap' of the mother. The word 'lap' was, in times past, used as a euphemism for the vulva or womb, for the birthplace. In the context of this poem, it may be seen as symbolising a female creative potential, a potential capable of recognising and including the dark side: the unconscious, the non-sensical, the instinctual, the sexual female body – and as acknowledging the threatening Dionysian shadows of flux, change and death. Yet, as Cixous suggests, this inspirational maternal focus invested with so much potential is but a metaphor:

The mother, too, is a metaphor. It is necessary and

sufficient that the best of herself be given to woman by another woman for her to be able to love herself and return in love the body that was 'born' to her. Touch me, caress me, you the living no-name, give me my self as myself.[34]

This metaphoric reclamation of 'my self as myself' through the body of the mother, through *the best of herself . . . given to woman by another woman,* Cixous extends to the textual body of language. It is the 'no-name' of the living (textual) body that she asks to 'touch me, caress me' – that is, that of woman which has yet to be named, the transformed and transforming 'I' of the singing female body. This body has yet to find its forms within language: 'Text: my body – shot through with . . . song' which 'urges you to inscribe in language your woman's style' (p. 252). Running through 'Transcendental Etude' are repeated references to the woman's body, her senses, her touch, her flesh. This anchorage in the woman's body, in the 'lap' of the woman is of fundamental importance to Rich's work during this period. At the very centre of her critique of patriarchy is the idea of the reclamation of the woman's body. She comments forcefully in *Of Woman Born*:

> I have come to believe, as will be clear throughout this book, that female biology – the diffuse, intense sensuality radiating out from clitoris, breasts, uterus, vagina; the lunar cycles of menstruation; the gestation and fruition of life which can take place in the female body – has far more radical implications than we have yet come to appreciate. Patriarchal thought has limited female biology to its own narrow specifications. The feminist vision has recoiled from female biology for these reasons; it will, I believe, come to view our physicality as a resource, rather than a destiny. In order to live a fully human life we require not only *control* of our bodies (though control is a prerequisite); we must touch the unity and resonance of our physicality, our bond with the natural order, the corporeal ground of our intelligence.[35]

Reclaiming the bodies of women – and the body of the woman/ text – from patriarchal colonisation in all its multiform dimensions, means also reclaiming the (psychoanalytic) metaphoric mother who stands against separation. Here, the mother/

woman/lover who is both namer and named, is also the means to 'knock the wind out of the codes': she is

> *the lover and the loved,*
> *home and wanderer, she who splits*
> *firewood and she who knocks, a stranger*
> *in the storm,* two women, eye to eye
> measuring each other's spirit, each other's
> limitless desire

The women are both lover and loved, loved and lover – both are equal subjects in relationship and yet paradoxically are one and the same: 'I am the lover and the loved'; *'home* and *wanderer, she who splits/ firewood* and *she who knocks, a stranger'* (my emphasis). Here we find echoes resonant of the intensity of the relationship between mother and child: an erotic, sensual, sexual, libidinal connection. This energy sustains the mutually fascinating gaze: the infant's eyes 'steady on the face of love' of the mother – or the gaze exchanged between the 'two women, eye to eye'. It is not clear who is the actor, who is the acted upon, the subject as opposed to the object – who is the lover, who is the loved. In the end it is subject and subject – both/and rather than either/or – they are different and they are the same. Rich, again invites the reader to enter into a limitless play of paradox which disorganises the polarities between what is known and what is not-known, between self and another self, between lover and lover, between two women gazing at each other with the liquid intensity of love.

In my reading, 'Transcendental Etude' may be seen as a mythic mirror, in which the processes of transformation and change over time can be envisaged/enacted/experienced by women as they struggle to transform phallogocentric language. The poem dramatises the woman's courageous journey towards creating a new way of writing, thinking, acting, loving. This poem enacts the mythic return to the archaic pre-Oedipal depths – to face the dragon of primordial loneliness. Getting lost in the abyss of infantile desolation, re-experiencing the agony of loss and separation from the mother, discovering the nameless chaos, the flux and formlessness of loss of identity and meaning are all aspects of this terrifying space. There, in that lonely place, the poet seeks to erase the patriarchal imprinting of the symbolic and work on the re-visionary task of reconstructing meaning in female terms. For

Rich, the pre-Oedipal is a vulnerable but a potent space of possibility, but this metaphoric 'journey of return' can only ever be mythic, can only ever symbolise the poet's 'passage through' in her struggle to transform meaning *within* the (always slowly changing) symbolic order. This poem does not therefore seek to recall in words the preverbal imaginary state.

An actual (linguistic) return to the space of the archaic imaginary (which, by definition, is an impossibility!) would produce a very different scenario – comparable to Monique Wittig's projected fantasy in *The Lesbian Body*.[36] Jan Montefiore identifies Wittig's imaginary realm as engaging with 'the earliest and most primitive Imaginary fantasies. In particular, the oral sadism (a psychoanalytic term *not* a moral criticism) which Melanie Klein identified as characteristic of primitive infantile eroticism.'[37] Wittig's book 'is full of the passion to possess and devour, of anxiety . . . and of fantasies of omnipotence'. Montefiore reminds us that 'The Imaginary mode of being is archaic, dating from a time before the castration complex, and before language was acquired – the dual event which begins the history of the human subject' (p. 177).

Rich's attempt to create a poetry in which the sexual specificity of being female and the difference of being lesbian can be articulated is far from Wittig's fantasied return to these archaic and terrifying states of undifferentiation. Unlike Wittig, whose writing can be said to 'evade' the castration complex and the idea of sexual difference, Rich's poetic invocation produces a discourse which problematises sexual and libidinal difference in order to explore the *specificities* of female desire.[38] To claim a place as female *in other terms* is to have entered (or re-entered) the realm of the symbolic order. Rich is fundamentally concerned with the task of producing identificatory images that hopefully will work to consolidate lesbian identity and provide an imaginary stability and permanence to set against lack. As Grosz reminds us: 'the ego operates within an imaginary order, an order in which it strives to see itself reflected in its relations to others.'[39] In her poetry, Rich validates alternative networks of relations with others to those given within hetero-patriarchal society, and she produces representations invested with (lesbian) libidinal energy. These images, registers, inter-personal modes, social codes are produced within the symbolic order as a rebellion against patriarchal encoding of the symbolic order and they symbolise the lesbian rejection of any predesignated social place. They are imaginary representations in which the lesbian woman may come to terms with and for herself.

The poetic task here is not one of seeking to articulate an archaic female imaginary, but of re-valuing the codes and categories within which the (lesbian) woman, aware of her biological and libidinal differences from other women and from the male, may be conceptualised and spoken *within* the symbolic. As I read her then, Rich is not attempting to re-create a female archaic imaginary as such, but is rather affirming the Irigarayan project of 'challenging and deconstructing the cultural representations of femininity so that it may be capable of representation and recognition in its own self-defined terms' (p. 101).

Whilst I agree with Montefiore that 'sexual difference is irrelevant to the Imaginary mode of being'[40] it is not irrelevant to the later manifestations of polymorphous multiplicity which break through the barriers of repression to return to language. As Elizabeth Grosz puts it: 'because repression banishes and yet preserves what it expels, the repressed is liable to return through its re-evocation in current, often chance or contingent events which recall it .... The fluidity of pre-Oedipal maternal pleasures is *always already there* in any adult sexual pleasure (men's as well as women's).'[41]

The question thus moves on from – how does a female text/ body speak its pre-text/pre-Oedipal? – to how might a transformed understanding of female or lesbian sexual difference be articulated within language? And, in terms of lesbian sexual orientation – how is the repressed energy of lesbian desire made manifest in the lesbian text? All of this effort of reconstrual implies 'a profound and difficult reorganisation of the forms and means of representation – a reorganisation of language itself' (p. 109). Recognising that patriarchal knowledge and poetic forms have been produced from a sexually specific discursive position rather than a universal one, Rich's self-consciously aware poetry produces its meanings from another point of location, from a woman-identified position within language. Writing as a lesbian-identified woman, she offers a transformed understanding of the differences between one sex and another, between one libidinal trajectory and another – and Rich seeks overall to revalue traditional conceptions of the lesbian female.

153

In conclusion, I suggest that this poem, with its complex re-visioning of high Romantic forms, presents a powerful, specifically female mythic model which seeks to displace phallogocentric structures of language. Authoritarian, trans-cendent God/Father/I-am images of domination, majesty, power and dominion which have their sources in the classical formula-tions of the Judaeo-Christian tradition, give way to an ecologi-cally aware model of a valued earth as underpinning all forms of life. Rich seeks also to restore the validity (lost in patriarchal religious and psychoanalytic formulations) of a woman living in relation to other women as mothers/sisters/daughters/lovers without anywhere suggesting that Mother Nature or any other sort of earth-mother-god exists: in no sense is such a deity called upon poetically or otherwise. I suggest also that this poem is probably better not read as a template for feminist political action as such, but rather as an experiment in writing a holistic poetry from a woman's point of view, one which refuses to exclude or condemn women's traditional skills – the historical work of women's hands – even though that work was produced within women's patriarchally allocated sphere, very often under conditions of extreme rigour.

Despite her celebration of 'the difference' in this poem, it is worth pointing out that Rich has, elsewhere, explicitly distanced herself from any belief in the quality of care as being an essentially female attribute: 'it can be dangerously simplistic to fix on "nurturance" as a special strength of women, which need only be released into the larger society to create a new human order'.[42] With this proviso in mind, we may assume that her support of a tough-minded ethic of care for the earth is not grounded in any assumption of female moral superiority, but is, rather, a call to all to place greater value on this immediately present world of relation, this world in which all of life is experienced as intrinsically dynamic, inter-dependent, and in need of protection. Far from embracing inarticulateness, Rich, like McFague, calls for both women and men to espouse an ethic of 'responsibility and care' – for past, present and future – grounded in a logic of connection which does not merely use the other as object, but gives full respect to other forms of life.[43] This ethical model is the rock upon which this poem is founded.[44]

Part IV

PRIMARY INTENSITIES:

LESBIAN POETRY AND THE READING OF DIFFERENCE

10

VALIDATING THE
LESBIAN BODY

It is, after all, always the meaning, the reading of difference
that matters, and meaning is culturally engendered and
sustained. Not to consider the body as some absolute (milk,
blood, breasts, clitoris) for no 'body' is unmediated. Not
body but the 'body' of psychosocial fabrications of differ-
ence. Or again, of sameness. Or again, of their relation.
                    Rachel Blau DuPlessis, 'For the Etruscans'[1]

In this section, I explore the re-visionary strategies of a number of
women poets who are engaged in an attempt to construct a
language which adequately re-visions the body, sexuality and
libidinal trajectory of the lesbian. Coming to terms with lesbian
sexuality involves the poets in the political effort of devising a
pro-visional poetic strategy – as a means to make explicit what
has been excluded from patriarchal discourses. This rethinking
requires a major reorganisation of sexual, linguistic and socio-
symbolic systems, and in addition requires theorising the female
body as a positivity rather than a lack. I will draw on Elizabeth
Grosz's Irigarayan conceptualisations of the body as

> structured, inscribed, constituted and given meaning
> *socially* and *historically* – a body that exists as such only
> through its socio-linguistic construction. She [Irigaray]
> renders the concept of a 'pure' or 'natural' body meaning-
> less. Power relations and systems of representations not
> only traverse the body and utilise its energies (as Kristeva
> claims) but actively constitute the body's very sensations,
> pleasures – the phenomenology of bodily experience.[2]

Recoding the lesbian body involves the poets in a strategic and
transgressive effort to put in place new representations within

language. Their effort is frequently directed towards countering the negative terms of Freudian and Lacanian accounts of the formation of a gendered identity. If gendered identity is not necessarily 'the result of biology, but of the *social and psychical meaning of the body*', then the way is open to reconceive of lesbian sexuality in terms other than the patriarchally given. Rather than seeing the poems as encoding a language of authentic female being, I analyse the fabrication of meaning that takes place within the mythical body of a number of women's poems.

The language of poetry especially lends itself to the lesbian feminist poet's strategic and combative project, that is, the critique and revaluation of the coding of lesbian sexuality from different perspectives and locations within culture. Politically motivated lesbian poetry is interested in displacing inherited male models and myths through both a recoding of the relations between the self and 'the other' and a positive revaluing of a female body whose sexuality is lived *in other terms*. A poetry not necessarily concerned with the 'exclusion' of men as such, but rather, in Rich's words, with 'that *primary presence of women to ourselves and each other* first described in prose by Mary Daly, and which is the crucible of a new language'.[3]

As well as breaking through the cultural taboo against the depiction of an affirming lesbian sexuality in art, these poems render historically visible *reconstructed representations* which endeavour to treat the primary intensity of lesbian eroticism with respect and reverence. In effect, the poems offer a position for the lesbian woman subject with which it is possible, in delight and/or in anguish, to identify. The poet constructs a position or positions within language which offer lesbian women self-validating experiences. I see this poetry as offering a lesbian reader the validating experience of being able to recognise and realise her own position (or that of other women) *as an identity* in and through language. Again, I use the term 'identity' in this special sense: identity is to be viewed as a desired position for the subject, constructed here so as to legitimate and validate particular lesbian viewpoints.

The poems included in this section are chosen because they offer a legitimating, cleansing, recuperative version of lesbian erotic life and its corresponding dimensions of joy and loss. Crucially, they embody a refusal to collaborate with the coercive, almost palpable, interlocking construct of heterosexual ideology,

158

language and law which would deny and/or misrepresent the wholesome validity of the lesbian trajectory of desire, and attempt to delegitimate and harrass the lesbian subject.

Both black and white lesbian feminist poets, writing from a position of otherness, as from a different psychic economy, have strongly responded to the call, first voiced by Daly and Rich, to restructure language. The poets have especially tried to reorder the heterosexual codes that structure sexual difference – often in terms that are potentially disruptive to the social contract. Diana Collecott has spoken of the 'shared sense of difference' as well as of a 'sameness' between black and white lesbians.[4] Exploring her understanding of Audre Lorde's *Zami*, she suggests that ' "difference" is a sign of otherness that can be shared. Thus difference of colour may unite Black Women of different sexual orientation, while another difference unites lovers of the same sex.' Collecott, in speaking of this 'paradoxical sense of sameness within alienation', highlights for me the commonality of otherness shared by lesbians and black lesbians. Despite a different history, a different culture, these poets share a similarly marginalised libidinal economy.

In the transformed terms of the libidinal economy proposed/ experienced by lesbian poets, it is often and precisely the genital anatomical difference from the male which is celebrated and desired as an empowering source of pleasure, rather than being reviled as 'castrated'. In their diverse attempts to counter patriarchal heterosexual cultural codes, they have frequently tried to make real the possibility for a woman to keep in consciousness her deepest attachments to the mother, and have celebrated and mourned this attachment in the transformed and transforming context of one woman's love for another.

For women living within western patriarchy, this transformation requires women to undertake a difficult emotional and intellectual journey. In Olga Broumas' poem, 'Snow White', the only passions that the grandmother, mother, and daughter of this poem are 'permitted' to know in the symbolic 'marriage bed' of the heterosexual nuclear family, are those of mutual antagonism:

Later we fought so
bitterly through the peace
that father blanched in his uniform,
battlelined forehead milky
beneath the khaki brim.

We fought like mad–
women till the house–
hold shuddered, crockery fell, the bed–
clothes heaved in the only passion
they were, those maddening
peacetime years,
to know.[5]

In waking from an 'unspeakable dream' in which the mother and
daughter seem to be coming to terms with the break-up of the
daughter's marriage, the daughter strives to overcome the patri-
archal division between women and pleads for the mother's
acceptance: 'Receive/ me, Mother.' The daughter's desire is
depicted as a desire to return to the earlier, unconditional, pre-
Oedipal love bond with the mother:

> Defenceless
> and naked as the day
> I slid from you
> twin voices keening and the cord
> pulsing our common protest, I'm coming back
> back to you
> woman, flesh
> of your woman's flesh, your fairest, most
> faithful mirror,
>   my love
> transversing me like a filament
> wired to the noonday sun.
>
> Receive
> me, Mother.

Recalling the nakedness and vulnerability of the moments of
birth, the daughter affirms her sense of identification with the
mother; she names her mother's oppression and pain as like her
own, and their voices are presented as inseparable: they become
'twin voices keening'. The daughter reaffirms the link with her
mother (and all women) through the image, again, of the
umbilical cord – 'pulsing our common protest'. In this return,
the passionate desire of the daughter for the mother's presence
and body shows the poet again striving to recuperate the first
Other, the mother. She affirms her love and deep acceptance of

her mother by seeing herself as her 'fairest, most/ faithful mirror'. This reverses the Lacanian emphasis on the mother as the Other, making the daughter the Other for the mother.

In another poem, 'Artemis', Broumas addresses the problem of finding words and language to represent lesbian (sexual) bodily specificity and her different libidinal economy. 'Artemis' is one of a series of poems and paintings which were exhibited at the Maud Kerns Gallery, Oregon, entitled 'The Twelve Aspects of God'.[6] In many of the poems of this sequence, God herself is represented as at one with the woman's spiritual, physical (erotic) body. Broumas draws her inspiration from an (excised) pre-Christian mythology, re-creating it in terms that set it outside heterosexual patriarchal forms.

According to Broumas, Artemis was a deity traditionally sexually 'free' (from phallocentric organisation of her desire?). She tells us her virginity 'signified absence of matrimony, not chastity'.[7] A goddess, then, whose body escapes those 'psycho-social fabrications of difference'[8] that are inscribed within the logic of patriarchal language.

> Let's not have tea. White wine
> eases the mind along
> the slopes
> of the faithful body, helps
>
> any memory once engraved
> on the twin
> chromosome ribbons, emerge, tentative
> from the archaeology of an excised past.[9]

In these seductive opening lines, apparently addressed to her lesbian lover, the poet, at another level, also invites the presumed lesbian reader to participate. She invites her lover (and her reader!) to share (ceremonial?) 'white wine' with her – rather than the less intoxicating 'tea' – as an 'easing' agent, perhaps to inspire the spiritual and physical/erotic mind in the same reverent way that wine was used in ancient Greek cultures. The speaker/poet invites participation in her 'work' or craft: the task – to work in silver 'what tiny fragments/ survive' of the language of the body. Her desire, her effort is to re-collect the overwritten traces of an 'arkhe-logos' (ancient speech) locked within the body.[10]

Broumas' own childhood years were spent in Greece: she arrived in America as an immigrant, in 1967. We cannot know if this retrieval is also part of the poet's desire to re-invent the 'excised' language of her own mother-tongue, or her own cultural roots, or her own 'beginnings'. I see her project as comparable to the effort of invention described by Luce Irigaray in the following passage:

> If we don't invent a language, if we don't find our body's language, its gestures will be too few to accompany our story . . . . Continue, don't run out of breath. Your body is not the same today as yesterday. Your body remembers. *You* don't need to remember, to store up yesterday like capital in your head. Your memory? Your body reveals yesterday in what it wants today.[11]

Irigaray, like the poet/speaker, invites women to recognise the past in what the body 'wants today' – emerging from the biological (pre-Oedipal? pre-historical? genetic? cultural?) *memory* the poet finds a plurally meaningful inscription traced 'along/the slopes/of the faithful body'. I have suggested that Olga Broumas draws her inspiration from long suppressed Greek pagan mythologies. These speak of the Amazon moon-goddess, Artemis, known in ancient times as Mother of Creatures, as a Virgin Huntress. The poet's impulse to re-collect this 'excised past' also sets in motion a search for a particular forgotten 'significance' of the sexual body – one that 'defies decoding', but is, none the less, a significance that, the speaker claims, 'stirs in me':

>   I work
> in silver the tongue-like forms
> that curve round a throat
>
> an arm-pit, the upper
> thigh, whose significance stirs in me
> like a curviform alphabet
> that defies
>
> decoding, appears
> to consist of vowels, beginning with O, the O–
> mega, horseshoe, the cave of sound.
> What tiny fragments
> survive, mangled into our language

This significant 'memory', tentatively emerging, 'appears/ to consist of vowels, beginning with O'. The important symbol 'O' separates the stanzas of many poems, and the sectional arrangements of the book, as well as forming part of the title. Its meaning seems to me manifold. If we pursue the significance of this 'O' in patriarchal terms – as a sign for the female genital as a hole, a void, an empty space waiting to be filled – then we will be unpleasantly reminded of 'The Story of O', much discussed in radical feminist writings as an 'emblem of pornographic culture'.[12] This story relates how the ultimate victim O, whose orifice is continuously open to penetration, is pornographically and violently reduced to nothingness – how she is gradually schooled out of all knowledge of her bodily responses, and brought to the Omega of non-existence as degraded sexual object of male desire. In patriarchal terms, then, O is a metaphor for the utter negation of a woman's bodily integrity, for the psychic and bodily castration of the female, *'the horror of nothing to see'*.[13] The woman's body is encoded into a system derived from the pornographic scenario and ordered by dominant male patterns of desire. Irigaray asks –

> How can we speak to escape their enclosures, patterns, distinctions and oppositions: virginal/deflowered, pure/ impure, innocent/knowing . . . . How can we shake off the chains of these terms, free ourselves from their categories, divest ourselves of their names? Disengage ourselves *alive*, from their concepts?[14]

This speaker's stated commitment is to a 'methodology' that can 'transliterate' (or write in letters of another alphabet) an alternative poetic vision in which the desired 'suddenly possible shifts of meaning' may happen. Irigaray again, this time from *This Sex Which Is Not One*:

> As Freud admits, the beginnings of the sexual life of a girl child are so 'obscure', so 'faded with time', that one would have to dig down very deep indeed to discover beneath the traces of this civilisation, of this history, the vestiges of a more archaic civilisation that might give some clue to woman's sexuality. That extremely ancient civilisation would undoubtedly have a different alphabet, a different

language . . . . Woman's desire would not be expected to speak the same language as a man's; woman's desire has doubtless been submerged by the logic that has dominated the West since the time of the Greeks.[15]

Pursuing this movement between Irigaray and Broumas, and following Freud's directions, the search for the language of 'woman's desire' seems to have required Broumas to dig beneath 'the traces of this civilisation' for the earlier tracings of the Greeks. In the poem, symbolic references to the Greek culture, to the first and last letters of the Greek alphabet, the Alpha and the Omega, 'the O-/ mega, horseshoe, the cave [womb?] of sound' create and centrally inform the mythic re-visionary context in which these shifts might occur. According to Barbara G. Walker:

> Greeks assigned the yonic shape to the last letter of their sacred alphabet, Omega, literally, 'Great Om', the Word of Creation beginning the next cycle of becoming. The implication of the horseshoe symbol was that, having entered the yonic Door at the end of life (Omega), man would be reborn as a new child (Alpha) through the same Door.[16]

Broumas' transliterative strategy, then, involves the putting in place of new, tentative, somewhat uncertain representations in a transposed cultural and temporal setting. She fabricates a new code of representation in which the women's sexual difference may be symbolised, their desire articulated.

In her visionary relocation of the poem's socio-cultural and temporal situation, the poet also transposes its signifying field to a (selectively retrieved) world of Greek religious mythology. In this context it becomes possible/plausible to open up a different hieratic frame of reference in which the organising metaphor – the Ω, the Omega, the O – figuratively displaces or shifts the all too familiar metaphors of phallocentric pornography. The 'curviform' or 'yonic' letter, as key signifier displacing the phallus, takes the specific form or shape of the female body – in this context, imbued with the revered qualities of the circular; the cyclical; the open. The poet creates metaphors of/for the woman's body that open up the potential for a regenerative, labyrinthine and infinitely meaningful play of significance around the simulacrum or mental image of the Ω. This erotic field, having the Ω as locus of libidinal significance, in effect

164

displaces the negatory namings of phallocratic logic. Omega, the end, could become a new beginning, in that it may work towards engendering a female symbolic which sustains positive significances of the female libidinal and anatomical difference from the male.

Positive symbolisation of vulval or uterine imagery may indeed play a useful part in the construction of a new symbolic. Such symbolisation could work to affirm/encode the woman as having weight, substance and value in her sexual body, and thus strongly counter the discouraging effects of names called in contemptuous intimidation. These transformed codes for representing the woman's body may also play a part in reorganising the category and identity of the lesbian or bi-sexual woman, and the heterosexual woman, influencing in a complex way what identifications and disidentifications she may make.[17] Since the *woman-identified woman* is not, necessarily, lesbian, this crucial re-visionary strategy could open up a very different semantic, cognitive and symbolic space for representing all women:

> It is by writing, from and toward women, and by taking up the challenge of speech which has been governed by the phallus, that women will confirm women in a place other than that which is reserved in and by the symbolic, that is, in a place other than silence.[18]

This emphasis, fundamental to a number of French feminist theoretical, critical and poetic writers – as well as at the heart of American lesbian feminist political practice during the seventies and eighties – is articulated clearly, here, by Cixous. The *woman-identified woman* – whom I see as the woman who looks to the words of other women for meanings in which to identify her own position – does so out of her desire to know how to be, or not to be (for the daughter may define herself in opposition to the mother), what the m/Other desires. Yet, important as it is to show the direction of the woman's libidinal economy, perhaps it is even more important to reclaim the processes of writing and theorising the female body as a positivity rather than a lack. I see this as a crucial strategy for a lesbian poetics.

11

'WITHIN THE FOLD OF PURPLE'
H.D.'s argument with Freud

And on the other hand, when he said, *she is perfect*, he meant not only that the little bronze statue was a perfect symbol, made in man's image (in woman's, as it happened), to be venerated as a projection of abstract thought, Pallas Athené, born without human or even without divine mother, sprung full-armed from the head of her father, our-father, Zeus, Theus, or God; he meant as well, this little piece of metal you hold in your hand (look at it) is priceless really, it is *perfect*, a prize.

H.D., *Tribute to Freud*

I think of the words of Sappho as these colors, or states rather, transcending color yet containing (as great heat the compass of the spectrum) all color. And perhaps the most obvious is this rose color, merging to richer shades of scarlet, purple or Phoenician purple.

H.D., *Notes on Thought and Vision*[1]

Lesbian or bi-sexual poets, writing from a position of extreme marginality, as well as from a specific libidinal economy, locate themselves and are located as antagonistic to the cultural symbolic. In destabilising the ordering of patriarchally gendered codes, their words can be seen as already engaged in the work of creating a new symbolic. In tracing this re-visionary trajectory in women's poetry, I want to consider an important poem of H.D.'s, much discussed by feminist critics, entitled 'The Master', which was written in 1933-34 (*CP* pp. 451-461). It seems to me that this poem, which H.D. withheld from publication fearing that her analysis with 'Professor' Freud might be jeopardised, engages directly with the fundamental issue of the representation of the woman's body within the symbolic - which, as DuPlessis

166

reminds us, is 'not body but the "body" of psychosocial fabrications of difference'.[2]

Rachel Blau DuPlessis and Susan Friedman introduce 'The Master' as a poem in which H.D.'s differences from Professor Freud 'are precisely and frankly the subject'.[3] The title of their article, a phrase from the poem, encapsulates H.D.'s angry poetic counter-proposal to the scientific Freud, 'with his talk of the man-strength' (*CP* p. 455). In encoding her reactive and oppositional stance, H.D. constructs her 'emblematic proposition': woman is not to be named as castrated, deficient, without a penis (p. 420). Rather, the poet asserts: *'woman is perfect'*.

I was angry with the old man
with his talk of the man-strength,
I was angry with his mystery, his mysteries,
I argued till day-break;

O, it was late,
and God will forgive me, my anger,
but I could not accept it.

I could not accept from wisdom
what love taught,
woman is perfect.

(*CP* p. 455)

Claire Buck, in her article 'Freud and H.D. – bisexuality and a feminine discourse', takes DuPlessis and Friedman to task for assuming the autobiographical nature of 'The Master' and for reading the text as 'basically revelatory of the writer's psyche': they see the text as 'self-disclosure'; they slide from text to 'real author' and assume an identity free of division.[4] Buck raises the all-important question of the relationship of the text to the production/construction of sexual difference. She criticises Friedman and DuPlessis for their adoption of the idea of 'a feminine language' which suggests that 'H.D. was able to "translate" Freud's negative terms into a powerful feminine language of affirmation based on the female body and sexuality as "complete" ' (p. 58).

It will be evident that my interpretive strategy compels me towards a significantly different reading. Rather than looking for an author anterior to the text, or to the woman's real 'essential' body (for the body is always already mediated), or to some fantasied feminine language or to some imaginary register prior to culture – I seek to explore its trajectory *posterior to the writing*, recognising that this writing is open to endless reinterpretation by successive readers. Whilst the written text will continually displace and defer meaning, meaning and identity are not, absolutely, dispensed with . . . rather, they are endlessly re-created out of the plurality and polyvalency of the text. Thus the text can never give us access to the real exchange between Freud and H.D., or disclose the real author to us. It is possible, however, to indicate how H.D. did construct the text: we can also fruitfully explore the forms, the metaphors, and the symbolic mediations employed by H.D., *as readers*. But Buck does ask crucial questions for any study concerned with the revaluation of the terms instituting sexual difference.

In raising the problem of 'how a language premised on female inferiority can be simply countered by the erection within it of an image of woman's perfection', Buck points to castration as universally instituting sexual division, as a necessary aspect of entry into the symbolic (p. 59). She notes particularly the difficulties encountered by Friedman and DuPlessis in theorising bi-sexuality, arguing that H.D.'s project is, rather, 'founded on an imaginary self-reflexiveness dependent on the erection of the female self as phallus' (p. 62). Buck follows the master, Lacan, closely, even dutifully, in asserting that in H.D.'s poem the female body has 'become phallicised as a result of the disavowal of castration rather than being able to achieve a powerful female sexuality' (p. 63). But this poem and this phallus may be read differently, as I hope to show.

Castration in the Freudian sense is a foundational term: Mitchell says that Freud 'made it the focal point of the acquisition of culture; it operates as a law whereby men and women assume their humanity and, inextricably bound up with this, it gives the human meaning of the distinction between the sexes'.[5] This nexus of events in the child's life, which psychoanalysis has chosen to call the castration complex, is considered unavoidable if a child is to become a sexed speaking participant in culture. During this process of identity formation, the child must repudiate the mother as love object and participate in the cultural prohibitions of the Law of the Father in order to take up a speaking position independent of her. In effect, the girl child does take up a symbolically castrated position in that she is deprived of the power that is automatically authorised within hetero-patriarchy to possessors of the male organ, the penis – a power that is symbolised by that content nebula, the phallus (which, it must be stressed, has no given signified.) Castration for the girl child within patriarchal systems involves a giving up, a sacrifice of the mother, but, unlike the male child, she is designated a less powerful, more passive, more marginal position in relation to the symbolic – and assigned to be more an object of desire for men than a desiring subject in her own right.

The symbolic phallus is crucially implicated in the organisa-tion of sexual difference in that it becomes the 'differential mark of sexual identification (boy or girl, having or not having the phallus)'.[6] Like the symbolic term castration, it is a term which is socially produced within the systems of definition of psycho-analysis. Jacqueline Rose reminds us that possessing or not possessing the phallus

> means not that anatomical difference *is* sexual difference, (the one as strictly deducible from the other), but that anatomical difference comes to *figure* sexual difference, that is, it becomes the sole representative of what that difference is allowed to be. It thus covers over the complexity of the child's early sexual life with a crude opposition in which that very complexity is refused or repressed. The phallus thus indicates the reduction of difference to an instance of visible perception, a *seeming* value.
>
> (p. 42)

Lacan's valorisation of what is visible or not visible, his division of the sexes on the basis of an assessment of the male organ as present or not present, in its effect privileges the male body as phallic and names the female body as minus the phallus. The differences between male and female genitals in his thought become spoken in terms of the positive presence of the phallus as opposed to its negative absence – in a dualist hypothesis that is constructed entirely in male-centred oppositional terms. Vagina, clitoris, vulva, womb, breasts, all that which constitutes women's sexual difference from men in the real (and which could have been described in contrary rather than oppositional terms) becomes effaced, defined negatively as an absence. This con-stitutes an astonishing disavowal entirely consistent with his theories: it is a studied denial in that he steadfastly refuses, like the little boy, to believe in what is manifestly there, or to acknowledge the sexual differences of the real body. Lacan seems to be bound up in his own socially and politically motivated fantasy, when he gives this explanation for choosing to use the phallus as a symbolic term:

> The phallus is the privileged signifier of that mark where the share of the logos is wedded to the advent of desire. One might say that this signifier is chosen as what stands out as most easily seized upon in the real of sexual copulation, and also as the most symbolic in the literal (typographical) sense of the term, since it is the equivalent in that relation of the (logical) copula. One might also say that by virtue of its turgidity, it is the image of the vital flow as it is transmitted in generation.[7]

Lacan's playful (and deliberately provocative) fantasy of wedded union between desire and logos finds its metaphors of gener-ativity in the erectile, 'turgidity' (turgid: swollen, extended beyond the natural size) of the male organ, the virile, ejaculating penis. The phallus and the penis that 'stands out as most easily seized upon in the real of sexual copulation' are in this instance as conflated in Lacan's thinking as in the socio-symbolic network he describes. In constructing his position within the symbolic, and in producing a dualist logic that systematically excludes women from any kind of positive term, Lacan invests his 'vital' energy of transmission in promoting and perpetuating phallogocentric language. This passage, in which Lacan himself slips between signifier and signified, phallus and penis, can be read as a valiant symbolic effort to ward off lack. This, in effect, shields him from the vulnerability and anxiety bound up with the fear of impotence and loss. (Is this also a (self-displaying) demand to be loved for having one?) But being male and possessor of the phallus does not necessarily ensure that the other will always affirm its valorised position. I for one refuse to affirm it, for the phallus is only a signifier after all!

For those who have not got one, a similar slippage frequently occurs: women, especially the mother, seen to 'lack' the phallus, become devalued in this paradigm – hence Irigaray's ironic emphasis on the mother as a 'reviled' castrated figure. Given this slippage within the language of psychoanalysis, which occurs regardless of the real anatomical difference, it is (illusorily) assumed that what the mother lacks – owing to the 'fact' of her castration – is the real organ, the penis, which becomes confounded in the (Lacanian) imagination with the phallus as 'key signifier': she lacks power because she lacks the penis. Thus, phallocentric theory not only can assume a castrated (yet phallic) mother, constructed as subject to the determinative intrusions of the paternal symbolic (inasmuch as the penis assumes the role of the phallus) it can also, by virtue of this slippage, depict her as heterosexually subject to the penetrations of that turgid organ, the penis; and thus easily imagine her as compliant and receptive to the libidinal desires of the male. In the passage from Lacan quoted above, though she is not mentioned, the woman is implicitly there as, to borrow a phrase from Irigaray, 'a more or less obliging prop for the enactment of man's fantasies'.[8] Lacan's investments in his own (presumed superior) masculinity, his overvaluation of the phallic penis and the slippages, projections and disavowals of his position as a male theorist prevent him from recognising resistances and refusals to his masterly theory.

Lacanian psychoanalysis has traditionally presumed an already constituted heterosexual mother, and has contructed its theoretical (fading) subject out of her articulations. But what of the lesbian woman (or, even more unimaginable, the lesbian mother) whose libidinal economy is not named or is negatively named within the cultural symbolic, who experiences her self as utterly other to and different from the symbolic representations, the signifiers, of patriarchy? If representation governs the limits within which she can experience her sexual life, how is *her* specific nature 'woven by effects in which we can find the structure of language, whose material he [she] becomes' ?[9]

How, indeed, is that 'unconscious position [the symbolic phallus] without which he [she] would be unable to identify with the ideal type of his [her] sex' – constructed (p. 75)? What relation can she have to the turgid ejaculatory organ Lacan posits as privileged – that apparently tumescent, erect signifier the phallus? As we have seen, the phallus, according to Lacan, is privileged 'by virtue of its turgidity . . . is the image of the vital flow as it is transmitted in generation'. What happens then if women, having entered the symbolic, refuse the 'vital flow' of masculine Lacanian metaphors, afford little *value* to the normative, paternal law, defy the prohibition on incest and find that their pleasure lies 'elsewhere' (p. 82)? Well, Lacan can in his own terms shrug his shoulders at her heroic defiance, claiming that, yes, what she wants is to become the phallus and devote herself to her lady-friend.[10]

But it seems to me that in the case of the lesbian, this Lacanian 'phallus' is suspect. It is enigmatic and heavily veiled in mystery, for what is its role in the construction of lesbian identity? True, she must differentiate herself from her mother in order to identify her own boundaries, she must submit to the anatomical ordering that defines her as not possessing a male organ (that is, as actually possessing a female body) and in this sense must work some way through the castration complex. But her self-conscious repudiations of the orderings of the paternal symbolic disrupt the inevitability of the construction of sexual identity according to pre-ordained psychoanalytic models. We might well ask in this context: what does the lesbian (or bi-sexual) mother want – and what effect does that have on her daughter?

Indeed, we might also ask what different symbolic term is needed to institute the lesbian relation to the symbolic, in that she consciously resists the economic organisation, the political ordering, and heterosexual identity as woman, of normative phallocentric logic? Must the phallus, as signifier of her different desire, continue to act as organising intrapsychic metaphor? Must her desire remain undifferentiated, unidentified in its specificity, unquestionably bound up in the Lacanian slippages that lead as if inevitably back to the penis?

Given that the phallus/penis metonym is also bound up with the historical fact of male dominance, and continues to function within a symbolic order that is constructed and organised in the interests of men, it is surely politically necessary that this signifier as a signifier of desire should be written and thought otherwise. Women need not be thought of as not-male, they may also be thought of as positively female. As Teresa Brennan has pointed out, in its present figuration the phallus is hardly a neutral term: the male organ is valorised, masculinity is privileged, hetero-patriarchy is sustained.[11] In that some women and men do take up positions of refusal of its symbolic ordering, its specific function of assigning a position within language at times falters, even fails. Even given the biological differences between male and female, the positions taken up by men and by women within the symbolic order are many and various: histori-cally speaking, individuals have taken up positions far from those traditionally assigned to their class, sex, gender, orientation, ability or race.

It is not useful to imagine a return to pre-symbolic space, nor is it possible to remain outside the symbolic orderings of language without falling into psychosis – but it is possible to transform the terms in which such concepts as 'the phallus' are thought and spoken. As Brennan suggests, 'assuming it is true that psychosis is the alternative to the symbolic, this need not of itself be an unsurpassable obstacle, providing one can conceive of a symbolic that is not patriarchal. The real problem is that Lacan's symbolic makes patriarchy seem inevitable' (p. 3). How disturb that seeming inevitability? How construct a symbolic that is not patriarchal? How is an effective strategy for change to be imagined?

Given the feminist social and political necessity to work towards a different future, the relation between the psychic and the social undoubtedly needs to be rethought. Perhaps a valid place to begin this task is to re-symbolise 'the phallus' which is, after all,˙ simply an expedient metaphor for a complex of designations which could be differently organised socially, politically and psychically. Different social positions may be taken up; parenting practice may change; the distribution of power may be altered, authority democratised; the networks of exchange and ritual transactions, the social codes, norms and values that embody the Law of the Father do already change over time just as the language that sustains the Law is continually transforming and being transformed. Indeed, in that many objects, organs and bodies may become 'phallicised' this polyvalent term, which is both full and empty, should never be fixed in one orientation, reduced to one libidinal trajectory of desire.

In this context, Teresa Brennan's suggestion that 'Irigaray's renowned explicit attention to the female body can be read, not as a celebration of the body for its own sake, but as a psychoanalytically informed argument, intended to counter the centrality of the penis in psychical differentiation' seems to me relevant to this discussion (p. 5). As a motivated combative strategy, it strikes against the logic of privilege sustained by the terminology used by both Freud and Lacan. Luce Irigaray, in the following (auto-erotic?) passage, strives to articulate a post-dualist, post-patriarchal ideal relation between women: it should be noted that this

173

proposed interdependent relation between woman and woman strives to be convention-free, balanced, reciprocal: embodied subject and embodied subject in a relationship in which neither is consigned to the negative pole or excluded as other to the self.

I love you: our two lips cannot part to let *one* word pass. One single word that would say 'you' or 'me'. Or, 'equals': she who loves, she who is loved. Open or closed, for one never excludes the other, our lips say that both love each other. Together.

Let's be neither husband nor wife, do without the family, without roles, functions, and their laws of reproduction. I love you: your body, here, there, now. I/you touch you/me; it's quite enough for us to feel alive.[12]

Speaking of a similar passage from Irigaray, Jan Montefiore has stressed that 'this metaphor of "two lips" is *not* a definition of women's identity in biological terms: the statement that they are "continually interchanging" must make it clear that Irigaray is not talking about literal biology'.[13] Similarly, the metaphor of the two lips as a different symbolic term (replacing the terminology and meaning of the phallus in theory, rather than intrapsychically) is not derived from the female body as such, but is a discursive construction within language: vulval lips do not literally 'speak'! This has to be acknowledged as a mediated relation to the body as metaphor. We are not nostalgically returned to the polymorphously perverse world of the child 'in which the erogenous zones would lie waiting to be regrouped under the primacy of the phallus'.[14] Rather, we are located in a world of future becoming – not of let's remember or let's pretend but of let's be, let's do, in and through the articulations of our lives, and through exploring the polysemic, unlimited possibilities of being a woman in relation to other women. We enter the world of myth – as of strategy – in a newly symbolised space using the potential within the symbolic itself to construct a location outside the social codes and mechanisms of control of the patriarchal symbolic.

Irigaray presents a mythic world in which women may love and embrace each other in a multivalent movement of lips touching, a being in touch, in which both are radically open to each other's (possibly painful) difference. She constructs a different discursive field as a representational challenge not only to the symbolic coding of the phallus, but also to the coding of socio-economic organisation, heterosexual power relations, and the codified ordering of intersubjective relations. Not an imaginary world as such, though the repressed (of the unconscious, as of theory) is always likely to break through – but a world deliber-ately constructed according to the necessities of her political strategy, 'an ambitious project' which Margaret Whitford sees as 'to dismantle from within the foundations of western meta-physics'.[15] In her fine critique which addresses itself to the task of 'Rereading Irigaray', Whitford comments: 'I take her to be talking about feminine specificity at the level of the symbolic, or representation . . . my view is that, in everything she has written, she has been addressing herself to the symbolic and not to the innate' (p. 114).

This Irigarayan strategy is very relevant to the concerns of a lesbian or bi-sexual poetic committed to the work of re-vision. To attempt to replace or revalue the phallic metaphor at the level of the text, and to disrupt the codes and categories in which lesbian sexual relations are thought and spoken – as to expose the underside of Lacanian theories – is a comparable 'ambitious' project. Though this effort may not transform already established unconscious intrapsychic patterns wherein the Power of the Father to 'castrate' may go unchallenged, who can tell what a new figuration of the phallus, what a new logic of difference will do? As Whitford suggests, it is a practical ques-tion, and one, I believe, that has already been extensively addressed by lesbian and bi-sexual poets: the question is 'how to construct a female sociality (*les femmes entre-elles*), a female symbolic, and a female social contract: a horizontal relation *between* women' (p. 109).

I will now return to H.D.'s 'The Master', reading it as a re-visionary poem which makes a very clear attempt to displace and revalue the phallic metaphor at the level of the text, and which manifestly disrupts the codes and categories of Freudian theory.

Ambiguously (or, perhaps, subtly sardonically) the poem has opened with the poet identifying the 'wisdom' of 'the old man' as his understanding of her. It is his wisdom *as guide* through the world of dream, which enables the poet herself to know 'small wisdom'. She comments: 'I found measureless truth/ in his words' (*CP* p. 451). This expression of gratitude is, however,

deeply undercut by the ambiguous word 'measureless': the ratio-
nal, scientific truth of his words have no measure, no music, no
dance, no poetry in them. It is his commanding scientific
knowledge, his Godlike authority as the master of his own (in
fact vulnerable) phallocentric discourse that, indirectly and hesit-
antly – but knowingly – is challenged by H.D.(*CP* pp. 452–453):

> I don't know what to suggest,
> I can hardly suggest things to God
> who with a nod
> says, 'rise Olympos,
> sink into the sea,
> O Pelion
> Ossa,
> be still'

It is through the hesitancies, displacements and ambiguities
made possible within the poetic text that H.D. seeks to destabilise
the certainties of the phallocentric 'wisdom' of Freud. Despite her
love and respect for Freud the man, H.D. undoubtedly recognised
his work on women's sexuality as instituting an authoritative
and, for her, ultimately unhelpful, canon within (patriarchal)
culture from which she is determined to escape:

> they will discuss all his written words,
> his pen will be sacred
> they will build a temple
> and keep all his sacred writings safe,
> and men will come
> and men will quarrel
> but he will be safe;
> they will found temples in his name,
> his fame
> will be so great
> that anyone who has known him
> will also be hailed as master,
> seer,
> interpreter;
>
> only I,
> I will escape.

(CP pp. 457–458)

How does she *escape* the psychic assault of Freud's written words? His negatory definitions of the female body? It will be recalled that Freud had spoken in the following terms of the horrors of the female genital, its terrifying malevolent effects on the male viewer (voyeur):

> We know, too, to what a degree depreciation of women, horror of women, and a disposition to homosexuality are derived from the final conviction that women have no penis. Ferenczi (1923) has recently, with complete justice, traced back the mythological symbol of horror – Medusa's head – to the impression of the female genitals devoid of a penis. [16]

Freud notes how men depreciate the horrible and fascinating abomination that is the woman's body. This (male-centred) representation of the maleficent Medusa head as metaphor for 'castration', has to be recognised as emerging out of masculine economies of defensive anxiety – out of the male fear of being mutilated himself, out of his fear of the loss of potency – and no one recognised this more clearly than Freud himself. Obviously, masculine virility is at stake in any encounter with the female genital.

In 'The Master', as Blau DuPlessis and Friedman have pointed out, the bi-sexual 'H.D. confronted the misogyny of Freud's theory with directness and high verve by affirming the perfection of woman'. [17] H.D., in her poem, constructs an ideal – but not static – metaphor for the lesbian (rather than bi-sexual) trajectory of desire. She visualises a perfect, 'frail yet strong' woman, an embodied symbolic Other charged with spiritual value and physical substance, her sexual meanings (almost) made explicit. The verbs of the poem indicate the dancer's physical immediacy and presence *as woman* whose restricted yet all powerful meanings are mobilised and acted out through time and space simultaneously, in the metaphoric figure of the dancer:

> she is woman,
> her thighs are frail yet strong,
> she leaps from rock to rock
> (it was only a small circle for her dance)
>
> and the hills dance,

she conjures the hills;
'rhododendrons
awake,'
her feet
pulse,
the rhododendrons
wake
there is purple flower
between her marble, her birch-tree white
thighs,
or there is a red flower,

there is a rose flower
parted wide,
as her limbs fling wide in dance
ecstatic
Aphrodite . . .

(*CP* p. 456)

This celebratory rhythmic movement of the dancer – an image situated at the conjunction of the body and music – articulates the harmonic patterns of lesbian desire in language which ecstatically replaces the representations of castration used within Freudian psychoanalytic theory. By her use of contrary (rather than oppositional) metaphors, the flowering of sexual exuberance – the 'rhododendrons' (from the Greek: Rhodon – rose, rose coloured, associated with sensuality and emotion); the 'purple flower/ between her marble, her birch-tree white/ thighs'; the 'rose flower/ parted wide' – H.D. opens up the discursive field to the hitherto non-spoken, non-symbolised realms of lesbian desire (*CP* p. 456).[18] Her restorative metaphors transform the woman's relation to the symbolic and dissolve, deform, shift, displace male-defined categories. They bring lesbian desire out of the nameless silence of frustrated meaning, and the Freudian oppositional terms, phallic/castrated are called into question. The woman's difference is no longer identified in terms of a male projection, but is symbolised in terms of positive metaphors bearing some relation to the specificities of the real body. In *Speculum*, Irigaray offers this critique of the concept of 'castration': 'the "fact of castration" has to be understood as a definitive prohibition against establishing one's own economy of the desire for origin. Hence, the hole, the lack, the fault, the

178

"castration" that greets the little girl as she enters as a subject into representative systems.'[19] Here too, the poet has refused to accept the Freudian metaphor for 'castration', or indeed any kind of negative naming, and seeks to establish what Irigaray calls the *primary metaphorisation* of her own economy of desire, both for the 'white Mother/ of green/ leaves/ and green rills/ and silver' and for the daughter/dancer/lover (*CP* p. 453) (*Speculum*, p. 84).

The jubilatory emergence of the wo(man) of section v, allows the lesbian/bi-sexual woman reader the possibility of identification with this lyrical construction in language – of an 'ideal type' [20] for her sex – a woman who is a new creation grown out of the earth, a transformed mythic Eve 'alone in a forest' (and thus created first?), who embodies attributes of both sexes (*CP* p. 456).[21] The bi-sexual H.D., in effect, 'finds the signifier of her own [bi-sexual/lesbian?] desire in the body of the one to whom she addresses her demand for love'.[22] This specific libidinal trajectory is marked in and through an (impossible) desire for this perfect wo(man), Aphrodite, goddess of desire.[23] In H.D.'s vision, this wo(man)'s body, represented as ideally complete in itself, incorporates the paternal metaphor *penis/phallus* at the level of the text (yes, Lacan, it comes back . . .) – but in terms that imply a radical transmutation. H.D.'s 'dart and pulse' bears little relation to Lacan's turgid signifier transmitting its 'vital flow'. We do not encounter the dominating, oversized erectile penis – rather, a more delicate metaphor of masculine creative 'generation' is subsumed within this moving icon of female desire:

> her feet are the delicate pulse of the narcissus bud,
> pushing from earth
> (ah, where is your man-strength?)
> her arms are the waving of the young
> male,
> tentative,
> reaching out
> that first evening
> alone in a forest
>
> (*CP* pp. 455–456)

The woman's body includes the masculine in much the same way that a *vierge ouvrante* opens to reveal a subordinate Christ figure within her body.[24] In H.D.'s poem, what the the woman needs, what she must have in order to be satisfied, specifically excludes the male. The sexual body of woman is sufficient-unto-herself: 'for she needs no man,/ herself/ is that dart and pulse of the male,/ hands, feet, thighs,/ herself perfect' (*CP* p. 456). Like Irigaray's two lips, 'they require nothing external to be satisfied. The *penis* may be the object of women's desire but need not be.' [25] Legitimating a female trajectory of desire, this perfection in dance of the gynandrous sexed subject is an affirming divine image, which not only sets psychical and symbolic metaphors (phallus/rhododendrons) in tension with each other, it also offers a specifically lesbian (or bi-sexual) point of location for the ego-identifications of the reader. The ideal/perfect image (which is both fixed and in movement) lends itself to the processes of social identification, and disorganises socially ordained, opposit-ional divisions: male/female, masculine/feminine. Drawing on Freud's account of the role of the ego-ideal in *Group Psychology and the Ego*, Brennan takes the view that 'one's ego needs its fix: it is fixed in relation to given points of identification, tied up in associations'.[26] Following Brennan, I would suggest that just as 'we can postulate that an ego-ideal identification with feminism, in the form of a person, people, or a body of writing, suspends the ego-ideal's existing prohibitions, that it *permits* different thinking', so too is it possible to suspend existing prohibitions against lesbian sexuality, permitting 'different thinking' in rela-tion to the associations which cluster around the lesbian and bi-sexual woman – in the poem, as in society (p. 10).

Freud himself, as healer, has made 'feasible' this disordering of the gendered codes of sexual difference, a fact acknowledged by H.D. in her poem (*CP* p. 459). Norman Holmes Pearson comments that what H.D., as analysand, got from Freud was the guidance that enabled her to reach 'her own cohesion, her own frame of reference, the rounding out of her own personality and psyche'.[27] But as her *Tribute to Freud*, and the poem 'The Master', show, H.D. and Freud were deeply divided on the issue of the lesbian aspects of her sexuality.

In 'Advent' this difference becomes painfully overt:

> When I told the Professor that I had been infatuated with Frances Josepha and might have been happy with her, he said, 'No – biologically, no.' For some reason, though I had been so happy with the Professor (Freud – *Freude*), my head hurt and I felt unnerved.[28]

180

None the less, Freud's associative techniques were what had made it possible for the poet to reach into the unknown, the 'hieratic', the unconscious – to explore, and bring to articulation in the symbolic, her 'whole miracle' (*CP* p. 454). What the 'old man' has made 'tenable' to her conscious understanding allows her to write: H.D. is now able to create a re-visionary figure, a metaphoric image in which her lesbian desire can be imagined, and thus represented. This figure of and for her desire becomes symbolised in the rhythms, gestures, words, movement, perfection of the dancer. Words 'scrawled' (unclear) and words carefully written; words separate and words interconnecting with other words create a pattern or gestalt made up of both legible and illegible traces, of similar and different parts, which, despite their diversity, become a recognisable, rhythmic whole, 'till now unguessed at/ unknown':

> how could he have known
> how each gesture of this dancer
> would be hieratic?
> words were scrawled on papyrus,
> words were written most carefully,
> each word was separate
> yet each word led to another word,
> and the whole made a rhythm
> in the air,
> till now unguessed at,
> unknown.
>
> (*CP* p. 454)

H.D. is grateful that Freud was able to help her differentiate her 'two loves separate': as she tells us, the 'old man' 'made this possible' for her (*CP* p. 453). The 'whole miracle' answers the riddle of the woman's desire, which is symbolised initially as volcano, as fire-mountain wrapped in snow, anemones, violets (*CP* pp. 453–454). The riddle of the volcano is solved when the realisation occurs that without the experience of her many different loves – for God's daughter/*earth* Mother (and powerful woman) as for her dancer/lover – there can be no experience of identity, of unity, of oneness in diversity. H.D. must recognise similarity and differences between the heterogeneous images of 'purple fire' and 'red heat' of passionate *jouissance* and the pain of separation or loss, the 'cold/silver/of her [the Mother's?] feet'.

181

Nevertheless, the mother's (earth) substance is 'like' the daughter's own (volcano) substance; they are part of one another and yet are separate, for, directed by the Father God, the Mother must '*send* peace/ and surcease of peril/ when a mountain has spit fire' (my emphasis). She is thus obedient to the Father and set at some distance from the daughter (*CP* p. 453). Bound up with this earth/mountain/volcano/hill metaphoric chain is the woman/dancer who, as she 'leaps from rock to rock', causes the hills to dance: 'she conjures the hills' (*CP* p. 456).

The danger of using these metaphors, which do not clearly differentiate one woman from another is anticipated by H.D., who is at pains to symbolise the hostility and ambivalence (the heat and cold, the fire and ice) between mother and daughter and between women lovers – there is no denial of the love, or of the pain of differences and distances between them. A woman must recognise not only her separation and individuation from the mother/lover, but also her continuing attachment to her. Equally, she must learn to distinguish and recognise her different (lesbian) desire for a woman. H.D. makes art out of her struggle to differentiate the likenesses and the differences between the women, as 'between volcanic desire,/ anemones like embers/ and purple fire/ of violets/ like red heat,/ and [like] the cold/ silver/ of her feet' (*CP* p. 453).

In section iii, H.D. symbolises the answer to her difficulties: in her writing, she produces an 'impossible' mystic statement which disorders dualist phallogocentric logic just as it confounds the dichotomising principle of gender organisation. She identifies an ideal woman who is (rather than is like) all things: she is represented in her symbolic (and spiritual) perfection as snow-flake, pure amethysts, clear water (*CP* p. 454).

for a woman
breathes fire
and is cold,
a woman sheds snow from ankles
and is warm;
white heat
melts into snow-flake
and violets
turn to pure amethysts,
water-clear

182

Snow-flakes can change state, water is totally unfixed, fluid; amethysts hard, unchangeable: as woman she is 'cold', she is 'warm'. Even in her metaphors for and of perfection, H.D. refuses to freeze an ideal moment into something fixed and unchanging, either one or the other. The mountain/volcano; mountain/ woman; subject/object; heat/cold; fire/ice – the white heat that melts(!) into snow-flake – are represented in a logic of both/and, a logic of multiplicity in which a woman is both undivided (perfect, identified, firm and fluid ego-boundaries) and multiple (two loves separate, multiply desiring), accepting not only the divisions within her own identity and between herself and others, but also finding/founding a unity in their diversity. This disorganisation of the logical categories of binary division is a necessary strategy if the poet is to shift phallic patterns of dominance and put in place her new representations at the level of the symbolic; but it is also a strategy which can be read against, for it may be seen as an apparent merging, fusion or confusion in relation to identity, a collapsing of difference into a regressive nostalgia for wholeness. This perhaps is the ultimate difficulty of differentiation – that between a synthetic wholeness founded on a collapsing of differences, a merging, and a profound ideal of a unity despite multiplicity which fully recognises difference, diversity and division within it.

In situating herself with respect to the God/mother and the daughter/lover/icon, and seeking to symbolise the sameness and differences of the relation between them, H.D. here parallels the Irigarayan project of striving to create a cultural discourse to articulate adequately this relation. Whitford comments: 'Irigaray writes repeatedly and consistently that the problem for women lies in the *non-symbolisation* of the relation to the mother and to the mothers body, and that this threatens women with psychosis.' [29] The threat of psychosis in these terms becomes the product of 'foreclosure', of the non-symbolisation of the mother/ woman's body, the girl child having 'no representation of what she might fear to lose'.[30] Thus Irigaray suggests that:

> symbolising the mother/daughter relationship, creating *externally located* and *durable* representations of this prototypical relation between women, is an urgent necessity, if women are ever to achieve ontological status in this society.
>
> (p. 120)

For similar reasons, it is also an urgent necessity to create and sustain representations of lesbian relationships within cultural forms. I want to turn now to a closely related poem: 'The Dancer', in which the problem of sexual differentiation and desire between two women is acutely rendered (*CP* pp. 440–450). When, in their sexual meeting, symbolised in the poem as the flowering of rhododendrons, 'fire flashes through clear ice', it is impossible to assign gender or to recognise the women's difference from each other (*CP* p. 442). The line 'which is which?/ either is either' leaves the tendentious question of gender division open to interpretation (*CP* p. 440). The 'you' and the 'I' may embody both male and female roles interchangeably: 'I am a priestess;/ I am a priest,/ you are a priest,/ you are a priestess': both are male, both are female. Yet, when fire and ice meet, the perfection, the wholeness of woman is 'more than human', 'more than fire', 'more than ice': in their unity despite diversity, the women find 'we are more than we know'. This 'miracle of beauty' (*CP* p. 443) occurs within the love and hostility, sameness and difference of a woman–woman relation: 'I came far,/ you came far,/ both from strange cities,/ I from the west,/ you from the east;/ but distance can not mar/ nor deter/ meeting' (*CP* p. 440). Again, this miracle is represented as a miracle of gynandrous vision – the male, as in 'The Master', incorporated within the female:

> miracle,
> miracle of beauty returned to us,
> the sun
> born in a woman
>
> (*CP* p. 443)

This redemptive 'miracle' of 'the sun/ born in a woman', which parallels the phrase 'Lord become woman' of 'The Master', signifies woman's jubilant enigma, the *gynocentric* (rather than androcentric) bringing together of male and female (*CP* p. 461). Again, the woman's body has the phallus, she is the phallus – as poet; but as poet who chooses not to claim precedence, greatness, the legitimating laurel, the meaningful judgement, the mastery of rationalist, phallogocentric logic. The arrow, rather, dares to follow desire, the mystic flame, the passion of the sexual body, the quest for spiritual transcendence. She would pursue the *jouissance* of the visionary – 'your twin arrows,/ you then pulse

into one flame/ O luminous' (*CP* p. 444). As in 'The Master',
H.D. again re-identifies the phallic figure – 'you are wind in a
stark tree,/. . . you are a strung bow, you are an arrow,/ another
arrow' – as lesbian, and constitutes it differently within the
symbolic (*CP* p. 443).

The indeterminacy of the countering voice – apparently the
voice of the omnipotent phallic 'Father,/ burning sun-lover' –
may instruct the sullen, silent poet to 'dance'; to service him as
his mistress; to write his message for him: 'you are my stylus' (*CP*
p. 445). This father/lover claims and may name as his the hand,
body, poetry, beauty and desire of woman: 'your taut frame/ is
one arrow,/ my message'. He may also claim the 'arrow' of
woman's mystic *jouissance* as his own flame, striving to appro-
priate in order to control the pleasure that belongs to the woman.
The woman, however, may retain her integrity against this
claim, against his seizing of the power of naming.

Renunciation, chastity, silence: resistance to the aggressive
agency of his words must defensively ensure the fundamental
integrity of the woman's word against his appropriations. The
poet defends the integrity of the woman's body as text, retrieves
her words, as belonging to her and to her woman lover, against
the crushing power of the god (father's) dominating forces:

> O let us never speak, my love,
> let us never utter
> words less than my heart-beat
> words less than your throbbing feet;
>
> white cygnet,
> black missel-thrush
>
> let us never crush
> breast to breast,
> let us never rush
> purple to purple fire,
> wide flowers,
> crushed under the glory
> of god in the whirl-wind,
> of god in the torrent.
>
> O chaste Aphrodite,
>
> let us be wild and free,

let us retain integrity,
intensity

(CP p. 446)

This move towards chastity/silence/body language offers a temporary, containing strategy which must function until men recognise the validity of the lesbian trajectory of desire. Both phallic and vulval metaphors co-exist in this text – but, as we move through the narrative structure, H.D. progressively privileges the not-spoken of lesbian eroticism, subordinating the phallus and re-presenting (and repeating) her vulval metaphors. In this poem, the wide open flowers – rhododendron, rose – become more insistently re-invoked, the phallus/penis more definitively displaced:

> Rhododendron,
> O wild-wood,
> let no serpent
> with drawn hood,
> enter,
> know the world we know;
>
> rhododendron,
> O white snow,
> let no mortal ever know
> mysteries
> within the fold
> of purple
> and of rose
> and gold

(CP p. 449)

The serpent: symbol of healing, of wisdom, of resurrection – but also of death, H.D. tells us in *Tribute to Freud* (p. 65). Perhaps, given the Freudian context, we might also understand this serpent as a not so concealed reference to the phallic Freud himself ('S for *seal, symbol, serpent* certainly, *signet, Sigmund*' (*CP* p. 88) who is refused entry to the 'world we know'. 'The Master' repeats this pattern of exclusion of the deluded, blind, weakened male – made weak through the self-deception of the 'man-pulse' (*CP* p. 460) and his sad failure to see the perfection of woman – from these female mysteries:

186

no man will be present in those mysteries,
yet all men will kneel,
no man will be potent,
important,
yet all men will feel
what it is to be a woman

(CP p. 460)

In her effort to put in place a lesbian sexed subject – to organise desire differently within the symbolic – H.D. privileges vulval metaphors that link her poetic to the real of the woman's body – to that real which is, by definition, outside all symbolism, all representation. In this way 'she finds the signifier of her own desire in the body of the one to whom she addresses her demand for love'.[31] Can this decensored vulval metaphor circulating in the systems of representation of the symbolic eventually displace the imaginary phallus from its privileged position as key signifier in the unconscious?[32] I would suggest that perhaps even the intrapsychic metaphor may become modified, once this transformed symbolic can be said to precede the child's entry into language. H.D. represents, not the archaic pre-Oedipal metaphor but restorative re-visionary or prophetic representations articulated within the symbolic order, the poet figuring in her phrasing the dance of that (real) woman's body whose representations engender pleasure as both a cosmic and a sexual mystery.

The signifying field of this Other woman plays a necessary role in the identifications of the lesbian and bi-sexual sexed subject. The Other woman must be enabled to speak, so that she may validate the identity of her lover and bring the lesbian relationship out of the silences of negation to become positively, nay rhapsodically, inscribed within language:

Rhododendron,
O strong tree,
sway and bend
and speak to me;

utter words
that I may
take
wax
and cut upon my tablets

187

words to make men pause
and cry
rhododendron
to the sky;

words that men may pause
and kneel,
broken
by this pulse we feel

(*CP* p. 448)

'The Dancer' also strives to 'teach men' – to ask men to 'dare further,/ stare with me/ into the face of Death,/ and say,/ Love is stronger' (*CP* pp. 447–448). Here the man/phallus is 'broken' in the face of the words of women, 'the pulse' of their desire, the flowering body of their love. In 'The Master', H.D. sought to inscribe her figuration of the woman's body within language as participating in the sacred, the holy, this inscription displacing the old man's 'talk of the man-strength . . . his mystery, his mysteries', within the poem *(CP* p. 455). In the culture, however, his potent, 'sacred' written words, will, none the less, be safely preserved in socially sanctified 'temples', from which 'Only I,/ I will escape' (*CP* pp. 457–458).

What this analysis shows is that, fundamentally, the problem of sexuality is a problem of representation – of contesting representations in dispute over the same biological body. H.D., in her encounter with Freud, the one who is supposed to know, could not accept what he said, what he hinted at, what he brought out as meaning: she cannot realise her self in his truth and refuses to be subject to his logic, his words. The unsettled H.D., rather, looked to the Other woman – to her gestures, her rhythms, her dance, her metaphoric *body*, for words and meanings in which to identify herself.

What this means is that there is no necessary representation of the anatomical difference between the sexes – that Freud's article of faith, the hypothesis of the castration complex, may be written otherwise. It shows also that there is no necessary subjection to the signifying field of one particular Other – even when that Other is Sigmund Freud! Difference and conflict, rather, open to each what is not contained within the limits of the other identity, or theory.

What H.D.'s *illicit* poetics decensors (or decensures) is another locus, field (or body) of significance in which she may realise her sexuality, her identity – and that of the Other woman – as body of the mother called back to her, renewed. This position of challenge to the phallocentric logic of castration is taken up, somewhat less reverently, by Hélène Cixous:

> Let the priests tremble, we're going to show them our sexts! Too bad for them if they fall apart upon discovering that women aren't men, or that the mother doesn't have one. But isn't this fear convenient for them? Wouldn't the worst be, isn't the worst, in truth, that women aren't castrated, that they have only to stop listening to the Sirens (for the Sirens were men) for history to change its meaning? You only have to look at the Medusa straight on to see her. And she's not deadly. She's beautiful and she's laughing.[33]

The textual strategy is clear. Metaphors of and for the specificity of the woman's body, undetermined by any masculine or heterosexual libidinal economy, disavowal or negatory system of representation, become crucial to the process of identifying the woman, of designating her subjectivity – in other terms. H.D.'s text shows that these metaphors, whilst they have to do with female physiology, female anatomy, are still specific individual representations *in language* (rather than universal, biological, *natural* givens), whose effects may yet be seen in the weaving, in the construction, of a new identity for women.

12

'GOD CLAPS AND CLAPS/HER ONE HAND'[1]

In actual, lived practice, the process of identification – through naming and claiming an identity, through revealing the lesbian trajectory of desire and thus bringing the unspoken to speech – is far from easy. Susan Griffin's poem 'The Woman Who Swims in Her Tears' explores the painful soul-searching and self-questioning that accompanied this lesbian relationship of the early seventies. Rich, speaking of this poem and commenting on the difficulty of 'getting away' from male-defined language, of naming *for the first time*, indicates the challenge and struggle it was, then, to find an appropriate language for lesbian sexuality: 'That poem has just never been written before; it condenses in one poem so much of a very long process that two women may go through in order to come together at all.' [2]

> The woman
> who slept beside the body of one
> other woman weeping,
> the women who wept.
> the women whose tears wet
>   each other's hair
> the woman who wrapped her legs
>   around another woman's thigh
>   and said I am afraid.
> the woman who put her head
>   in the
> place between the shoulder and breast
> of the other woman and
> said, 'Am I wrong?' [3]

An impersonal voice tells of 'the woman', 'the other woman', 'the body of one other woman'. This voice, used to speak of this sexually intimate context, creates tension at different levels: privacy/revelation; proximity/distance; private/public space; concern/reluctance to intrude. There is tension too in the vague reference to other 'women'. There may be an inclusive movement outwards to indicate a community of like women, but where, how many, is not clearly defined. Who speaks? Why is there this distancing, this difficult, effortful repetition, this mode of anxiety, distress, self-questioning? These tensions gesture towards a struggle against muteness; a struggle to overcome the impediments to speech, the doubts, resistances, uncertainties; the struggle of dealing with raw conflict, of contradiction; and indicate also the especially intense process of honestly bringing to language that which has been rigorously excluded from it:

> So much defiance needed for the possible. All the labour of feminism. Casting away all the denials of female experience. The denial of what we *know* to be true. Unwrapping yards of bandages. Like the bandages wrapped around the dead. From our eyes. Ears. Hands. Skin. All we are complicit in hiding.[4]

To come out of hiding and cast away 'all the denials' requires validation of lesbian identity at the deepest levels. To accept and to claim an identity, a lesbian 'I', that culture has taught everyone to despise, requires a major revaluation of both personal and cultural values. How is this defiant 'I' to be constructed so as to emerge from the silences of self-censorship and cultural exclusion? Perhaps this extract from Olga Broumas' 'Rumpelstiltskin' shows how, through one woman's love for another, this revaluation can begin:

> Did anyone
> ever encourage you, you ask
> me, casual
> in afternoon light. You blaze
> fierce with protective anger as I shake
> my head, puzzled, remembering, no
> no. You blaze
>
> a beauty you won't claim. To name
> yourself beautiful makes you as vulnerable
> as feeling
> pleasure and claiming it

makes me. I call you lovely. Over

and over, cradling
your ugly memories as they burst
their banks, tears and tears, I call
you lovely. Your face
will come to trust that judgement, to bask
in its own clarity like sun.[5]

Drawing on Irigaray's account of the female psyche, I have suggested that the lesbian realises the possibility of renewing her first earliest libidinal attachments by displacing them onto a lesbian Other. To theorise this further, I must again (briefly!) refer to Lacan. In his earlier exposition, Lacan proposes two fields which together give birth to the subject: 'the subject in the field of the drive and the subject as he [she] appears in the field of the Other'.[6] The Other, in articulating the chain of signifiers which govern 'whatever may be made present of the subject', thus plays an essential part in the construction of subjectivity in relation to the drive or libido.[7] Lacan stresses that the process of *'making oneself'* necessitates *'loving oneself through the other'*. By 'making oneself heard' and 'making oneself seen',[8] one is involved in 'subject making' – that is, working towards but never actually unifying the one, the one who is the (always divided) and constantly fading 'I' of apparent identity, appropriated out of and constituted within language.[9]

If we pursue the logic of Lacanian psychoanalysis to a point beyond Lacan's own emphasis, the reciprocal articulation of their desires of/for each other should play a part in the construction of the lesbian 'I'. I see the lesbian as learning to love and identify herself in the affirming field of meaning of the lesbian Other. I want to make the further suggestion that it is, at deepest levels, the mirroring discourse of the lesbian *lover* which enables the lesbian subject to *make* her self, to identify herself so as to be seen and to be heard – defiantly to accept the costs and take the risks.

It is through receiving the deep acceptances of the reciprocal pleasures of lesbian love – that is, in the fullest dimensions of the physical, spiritual and sexual responses of her lover – that the lesbian is able to confirm the validity and integrity of her lesbian identity. In the context of poetry, this mirroring discourse may be seen as conveyed in the language of words; it may be conveyed in the gestural languages of the body or, non-verbally, through the use of sexually or emotionally charged images.

Olga Broumas' fine poem 'Innocence' is especially interesting in this respect.[10] This poem draws its inspiration from body spirituality being developed by feminist women of many different faiths, who are exploring their spirituality and sexuality in theological terms.[11] In this poem, the 'mirroring' symmetrical relation between (unlike) lesbian lovers, that is, in the reciprocal and (a)symmetrical relation between 'Love, Love' and their 'merging shadows', Queen and Jester, the lesbian sexual relation is ecstatically celebrated. This poem specifically validates each woman's lesbian sexuality, each woman's lesbian body, as being in and of God, the women's bodies being created in the image of God.

The poem images God herself as participating in the lovemaking between the two women, the inventive and physically embodied hand of God appearing to produce *extra pleasure*. This manifest hand that is itself active in the sexual communion of the women, both is, and is not, in and of them. She, God herself, is imaged as also around them, as the wind. This theology of the body dramatically counters fundamentalist (heterosexual and patriarchal) Christian pieties by representing religious ecstasy as of the body as well as the spirit, and – by representing the sexuality of the lesbian women as not merely without sin, but as divine and sacred in itself – as an aspect of God incarnate.

> God
> appears
>
> among us, elusive, the extra
> hand none of us – Love, Love, Jester, Queen –
> can quite locate, fix, or escape. Extra
> hand, extra
> pleasure. A hand
> with the glide of a tongue, a hand
> precise as an eyelid, a hand with a sense
> of smell, a hand that will dance
> to its liquid moan.
> God's hand
>
> loose on the four of us like a wind
> on the grassy hills of the South.[12]

God is Love, physically embodied in, around and between these lesbian women as they reciprocally give and receive the pleasures of sexual love:

Manita's Love

opens herself to me, my sharp
Jester's tongue, my
cartwheels of pleasure. The Queen's own pearl
at my fingertips, and Manita pealing

my Jester's bells on our four
small steeples, as Sunday dawns

In this playful and complex reworking of the idea of church bells ringing in celebration, the nipples? clitoral bodies? of the women, as it were, become the 'small steeples' of the church of love where God herself is worshipped.[13] In mutual joy, the 'Jester's bells' ring out their sexual ecstasy for all to hear 'as Sunday dawns'. In the closing lines of this challenging poem, God herself affirms and applauds the innocence of this spiritual/sexual relation by clapping with her one hand, that is, by making an 'audible' sign from an approving Other, as one who herself participates in creating their lesbian identity, and who signals her acceptance and recognition of their sexual pleasure. Broumas, in using this 'impossible' Zen figuration, the 'sound' of one hand that 'claps and claps', creates a paradox within her poem: the sound, like lesbian sexuality itself, is both there and not there. Lesbian sexuality has been one of the most deafening silences of history, and, even now, when it is spoken out and celebrated, it is a voice that is frequently simply *not heard*. A wry twist then, given the paradoxical hypocrisy of our cultural forms.

In the poem, this one hand seems to signal unconditional acceptance of lesbian sexuality, and is imaged by the poet as a part of God's creative 'making' of the lesbian sexual relation. This unconditional acceptance is also part of the poet's reconstruction of lesbian identity – in her creation of an affirming field of meaning for the lesbian reader, whether she is sexually active or not.

I want now to consider the different position of black lesbian women. An affirming field of meaning is important to the white lesbian – but even if she suffers discrimination at work, at home, in social life, in religious life and elsewhere she at least has access to 'skin privilege'. It must be even more important to the black lesbian woman who experiences, in addition to all the oppressive situations that can arise for the white lesbian, pernicious, systematic racial and economic discrimination, sexual devaluation specific to black women, and manifold overt and covert exclusions from certain fields of work, education and health care. There are no easy parallels to be drawn between black and white lesbian experience, though certain overlapping areas of oppression can be discerned.

It is also difficult to engage in any discussion of the dynamics of the bond between black mothers and their daughters according to the white western models formulated by Freud, Lacan and white French feminists. The limitations of this body of theory begin to be acutely felt wherever child-rearing practice does not conform to the typical western patterns of the patriarchal nuclear family. Black women, as mothers, have a pivotal and powerful role in many black families, but the mother is rarely sole carer for the child as in the white middle-class pattern. Black family networks have taken very different forms. In America, the extended family systems of Africa could not survive in their old patterns through the centuries of slavery and then through sustained racial and economic oppression. In the situations typical of today, the black mother is, of necessity, called upon to work to support her family – the grandmother, aunt, sister, cousin or any significant other of the extended family or circle of friends may well be the one, or the one among many, to take care of her children. The child's relation to the mother is thus altered in important ways. The words of Audre Lorde, black lesbian poet, point to this different mode of relating which throws Lacanian theories into disarray. She offers these comments about her family and its particular situation in relation to the construction of her 'I'. The extract is from her biomythography, *Zami: A New Spelling of My Name*:

> I have felt the age-old triangle of mother father and child, with the 'I' at its eternal core, elongate and flatten out into the elegantly strong triad of grandmother mother daughter, with the 'I' moving back and forth flowing in either or both directions as needed.[14]

None the less, in her poem 'Black Mother Woman', Audre Lorde examines the nature of the conflict between herself and her own very powerful mother as a key figure in the relational process of self-definition.[15] The poet does not deny the difficulties of the relationship and it is clear that the political stance taken up by Audre Lorde is very different to that of her parents.

As daughter, the poet acknowledges the sharp edge of the mother's discipline: 'I cannot recall you gentle.'[16] Despite this, through the mother's pride, the daughter is able to recognise the love that is hidden in the silence of the not spoken, but which is none the less conveyed to her in more subtle ways. The poet acknowledges both the centrality of her respect and love for her mother's 'aged spirit', as well as her sense of distance and difference from her. She bears witness to her mother's long-suffering acceptance of oppression in these ambivalent lines:

> When strangers come and compliment me
> your aged spirit takes a bow
> jingling with pride
> but once you hid that secret
> in the center of furies
> hanging me
> with deep breasts and wiry hair
> with your own split flesh
> and long suffering eyes
> buried in myths of little worth.

In effect, the poet defines herself as other to her mother, in taking up a position very different from any her mother might have chosen. Yet, despite this, the daughter recognises the 'core of love' that enables the daughter to stand *as herself*:

> . . . I have peeled away your anger
> down to the core of love
> and look mother
> I Am
> a dark temple where your true spirit rises
> beautiful
> and tough as chestnut
> stanchion against your nightmare of weakness
> and if my eyes conceal
> a squadron of conflicting rebellions
> I learned from you
> to define myself
> through your denials.   (p. 53)

Alicia Ostriker has noted that 'this pattern of angry division and visionary reunion is especially important, in fact almost universal, among black and third-world women poets'.[17] She locates its source in the 'ambivalence of maternal attachment, associated with ambivalent views of the mother as power figure'.[18] The 'magically strong' bond between mother and daughter gives rise to these moving tributes to the black mother's strength and powerlessness. As a poet, Audre Lorde resists glossing over the anger, pain and sense of difference experienced by black people: *I have a duty to speak the truth as I see it and to share not just my triumphs, not just the things that felt good, but the pain, the intense, often unmitigating pain.*[19] This pain she experiences as the outcome of white supremacist racism, and of sexism, heterosexism, and homophobia – some of which, most hurtfully, emerge from black culture itself. We can discern something of this homophobic voice emerging from within black culture in this extract from Johari M. Kunjufu's poem:

> when we was real
> we never had women lovers
> we *always* knew what Man meant
> and *that* was natural
> we wont build a nation with
> trippers out on smoke and
> lesbians wishin they wore pants and
> teachin our daughters to
> close up their centers before they
> are even old enough to give out life.[20]

However, Lorde suggests that the courage to stand against all oppressive definition must come from love; 'what was beautiful had to serve the purpose of changing my life, or I would have died'.[21] Lorde affirms the necessity to feel deeply, to feel joy, to love deeply as a crucial element of social protest: she bears witness to love above all:

> We define ourselves as lovers, as people who love each other
> all over again; we become new again. These poems insist
> that you can't separate loving from fighting, from dying,
> from hurting, but love is triumphant. It is powerful and

strong, and I feel I grow a great deal in all of my emotions, especially in the capacity to love.

The love expressed between women is particular and powerful, because we have had to love in order to live; love has been our survival.

In her poem 'Recreation', Audre Lorde affirms the possibility of identity re-creation through lesbian love-making: the lovers, 'moving through our word countries', affirm the 'coming-together' of each other's body – which is a poem.[22] This 'coming-together' is crucial to their creativity and writing, as to poetry, but is also crucial to the process of identifying each subjectivity to the other – through the signifying body of words. The categories: woman/poem/flesh; you/me; earth/body; outside/inside, fuse. Boundaries between them collapse into each other and lose their categorical specificity: the poem creates a woman-identified locus/field/'country' where the erotic 'flesh' may 'blossom' into 'the poem/ you make of me':

. . . as your body moves
under my hands
charged and waiting
we cut the leash
you create me against your thighs
hilly with images
moving through our word countries
my body
writes into your flesh
the poem
you make of me.

Touching you I catch midnight
as moon fires set in my throat
I love you flesh into blossom
I made you
and take you made
into me.

Lorde, in her essay, 'Uses of the Erotic: The Erotic as Power', sees the erotic as a powerful resource, one that is 'firmly rooted in the power of our unexpressed or unrecognised feeling'.[23] As in the work of Olga Broumas and Adrienne Rich, the deepest erotic passion of love is not merely a sensual, but is also a spiritual joy.

198

For Lorde, the erotic is 'a well of replenishing and provocative force' (p. 54) and 'a considered source of power and information' (p. 53) – the sharing of its joys being a provocative 'assertion of the lifeforce of women' (p. 55). Lorde comments: 'Our erotic knowledge empowers us, becomes a lens through which we scrutinize all aspects of our existence, forcing us to evaluate those aspects honestly in terms of their relative meaning within our lives' (p. 57). Representing the lesbian sexual body, the sensual-emotional relationship, the material geography of female pleasure in positive terms, becomes a political strategy – the poet strives to generate a celebratory mode of writing in which this empowering significance may be found.

Thus it is at the level of erotic sexual pleasure that lesbian difference makes itself most clearly apparent. The lesbian libidinal economy is neither identifiable by a man nor can it be seen as referrable to any masculine economy. Informing all of Adrienne Rich's *The Dream of a Common Language*, is her understanding of the political – and spiritual – importance of this libidinal connection between women at the level of the (textual) body:

> I want to travel with you to every sacred mountain
> smoking within like the sibyl stooped over her tripod,
> I want to reach for your hand as we scale the path,
> to feel your arteries glowing in my clasp,
> never failing to note the small, jewel-like flower
> unfamiliar to us, nameless till we rename her[24]

Libidinal difference, the 'smoking within' of lesbian sexual desire, is at the heart of this poem. The lesbian desire for physical connection to the other woman; the wish 'to feel' the (arterial) pulsing life of her blood; her body; the wish 'to travel' together; to 'scale the path' together. Again, in representing the contiguities and reciprocities of the woman–woman relation, in making visible the lesbian libidinal difference from the heterosexual trajectory, the poet's words 'burn' with the energy of libidinal and spiritual commitment to the lesbian 'path' which is to be undertaken outside the libidinal economies of the masculine symbolic order. It is the bodily presence of each to the other that empowers the women to rename 'the small jewel-like flower' of Poem XI, a flower that recalls Lorde's image of 'flesh into blossom';[25] and Olga Broumas' exotic lines from her revised myth, 'Leda and Her Swan': 'Scarlet/ liturgies shake our room,

‚maryllis blooms/ in your upper thighs, water lily/ on mine, fervent delta'.[26]

In 'The Floating Poem, Unnumbered', from Adrienne Rich's *The Dream of a Common Language*, the image of the vaginal 'rose-wet cave' takes on a comparable value to Lorde's 'blossom'; and Broumas' 'amaryllis' or 'water lily' – as signifier of perfection, of the 'innocence and wisdom' of a sanctified and holy place. The 'Floating Poem', like Broumas' poem 'Innocence', is much influenced by the women's spirituality movement.[27] Its title is taken from the zero card of the Tarot. This card, with no number and no specific place on the path, is, in effect, a floating card designated O, which, according to Vicki Noble, 'represents innocence, without ideas of sin or transgression' and is 'free to speak the truth without punishment or censorship, because we trust in the absolute innocence of her motivation'.[28] The poem, like the card, is resonant with infinitely joyful, carefree spontaneity. Just as in Broumas' poem 'Innocence', it finds the route to 'pure wisdom' – here, to the 'innocence and wisdom' of the body of woman:

> Whatever happens with us, your body
> will haunt mine – tender, delicate
> your lovemaking, like the half-curled frond
> of the fiddlehead fern in forests
> just washed by sun[29]

This superbly erotic language of touch, of tongue – of searching for and of reaching – which recognises the tender mutuality of the women, names, validates and dignifies the lesbian sexual bodily relation. Rich not only makes available what was previously 'unspeakable', censored, unwritten, and named only in patriarchal terms but also transforms the codes in which this relation is signified, as a vital part of her re-visionary poetic. Once published and public, despite its apparent spontaneity, this poem again becomes a self-conscious and urgent breaking through of the cultural taboo against the depiction of lesbian sensuality/sexuality in art. This language functions to displace the homophobic messages of obscenity, of disgust that bombard the lesbian from masculist (and pornographic) culture. Viewed unromantically as an artistic revaluation of an always already socialised bodily relation, the poem renders historically visible a reconstructed representation concerned with treating the primary intensity of lesbian eroticism with respect and reverence. In this context, Lorde's vulnerable and courageous 'Love Poem', eventually published in 1971, is comparable in its strategy, a strategy Rich recognises. She identifies (draws attention to) Lorde's poem, thus differentiating and confirming her position, and identifies with it as a self-conscious choice. Rich comments in 'An Interview: Audre Lorde and Adrienne Rich', 'It was incredible. Like defiance. It was glorious.'[30]

> Speak earth and bless me with what is richest
> make sky flow honey out of my hips
> rigid as mountains
> spread over a valley
> carved out by the mouth of rain
>
> And I knew when I entered her I was
> high wind in her forests hollow
> fingers whispering sound
>
> honey flowed
> from the split cup
> impaled on a lance of tongues[31]

In reading this poem, Diana Collecott places it alongside Monique Wittig's *The Lesbian Body* and comments that 'the lesbian reader will recognise a shared eroticism that the heterosexual reader might categorise as violence'.[32] This 'violence', when placed in the very different context of African mythology, gathers to it further meanings. The warrior woman is an image very dear to Lorde, from which she derives the evocative symbolism of the mouth/tongue/word/speech – imagery which is intrinsically linked to the warrior imagery of the lance/sword/knives. Often in her work, words and language become 'weapons' which are employed in the fight for the survival of black integrity. Ancestral myths and images drawn from black African folklore form a vital part of afro-american culture – and Audre Lorde powerfully develops this cultural project of reclamation in a feminist direction. Her use of these symbolic images gathers significance as we read, creating a symbolic network which resonates through many poems. In the poem 'Dahomey', for instance, we find the *fas* of the Nigerian god Shango, spelled out by a woman: 'I speak/ whatever language is needed/ to sharpen the knives of my tongue.' [33]

201

These images also link to Lorde's political desire to retain the concept of intrapsychic bi-sexuality: '*I have always wanted to be both man and woman, to incorporate the strongest and richest parts of my mother and father within/into me - to share valleys and mountains upon my body the way the earth does in hills and peaks.*'[34]

These poets' refusal to submit to the coercive force of a condemnatory community, the challenge they offer to the pejorative clinical terminology of deviance, as well as their resistance to heterosexual ideology and practice, mark a particular choice - to publicly and defiantly identify as lesbian, despite that identity being socially stigmatised. Perhaps inevitably, their challenge to heterosexual (medical or psychoanalytic) discursive practices finds as its locus or field the woman's erotic body - as the site of representation to be contested. These poets take responsibility for rewriting the codes informing lesbian social and sexual relations; for reformulating how 'the body', as locus in a network of relations, may be articulated. Thus, rather than accepting the conferred (despised) identity given within hostile but normative prescriptive discourses, the poets transform the codes, the categories: they change the rules. They offer another position for the lesbian subject to take up, to identify with, as a self-conscious cultural choice. Representing lesbians as normal rather than deviant; as sexually healthy rather than sexually 'sick'; as women whose behaviour is permissible rather than illegitimate - the poems, in effect, protest the privileged status of much judgemental prohibition concerning the lesbian and her 'unacceptable' erotic drives. Instead, they offer a legitimating, cleansing vision of her erotic life and its corresponding dimensions of joy and pain. The poets are involved in a process of producing, out of the erotic body's libidinal difference, social and political meanings unpoliced, uncensored, by a heterosexual patriarchy. These validations are woven into their poetry.

CONCLUSION

It is plain that, in reading the work of lesbian poets, I can conceive of a symbolic that is not patriarchal, a symbolic that might work towards establishing a different legality, that already validates a different sexuality. If an alternative to patriarchal symbolic law is possible, if what I have found in the writings of lesbian poets can help to give lesbians generally a sense of their place in the world, the ability to speak and be understood by others in and through a particular relation to language – without falling into the abyss of psychosis! – then one alternative to the patriarchal symbolic is not only possible but is beginning to be articulated. This alternative to the symbolic emerges from an edge separating the heterosexual from the lesbian woman and begins in an *écriture féminine* elaborated where the desiring body and the external reality of experience come together. Upholding this entry into the symbolic as a space of meaning, of naming the 'unspeakable' biological and biographical life of lesbian women, invites the recognition (as acceptance) of this difference, of this otherness to patriarchal heterosexuality, as a reasonable place of identity to inhabit.

Lesbian work, in countering the visual privilege of the thoroughly natural, essentialist (non-essential) penis through making visible thoroughly natural, essentialist (desirable) – and specifically female – representations as the mark of a different sexuality, can be seen as making a disturbing intervention into the phallocentric logic of theories of sexual difference. Lesbian work points to a logic in which the social, the psychoanalytic and the biological play a part in the founding and in the sustaining of a different sexual identity. If the representation within culture of these metaphors can institute changes in the symbolic through overwriting earlier patriarchal traces laid down in infancy, then even the formative constructions of the mirror-phase may be wiped out, or at least partially erased, becoming overlaid by the palimpsest of a different experience.

Given changes in actual parenting practice, it is possible that the introjected parental image – *perhaps of the lesbian mother* – carries a different set of meanings and values, and these may become attached to the intervening third term (that is, the other mother in the equation!). Alternative parenting practices may well play an important part in instituting an alternative symbolic order. In the other mother's sameness and difference from the natural mother, which is not the visual difference of having or not having the phallus, but which may be a difference in power, status, race, class or ability – she may thoroughly destabilise the ordering of the symbolic according to hierarchies of power instituted by fathers. She may well play a part in constituting radically different patterns according to the particular relational codes operating between the mothers.

The children of lesbian mothers, and children who are brought up in alternative family structures may, like any other dissident living outside the frames of the normative white, healthy, heterosexual, affluent, middle-class, patriarchal nuclear family, self-consciously construct alternative codes for themselves and for the community they relate to. Even if the child grows up to be different from her parents, that is, s/he chooses to be heterosexual, or does not become disabled, or is no longer poor – in her/his empathic identifications s/he too may participate in the forming of a shared alternative symbolic system, one that emerges from the margins or outside of the parameters of patriarchal forms. Such children may also, incidentally, become able to speak out of a strongly affirmed and legitimated identity – an individual or a group identity – and be ready to stand against the injustices committed against the outsider, the 'other', be more ready to oppose injustices perpetrated by the powerful against the weak.

In this book, I have suggested that to mediate the primal relation between the mother and daughter in representations that confirm her *in an other place* is of paramount importance to any poetic concerned with the representation of woman–woman relationships. Not only does this involve difficult processes of differentiation – of recognising the otherness of the other woman, the complexity of her differences – it also involves recognising and legitimising her sameness. Given the dynamics of psychical differentiation whereby an individual may decide 'I am not like you', 'I will define myself against you', however, the outcomes I have suggested are by no means a foregone conclusion! I would expect that the thoughtful child of a lesbian or black or disabled mother could, at least, begin to see things in a different light. Identification with the mythic mirrors offered by writing-as-poetry or writing-as-theory will be socially flexible, because to perceive likeness also involves discerning difference. Merging and differentiation are but two poles of the same process. (It is evident that I have not yet escaped the confines of dualistic thought!) This process of identification will, at the same time, be bound by the necessity to survive within a hostile or, at best, tolerant patriarchy. For the lesbian as for the black or deaf/blind/disabled woman, it is bound by the necessity to create and/or sustain both a sense of her difference from other women as well as a vital sense of her unity with others within her particular community.

The poetic reconstruction of women's stories involves fundamental shifts in perspective and also involves a break with the characteristic patterns of mirroring and projection that occur within patriarchal cultural forms. It is clear that women need no longer be subject to the effects of myths and representations created by men (and by women loyal to patriarchal forms). Our thralldom to constructs of the heterosexual scenario, to the myths of romance, femininity and maternity may become unfixed once other possibilities become revealed as acceptable alternatives. This release opens up a vast field of possible becoming for women as we gradually free ourselves from deeply entrenched psychic restraints – the self-censorship, self-denial, self-sacrifice – the colluding out of fear. We can begin to shake off those convictions that mould and hold us to a self-abasing, guilt-producing ethic and perhaps can begin to recognise the damaging masochistic patterns that tie some of us to abusing men. As we ourselves 'knock the wind out of the codes', we may, in the long term, also be enabled to struggle out of the material, social, familial and legal chains that bind us.[1] Not into *freedom*, but into other responsibilities more consonant with the achievement of global justice.

The 'im/pertinent disclosures' that are provided by the thoughtful poet-as-witness, in her fidelity to and respect for the position of the other-woman – are vital to the ongoing process of constructing a non-patriarchal symbolic, as well as a non-patriarchal world. This work of constructing a new symbolic will inevitably contribute to a substantial repositioning of the 'I' within discourse. Poetry urges us all to pursue our desire to know and to know differently, to listen intently to those bodied-forth words which may indeed threaten and frighten us with their disturbing logic. The poets ask that we do not rest too secure in our justified patterns of belief, that we struggle with the contradictions, diversities and difference contained within the other for only thus can we expand into our own full humanity.

I hope that the protest and promise of the many voices woven into the fabric of this book will be handed on – as the orange is handed on, from woman to woman, as a gift to be passed on to those who come after. I hope too that these impertinent, disruptive voices will continually precipitate fresh beginnings, and will help to realise the promise that poetry holds – that of helping readers towards 'knowing more, understanding more, feeling more'. Poetry written by women will surely help us to experience a 'wonderful expansion' of that subversive pertinence which exceeds all limits, and all boundaries of patriarchal definition. Certainly, we will be continually surprised by the possibilities of the text for finding out what we do not know. It is my desire that we will be ready to begin and begin again our journeys of discovery and that we will choose to take up a position in relation to the text that actively works towards the doing of justice.

NOTES

INTRODUCTION

(Notes for pages 1-6)

1 Wendy Martin, *An American Triptych: Anne Bradstreet, Emily Dickinson, Adrienne Rich*, London, University of North Carolina Press, 1984, p. 169.
2 Adrienne Rich, *Of Woman Born: Motherhood as Experience and Institution*, London, Virago, 1977, p. 285.
3 Elizabeth Grosz, *Sexual Subversions: Three French Feminists*, Sydney, Allen & Unwin, 1989, p. 117.
4 Mary Jacobus, *Reading Woman: Essays in Feminist Criticism*, New York, Columbia University Press, 1986, p. 39.
5 Susan Sellers, intro., *Writing Differences: Readings from the Seminar of Hélène Cixous*, Milton Keynes, Open University Press, 1988, p. 7.

1 A SONG OUT OF SILENCE

(Notes for pages 9-21)

1 In *The Newly Born Woman*, trans. Betsy Wing, intro. Sandra Gilbert, Manchester, Manchester University Press, 1986, p. 65. Originally published in France as *La Jeune Née*, 1975, by Union Générale d'Editions, Paris.
2 Adrienne Rich, 'Notes Toward a Politics of Location', *Blood, Bread and Poetry: Selected Prose 1979-1985*, London, Virago, 1987, p. 215.
3 Alicia Suskin Ostriker, *Stealing the Language: The Emergence of Women's Poetry in America*, London, The Women's Press, 1987, p. 9.
4 Rosa Braidotti, 'The Politics of Ontological Difference', in *Between Feminism and Psychoanalysis*, ed. Teresa Brennan, London, Routledge, 1989, p. 90.
5 Mary Daly, *Gyn/Ecology: The Metaethics of Radical Feminism*, London, The Women's Press, 1979, p. 12.
6 Hélène Cixous, 'The Laugh of the Medusa', in *New French Feminisms: An Anthology*, ed. Elaine Marks and Isabelle de Courtivron,

trans. Keith Cohen and Paula Cohen, Brighton, Harvester Press, 1981, p. 249.

7 Adrienne Rich, 'When We Dead Awaken: Writing as Re-Vision', *On Lies, Secrets and Silence: Selected Prose 1966–1978*, London, Virago, 1980, pp. 33 and 35. My adoption of the term re-vision (as opposed to revision) derives directly from Rich and signals the importance of her contribution to the theorising of re-visionary mythmaking. It also signals its distance from Harold Bloom's theory of revisionism.

8 Rachel Blau DuPlessis, 'The Critique of Consciousness and Myth in Levertov, Rich, and Rukeyser', in *Shakespeare's Sisters: Feminist Essays on Women Poets*, ed. Sandra M. Gilbert and Susan Gubar, Bloomington and London, Indiana University Press, 1979, pp. 280–281.

9 Bonnie Zimmerman, 'The Politics of Transliteration: Lesbian Personal Narratives', in *Signs: Journal of Women in Culture and Society*, 1984, vol. 9, no. 4, p. 672.

10 Adrienne Rich, 'Power and Danger: Works of a Common Woman (1977)', *On Lies, Secrets and Silence*, p. 249.

11 Judith McDaniel, 'The Transformation of Silence into Language and Action', in *Sinister Wisdom* 6, summer 1978, p. 17.

12 Adrienne Rich, 'Power and Danger: Works of a Common Woman', *On Lies, Secrets and Silence*, p. 248.

13 Adrienne Rich, 'When We Dead Awaken: Writing as Re-Vision', in *On Lies, Secrets and Silence*, p. 37.

14 Mary Daly, *Beyond God the Father: Towards a Philosophy of Women's Liberation*, London, The Women's Press, 1985, p. 8.

15 Adrienne Rich, 'Teaching Language in Open Admissions (1972)', *On Lies, Secrets and Silence*, p. 67.

16 Adrienne Rich, 'Vesuvius at Home: The Power of Emily Dickinson', *On Lies, Secrets and Silence*, p. 181.

17 Adrienne Rich, 'To a Poet', (1974), *The Dream of a Common Language: Poems 1974–1977*, New York and London, W. W. Norton & Co., 1978, p. 15.

18 Adrienne Rich, *Of Woman Born: Motherhood as Experience and Institution*, London, Virago, 1977, p. 37.

19 Margaret Homans, *Women Writers and Poetic Identity: Dorothy Wordsworth, Emily Brontë, and Emily Dickinson*, Surrey, Princeton University Press, 1980, pp. 230–232.

2 THE POET AS WITNESS: IM/PERTINENCE, FIDELITY, RESPECT

(Notes for pages 22–33)

1 Audre Lorde, *Sister Outsider: Essays and Speeches by Audre Lorde*, New York, The Crossing Press, 1984, pp. 41, 43.

2 Adrienne Rich, 'Frame', in *The Fact of a Doorframe: Poems Selected and New, 1950–1984*, New York and London, W. W. Norton & Co.,

1984, p. 303. FRAME: to form, to shape, to articulate. A case made to enclose, border, or support anything; to make victim of a frame-up; a structure on which embroidery is worked. FRAME of reference; the structure of standards, arising from the individual's experience, and continually developing, to which s/he refers, in all cases from the simplest to the most complicated, when judging or evaluating. A. M. Macdonald, ed., *Chambers Twentieth Century Dictionary*, London, W. R. Chambers, New Edition, 1972. For a pertinent, if superficial, discussion of the theory of framing, see Marvin Minsky, 'A Framework for Representing Knowledge', in *The Psychology of Computer Vision*, New York, McGraw Hill, 1975.

3 Hélène Cixous: 'Extreme Fidelity', in *Writing Differences: Readings from the Seminar of Hélène Cixous*, ed. Susan Sellers, Milton Keynes, Open University Press, 1988, p. 11. It asks a great deal of the reader to give this quality of attention to every text, especially where 'otherness' is not only strange but also repugnant. I would have difficulty with the texts of fascism or pornography and would not wish to give them my attention and receptive love. I feel I would be unable to enter into that otherness, to imagine being that particular 'not-me-at-all. The criminal, the bourgeoise, the rat, the cockroach'. Yet Cixous seems to be asking just that.

4 Audre Lorde, 'My Words Will Be There', *Black Women Writers: Arguments and Interviews*, ed. Mari Evans, Sydney, Pluto Press, 1985, p. 262.

5 Simone Weil, 'Attention and Will', in *Simone Weil: An Anthology*, ed. Siân Miles, London, Virago, 1986, p. 231.

6 Gayatri Chakravorty Spivak, from her Translator's Preface to Jacques Derrida's *Of Grammatology*, Baltimore and London, The John Hopkins University Press, 1976. Derrida has it both ways: the trace 'track, footprint, imprint' of writing is deleted because it is inaccurate to the concept, and yet it is what permits the structure of reference to work and go on working: 'the value of the transcendental arche (or trace) must make its necessity felt before letting itself be erased' (p. 61).

3 UNSETTLING RATIONAL VIOLENCE: SUSAN GRIFFIN'S HOLISTIC 'KNOWING'

(Notes for pages 34–45)

1 Starhawk: *Dreaming the Dark: Magic, Sex and Politics*, Boston, Beacon Press, 1982, p. 47.

2 Susan Griffin, 'Poetry as a Way of Knowledge', *Made From This Earth: Selections from her Writing 1967-1982*, London, The Women's Press, 1982, p. 248.

3 Susan Griffin, 'Notes on the Writing of Poetry', in ibid., p. 226.

4 Evelyn Fox Keller, 'Gender and Science', in *Psychoanalysis and Contemporary Thought*, 1, 1978, pp. 409–433.

5 Jessica Benjamin, 'The Bonds of Love: Rational Violence and Erotic Domination', in *The Future of Difference*, ed. Hester Eisenstein and Alice Jardine, Boston, G. K. Hall, 1980, p. 63.

6 Susan Griffin, *Made From This Earth*, p. 248.

7 Ibid., pp. 287–290, 288.

8 Hilde Hein, quoted in Estella Lauter, *Women as Mythmakers: Poetry and Visual Art by Twentieth Century Women*, Bloomington, Indiana University Press, 1984, p. 221.

9 Susan Griffin, *Woman and Nature: The Roaring Inside Her*, London, The Women's Press, 1984, pp. 226 and xvi.

10 Sarah Ruddick, 'Maternal Thinking', in *Feminist Studies* 6, no. 2, summer 1980, p. 348.

11 Hélène Cixous, 'Castration or Decapitation?', trans. Annette Kuhn, in *Signs: Journal of Women in Culture and Society*, 1981, vol. 7, no. 1, p. 44.

12 Susan Griffin, 'The Way of All Ideology', *Made From This Earth*, p. 162.

13 Sylvia Plath, 'In Plaster', in *Collected Poems*, ed. and intro. Ted Hughes, London, Faber & Faber, 1981, p. 158.

14 Mary Daly, *Gyn/Ecology: The Metaethics of Radical Feminism*, London, The Women's Press, 1979, p. 341.

4 IDENTITY AND CRISIS: SYLVIA PLATH'S QUEST FOR INTEGRITY

(Notes for pages 49–65)

1 Sigmund Freud, *On Psychopathology: Inhibitions, Symptoms and Anxiety and Other Works*, trans. and ed. James Strachey, vol. 10, Harmondsworth, Penguin Books, 1983, p. 90.

2 Sylvia Plath, *The Journals of Sylvia Plath*, ed. Ted Hughes and Frances McCullough, New York, Ballantyne Books, 1982, p. 280. Henceforth shown as *J*.

3 Julia Kristeva, *Powers of Horror: An Essay on Abjection*, trans. Leon S. Roudiez, New York, Columbia University Press, 1982, p. 41.

4 Alicia Suskin Ostriker, *Stealing the Language: The Emergence of Women's Poetry in America*, London, The Women's Press, 1987, p. 124.

5 Luce Irigaray, 'Any Theory of the "Subject" Has Always Been Appropriated by the "Masculine" ', trans. Gillian C. Gill, in *Speculum of the Other Woman*, Ithaca, New York, Cornell University Press, 1985, p. 140.

6 Linda Anderson, 'At the Threshold of the Self: Women and Autobiography', in *Women's Writing: A Challenge to Theory*, ed. Moira Monteith, Brighton, Harvester Press, 1986, pp. 58–60.

7 Julia Kristeva, *Powers of Horror: An Essay on Abjection*, pp. 44–46.

8 As Linda Bundtzen has noted, the medusa is 'the immature form of the adult jellyfish, aurelia, so that it works as a code for her mother's

name; but it also applies to the child, to Plath as an immature medusa to the adult aurelia. The double meaning contributes to the symbiotic relationship Plath explores in "Medusa".' Linda K. Bundtzen, *Plath's Incarnations: Woman and the Creative Process*, Ann Arbor, University of Michigan Press, 1983, p. 94.

9 Anne Stevenson, *Bitter Fame: A Life of Sylvia Plath*, Harmondsworth, Penguin, 1989, p. 302. I agree with Eric Homberger when he calls this book 'lacking in human sympathy' and 'ungenerous'. See his review in *The Times Higher Education Supplement*, 1 December 1989, p. 16.

10 Julia Kristeva, *Powers of Horror: An Essay on Abjection*, p. 53.

11 Lacan argues that the Other, in the first instance – the mother (the m/Other) – plays an essential part in the construction of subjectivity. See his essay, 'The Phallic Phase and the Subjective Import of the Castration Complex' (in *Feminine Sexuality: Jacques Lacan and the école freudienne*, London, Macmillan, 1982, pp. 106–109) for a brief account of the role of the m/Other in the construction of identity. See also, pp. 2, 5, 30-31.

12 Aurelia Plath, *New York Times*, 9 October 1979.

13 Juliet Mitchell and Jacqueline Rose, eds, *Feminine Sexuality*, p. 38.

5 'WHAT GIRL EVER FLOURISHED IN SUCH COMPANY?'

(Notes for pages 66–79)

1 Title taken from Sylvia Plath, 'Magi', in *Collected Poems*, ed. and intro. Ted Hughes, London, Faber & Faber, 1981, p. 148.

2 See Susanne Juhasz, ' "The Blood Jet", The Poetry of Sylvia Plath', in *Naked and Fiery Forms: Modern American Poetry by Women, A New Tradition*, New York and London, Harper & Row, 1976, for a comparable feminist reading of these poems. Susanne Juhasz sees 'Tulips' as a war between life and death: 'the positive power of life (flowers, babies, redness, breath) overwhelms the negative pull of death (whiteness, winter, ice, snow, passivity, purity, emptiness, peacefulness, freedom); and the action of the poem is the battle that is waged' (p. 109).

3 George Stade, in Nancy Hunter Steiner, *A Closer Look at Ariel: A Memory of Sylvia Plath*, London, Faber & Faber, 1974, pp. 63-64.

4 Sandra M. Gilbert, 'A Fine White Flying Myth: The Life/Work of Sylvia Plath', in Sandra M. Gilbert and Susan Gubar, eds, *Shakespeare's Sisters: Feminist Essays on Women Poets*, London and Bloomington, Indiana University Press, 1979, p. 256.

5 Pamela J. Annas, *A Disturbance in Mirrors: The Poetry of Sylvia Plath*, London, Greenwood Press, 1988, pp. 73-74.

6 Adrienne Rich, *Of Woman Born: Motherhood as Experience and Institution*, London, Virago, 1977, p. 243.

7 Hélène Cixous, 'Castration or Decapitation?', trans. Annette Kuhn, *Signs: Journal of Women in Culture and Society*, 1981, vol. 7, no. 1, p. 51.

6 SEDUCTIVE SCENARIOS: FIGHTING BACK

(Notes for pages 80–90)

1 Simone de Beauvoir, *The Second Sex*, trans. and ed. H. M. Parshley, Harmondsworth, Penguin Books, 1981 (1949), pp. 174–175.
2 Hélène Cixous and Catherine Clément, 'The Guilty One', in *The Newly Born Woman*, trans. Betsy Wing, intro. Sandra Gilbert, Manchester, Manchester University Press, 1986, pp. 6–7.
3 Susan Bassnett, *Sylvia Plath*, London, Macmillan, 1987, p. 50.
4 Ibid., p. 59.
5 Mary Daly, *Gyn/Ecology: The Metaethics of Radical Feminism*, London, The Women's Press, 1979, p. 341.
6 Hélène Cixous and Catherine Clément, 'The Guilty One', in *The Newly Born Woman*, p. 5.
7 Jean-Paul Sartre, *Anti-Semite and Jew*, trans. George Becker, New York, Schocken Books, 1970, pp. 48–49.
8 Hélène Cixous and Catherine Clément, 'The Guilty One', in *The Newly Born Woman*, p. 5.
9 Luce Irigaray, *This Sex Which is Not One*, trans. Catherine Porter with Carolyn Burke, Ithaca, New York, Cornell University Press, 1977, pp. 10 and 17.

7 RE-CREATING 'MY OWN LEGEND': H.D.'s *HELEN IN EGYPT*

(Notes for pages 91–107)

1 *H.D.: Tribute to Freud, Writing on the Wall, Advent*, foreword by Norman Holmes Pearson, Manchester, Carcanet Press, 1985. Henceforth shown as *TF*.
2 Ibid., p. v.
3 *H.D.: Helen in Egypt*, New York, New Directions, 1961, p. 170. Henceforth shown as *HE*.
4 Susan Stanford Friedman, *Psyche Reborn: The Emergence of H.D.*, Bloomington, Indiana University Press, 1981, p. 9.
5 Ibid., p. 65.
6 H.D., *Notes on Thought and Vision* (includes 'The Wise Sappho', an essay), San Francisco, City Lights Books, 1982, p. 23.
7 Sigmund Freud, *The Interpretation of Dreams*, trans. and ed. James Strachey, Harmondsworth, Penguin Books, 1976 (1953), p. 153.
8 Jane Harrison, *Themis: A Study of the Social Origins of Greek Religion*, London, Merlin Press, 1963, pp. 110 and 315.
9 Sigmund Freud, 'Moses and Monotheism: Three Essays (1939, 1934–

38)', in *The Origins of Religion: Totem and Taboo, Moses and Monotheism and other Works*, vol. 13, Harmondsworth, Penguin, 1985, p. 248.

10 Speaking of *Helen in Egypt*, Rachel Blau Duplessis makes the important suggestion that an unacceptable incestuous desire for the mother underlies all male violence, especially aggressive sexuality: 'all kinds of contemptuous challenge and assault, all expressions of sexual hatred, desire to hurt women, H.D. shows are a shamed avoidance for an almost unspeakable depth of passionate attraction for the mother.' This may be so: it certainly accords with H. D.'s political and gender-conscious spirituality. *H.D.: The Career of That Struggle*, Brighton, Harvester Press, 1986, p. 115.

11 Diana Collecott, 'Remembering oneself: the reputation and later poetry of H.D.', *Critical Quarterly*, vol. 27, no. 1, spring 1985, pp. 8–9.

12 Sigmund Freud, 'Civilisation and its Discontents', in *Civilisation, Society and Religion*, ed. Albert Dickson, trans. James Strachey, vol. 12, Harmondsworth, Penguin, 1985, p. 260.

8 ON THE NEED TO GO TO THE SOURCES

(Notes for pages 111–125)

1 Juliet Mitchell, Introduction I, in Juliet Mitchell and Jacqueline Rose (eds), *Feminine Sexuality: Jacques Lacan and the école freudienne*, trans. Jacqueline Rose, London, Macmillan, 1982, p. 5.

2 Jacqueline Rose, Introduction II in ibid., pp. 30–31.

3 Julia Kristeva, *The Kristeva Reader*, ed. Toril Moi, Oxford, Basil Blackwell, 1986. Kristeva points to the importance of any intertextual exchange to the construction of the subject. She suggests that 'any text is the absorption and transformation of another. The notion of *intertextuality* replaces that of intersubjectivity, and poetic language is read as at least *double*. The word as minimal textual unit thus turns out to occupy the status of *mediator*, linking structural models to cultural (historical) environment' (p. 37). This account of intertextuality as a process of 'transposition' in which the 'absorption and transformation' of mediating words causes the subject to make a new articulation of her position, is so ordinary an experience that it has seemed invisible. Reading as a process may always have the potential to precipitate 'an altering of the thetic *position* – the destruction of the old position and the formation of a new one' (p. 111).

4 Jan Montefiore, *Feminism and Poetry: Language, Experience, Identity in Women's Writing*, London and New York, Pandora Press, 1987, p. 105.

5 Luce Irigaray, *This Sex Which Is Not One*, trans. Catherine Porter with Carolyn Burke, Ithaca, New York, Cornell University Press, 1985, p. 30.

6 For further very clear discussion of these issues see Betty McGraw,

'Splitting Subject/Splitting Seduction', in *Boundary* 2, vol. XII, no. 2, winter 1984. pp. 143–151.

7 Elaine Marks, 'Women and Literature in France', in *Signs: Journal of Women in Culture and Society*, 1978, vol. 3, no. 4, p. 841.

8 Hélène Cixous, 'The Laugh of the Medusa', in *New French Feminisms: An Anthology*, ed. and intro. Elaine Marks and Isabelle de Courtivron, trans. Keith Cohen and Paula Cohen, Brighton, Harvester Press, 1981, p. 249.

9 Teresa Brennan, ed., *Between Feminism and Psychoanalysis*, London, Routledge, 1989, pp. 6 and 7. Teresa Brennan makes the useful suggestion that Freud's account in *Group Psychology and the Analysis of the Ego* of the identifications of the ego, lends itself to understanding how the subject can be 'identified with others in an on-going social process', and thus can become 'permeable' to new influences. 'We can postulate that an ego-ideal identification with feminism, in the form of a person, people or body of writing, suspends the ego-ideal's existing prohibitions, that it *permits* different thinking' (p. 10). 'Misleading identifications' can be deconstructed, and another story can be written. Radical shifts in perspective can thus occur: 'it is through historical contextual work that imaginary associations can be undone, or actively forgotten, and a continuity of memory restored' (p. 13).

10 Ibid., p. 7.

11 Arleen B. Dallery, 'Sexual Embodiment: Beauvoir and French Feminism *(écriture féminine)*', *Women's Studies International Forum*, vol. 8, no. 3, 1985, pp. 197–202.

12 Hélène Cixous, 'The Laugh of the Medusa', in *New French Feminisms*, p. 254.

13 For further insights see Beverly Brown and Parveen Adams, 'The Feminine Body and Feminist Politics', in *m/f*, no. 3, 1979, pp. 35–49, esp. pp. 41 and 44.

14 See translator's notes to Jacques Lacan's Seminar of 21 January 1975, 'A Love Letter (Une Lettre D'Amour)', for further explanation of Lacan's four discourses – of the master, of the university, of the hysteric, of the analyst: 'What matters is the primacy or subordination given by each form of discourse to the subject in its relation to desire.' in Jacqueline Rose and Juliet Mitchell, *Feminine Sexuality*, p. 160.

15 Jacques Lacan, 'Thought is *jouissance*. What analytic discourse brings out is this fact, which was already intimated in the philosophy of being – that there is a *jouissance* of being.' Seminar *'God and the* Jouissance *of The Woman'*, in *Feminine Sexuality*. p. 142.

16 Toril Moi, *Sexual/Textual Politics: Feminist Literary Theory*, London, Methuen, 1985, pp. 114, 110.

17 Hélène Cixous, *Vivre l'orange* (Paris: Editions des femmes, 1979), pp. 14–18, quoted in Annette Kuhn, intro. to Hélène Cixous' 'Castration or Decapitation?', in *Signs: Journal of Women in Culture and Society*, vol. 7, no. 1, 1981, p. 39. The voice from Brazil is that of the experimental modernist Brazilian writer Clarice Lispector. Kuhn

informs us that, like Cixous, she has also been concerned to break with fixed forms and conventional modes of expression, and – again like Cixous – writes *the body*: 'in no sense an intellectual, I write with my body. And what I write is like a dank haze. The words are sounds transfused with shadows that intersect unevenly, stalactites, woven lace, transposed organ music.' From *A Hora da Estrela*, Rio de Janeiro, Livraria José Olimpio Editora, 1979. English version: *The Hour of the Star*, trans. Giovanni Pontiero, Manchester, Carcanet, 1986.

18 Melanie Klein, 'Envy and Gratitude', in *Envy and Gratitude, and Other Works, 1946–1963*, London, The Hogarth Press and the Institute of Psychoanalysis, 1975, p. 180.

19 Cixous, *Vivre l'orange*, quoted in Kuhn, op. cit., p. 39.

20 Hélène Cixous and Catherine Clément 'Sorties', *The Newly Born Woman*, trans. Betsy Wing, intro. Sandra Gilbert, Manchester, Manchester University Press, 1986, p. 89.

21 Hélène Cixous, 'La Venue a l'écriture', quoted in Toril Moi, *Sexual/ Textual Politics*, p. 116.

22 Hélène Cixous and Catherine Clément, 'Sorties', *The Newly Born Woman*, p. 86.

23 Ibid., pp. 90 and 91.

24 Annette Kuhn, intro. to Hélène Cixous' 'Castration or Decapitation?', p. 39.

25 Umberto Eco, *Semiotics and the Philosophy of Language*, London, Macmillan, 1984, p. 130.

26 For an account of the symbol as a 'content nebula' see Eco's Section 4, 'Symbol', in ibid., pp. 130–163, 162.

27 Ibid., pp. 121 and 127.

28 Hélène Cixous, 'The Laugh of the Medusa', *New French Feminisms*, p. 251.

29 Ibid., p. 246.

30 See section V, 'What the Thunder said', T. S. Eliot, *The Waste Land*, London, Faber & Faber, 1974, pp. 76–77.

31 Umberto Eco, *Semiotics and the Philosophy of Language*, p. 151.

32 Toril Moi, *Sexual/Textual Politics*, p. 116.

33 Hélène Cixous, 'The Laugh of the Medusa', *New French Feminisms*, p. 253.

9 MOTHER, DAUGHTER, SISTER, LOVER: ADRIENNE RICH'S DREAM OF A WHOLE NEW POETRY

(Notes for pages 126–154)

1 Adrienne Rich, *Of Woman Born: Motherhood as Experience and Institution*, London, Virago Books, 1977, p. 220.

2 Hélène Cixous, 'The Laugh of the Medusa', in *New French Feminisms: An Anthology*, ed. and intro. Elaine Marks and Isabelle de

Courtivron, trans. Keith Cohen and Paula Cohen, Brighton, Harvester, 1981, p. 252.

3 Luce Irigaray, interviewed by Diana Adlam and Couze Venn: 'Women's Exile', in *Ideology and Consciousness*, no. 1, 1977, p. 76.

4 Adrienne Rich, 'Origins and History of Consciousness (1972-4)', in *The Dream of a Common Language: Poems 1974-1977*, New York and London, W. W. Norton & Co., 1978, p. 7.

5 Nor does Rich collude with typically heterosexual patterns of femininity: the women she portrays are rarely passive or docile.

6 Luce Irigaray, 'When Our Lips Speak Together', trans. Carolyn Burke, in *Signs: Journal of Women in Culture and Society*, 1980, vol. 6, no. 1. p. 78. There is an intriguing similarity between these passages from Rich and Irigaray which, if it were not for the incompatibility of dates, would suggest a close influence. Alicia Ostriker tells us in *Writing Like a Woman* (Ann Arbor, University of Michigan Press, 1983, p. 110) that Rich was, by 1973, 'assuming an influential position in an intellectual movement which is coming to include not only Anglo-American writers such as Millett, Greer, Daly, Piercy and Olsen, but the contemporary French feminists Hélène Cixous, Monique Wittig, Luce Irigaray, and Marguerite Duras'.

7 Ibid., p. 78.

8 Adrienne Rich, 'Transcendental Etude', *The Dream of a Common Language: Poems 1974-77*, p. 72.

9 Dorothy Dinnerstein, *The Rocking of the Cradle and the Ruling of the World*, London, The Women's Press, 1987, p. 15.

10 Julia Kristeva, 'Motherhood According to Bellini: The Maternal Body', *Desire in Language: A Semiotic Approach to Literature and Art*, ed. Leon S. Roudiez, trans. Thomas Gora, Alice Jardine and Leon S. Roudiez, Oxford, Basil Blackwell, 1981, p. 239.

11 Kristeva's account of the semiotic disposition may be found in *Desire in Language*, pp. 133-137. See also *The Kristeva Reader*, ed. Toril Moi, Oxford, Basil Blackwell, 1986, p. 93, where Kristeva suggests that the semiotic *chora* orders the drives, and is a modality that is concerned with 'not only the *facilitation* and the *structuring disposition* of drives, but also the so-called *primary processes* which displace and condense both energies and their inscription'.

12 Julia Kristeva, *Desire in Language*, p. 165.

13 Adrienne Rich, *Of Woman Born*, p. 221

14 Adrienne Rich, 'It Is the Lesbian in Us', *On Lies, Secrets and Silence, Selected Prose 1961-1978*, London, Virago, 1980, p. 202.

15 Margaret Homans, *Women Writers and Poetic Identity: Dorothy Wordsworth, Emily Brontë, and Emily Dickinson*, Surrey, Princeton University Press, 1980, pp. 226-229.

16 In *Of Woman Born*, Rich speaks of the Great Mother, the female principle, in the following terms: 'only with the development of a patriarchal cosmogony do we find her restricted to a purely "chthonic" or tellurian presence, represented by darkness, unconsciousness, and sleep' (p. 109).

17 Homans comments: 'transcendence is the major term for poetry in the Romantic tradition, and if it is an evasion it is a splendid one'.

18 See *Chambers Dictionary*.

19 Sallie McFague, *Models of God: Theology for an Ecological, Nuclear Age*, London, SCM Press Ltd, 1987, pp. 8, 12, 117. Rosemary Radford Reuther, *Sexism and God Talk: Toward a Feminist Theology*, Boston, Beacon Press, 1983, p. 71.

20 Adrienne Rich, poem no. 18, 'Contradictions: Tracking Poems', in *Your Native Land, Your Life*, New York and London, W. W. Norton & Co., 1986, p. 100.

21 Adrienne Rich, 'Hunger', in *The Dream of a Common Language*, p. 12.

22 Cora Kaplan, *Sea Changes: Essays on Culture and Feminism*, London, Verso, 1986, p. 54. Kaplan also offers a vigorous critique of the essay 'Compulsory Heterosexuality' in which Rich problematises 'unexamined heterocentricity'. Kaplan argues that this essay constitutes a 'rejection of the political integrity of heterosexual feminism' and 'a denial both of the specifity and variety of female sexuality and the specificity and variety of feminism' (p. 55). In response, I would wish to point to the following statements made by Rich: 'I continue to think that heterosexual feminists will draw political strength for change from taking a critical stance towards the ideology which *demands* heterosexuality, and that lesbians cannot assume that we are untouched by that ideology and the institutions founded upon it' (*Blood, Bread and Poetry*, p. 25). Despite her disillusion and frustration with Marxist and leftist failures to address women's issues, Rich's work has always grounded itself in a politics of the dispossessed: for her, radical feminism 'never meant anything less by women's liberation than the creation of a society without domination' (p. 217).

23 Adrienne Rich, *Blood, Bread and Poetry*, London, Virago, 1986, p. 222. Rich quotes Cynthia Enloe, *Does Khaki Become You? The Militarisation of Women's Lives*, London, Pluto Press, 1983, ch. 8.

24 Kaplan, *Sea Changes*, p. 54

25 Rich, *Blood, Bread and Poetry*, p. 224.

26 Ibid., foreword, p. viii. Montefiore places Rich as 'a lesbian separatist' in her book *Feminism and Poetry: Language, Experience, Identity in Women's Writing*, London and New York, Pandora Press, 1987, p. 165. In *Blood, Bread and Poetry*, Rich adds further comments to her essay on 'Compulsory Heterosexuality and Lesbian Existence' (1986): 'I now think we have much to learn both from the uniquely female aspects of lesbian existence and from the complex "gay" identity we share with gay men' (p. 53).

27 Hélène Cixous, 'Castration or Decapitation?', trans. Annette Kuhn, in *Signs: Journal of Women in Culture and Society*, vol. 7. no. 1, 1981, p. 54.

28 Adrienne Rich, *Of Woman Born*, p. 274.

29 Adrienne Rich, 'Natural Resources', part 12, *The Dream of a Common Language*, p. 65.

30 Jan Montefiore, ' "What Words Say": Three Women Poets Reading
   H.D.', in *Agenda: H.D. Special Issue*, ed. Diana Collecott, vol. 25,
   nos 3 and 4, autumn/winter, 1987/1988, pp. 182-3.

31 H.D., 'The Walls Do Not Fall', in *Collected Poems: 1912-1944*, ed.
   Louis L. Martz, Manchester, Carcanet Press, 1984, p. 510.

32 Montefiore, op. cit., p. 183.

33 Rich, *Of Woman Born*, p. 81. Montefiore's suggestion in 'Feminism
   and Poetry' (see p. 145 and, tangentially, p. 151) that Rich 'does not
   assent to the psychoanalytic concept of *repression*' seems to me
   misleading. In *Of Woman Born* she cites Freud, Horney, Klein,
   Fanon, Mitchell, Neumann, Bettelheim, Brown, Marcuse. Wendy
   Martin notes, in a taped conversation with Rich during May 1978,
   that Rich intends that her writing record 'the process of going from
   the conflicts and strife of the unconscious into the sayable, into the
   actable'. Wendy Martin, *An American Triptych: Anne Bradstreet,
   Emily Dickinson, Adrienne Rich*, London, University of North
   Carolina Press, 1984, p. 169.

34 Hélène Cixous, 'The Laugh of the Medusa', *New French Feminisms*,
   p. 252.

35 Adrienne Rich, *Of Woman Born*, p. 39.

36 Monique Wittig, *The Lesbian Body*, London, Peter Owen, 1975.

37 Jan Montefiore, *Feminism and Poetry*, p. 157.

38 Montefiore stresses that there is 'no reason why' Monique Wittig's
   violent pre-Oedipal realm should be specifically female: 'it can
   indeed be argued that . . . Imaginary writing, far from transcending
   problems of gender, simply evades them' (ibid., p. 157).

39 Elizabeth Grosz, *Sexual Subversions: Three French Feminists*,
   Sydney, Allen & Unwin, 1989, p. xviii.

40 Montefiore, *Feminism and Poetry*, p. 178. I do not see Rich as
   oversimplifying 'the issues drastically, depending on a female nature
   (good) corrupted by patriarchal culture (bad) to submit itself to
   "compulsory hereosexuality" ' - as I hope my analysis through these
   pages demonstrates.

41 Grosz, *Sexual Subversions*, p. 117.

42 Rich, *Of Woman Born*, p. 283. See also Hester Eisenstein, *Con-
   temporary Feminist Thought*, London, Unwin, 1984, chapter 7 and
   overall, for her extended critique of Rich's theoretical writings.
   Lynne Segal also condemns the belief in women's moral superiority.
   She questions Carol Gilligan's argument (*In a Different Voice*,
   London, Harvard University Press, 1982, p. 172) that 'they display
   greater compassion and empathy: notions of a more concrete
   "responsibility and care" will always remain central in women's
   conceptions of morality. Always?' Such a belief may be descriptive,
   but becomes essentialist when seen as an intrinsic goodness which
   allies itself very comfortably with patriarchal myths of femininity.
   Lynne Segal, *Is the Future Female? Troubled Thoughts on Con-
   temporary Feminism*, London, Virago, 1987, p. 146.

43 Margaret Homans, *Women Writers and Poetic Identity*, Surrey,
   Princeton University Press, 1980, p. 229.

44 Another interesting reading of this contentious metaphor is offered by Marianne Whelchel who sees Rich as 'mining the earth-deposits of our history' ('Power', p. 3, *The Dream of a Common Language*). This reading interprets the earth-deposits as a metaphor for Rich's strategy of bringing to light 'women whose lives have been forgotten, undervalued, misinterpreted'. Marianne Whelchel, 'Mining the "Earth-Deposits"': Women's History in Adrienne Rich's Poetry', in *Reading Adrienne Rich: Reviews and Re-Visions, 1951–81*, ed. Jane Roberta Cooper, Ann Arbor, University of Michigan Press, 1984, p. 69.

10 VALIDATING THE LESBIAN BODY

(Notes for pages 157–165)

1 Quoted in Rachel Blau DuPlessis' essay, 'For the Etruscans' (1979), in *The New Feminist Criticism: Essays on Women, Literature and Theory*, ed. Elaine Showalter, London, Virago, 1986, p. 273.
2 Elizabeth Grosz, *Sexual Subversions: Three French Feminists*, Sydney, Allen & Unwin, 1989, p. 111.
3 Adrienne Rich, *On Lies, Secrets and Silence: Selected Prose 1966–1978*, London, Virago, 1980, p. 250.
4 Diana Collecott, 'What is not said: a study in textual inversion', *Textual Practice*, vol. 4, no. 2, summer 1990, 'A Special Issue, Lesbian and Gay Cultures: Theories and Texts', guest ed. Joseph Bristow, p. 242.
5 Olga Broumas, 'Snow White', *Beginning With O*, New Haven and London, Yale University Press, 1977, pp. 69–71.
6 Olga Broumas, 'Artemis', in ibid., p. 23.
7 Olga Broumas, ibid., p. 74, endnotes.
8 Rachel Blau DuPlessis, 'For the Etruscans', p. 273.
9 Olga Broumas, 'Artemis', p. 23.
10 Mary Carruthers, 'The Re-vision of the Muse: Adrienne Rich, Audre Lorde, Judy Grahn, Olga Broumas', in *Hudson Review*, vol. XXXVI, spring 1983, pp. 293–324. Mary Carruthers sees the word 'archaeology' as referring to *arkhe-logos* or 'ancient speech'. I have borrowed her term to insert into the rather different context of my analysis.
11 Luce Irigaray, 'When Our Lips Speak Together', in *Signs: Journal of Women in Culture and Society*, trans. Carolyn Burke, vol. 6, no. 1, 1980, p. 76. For the relation of Irigaray to intellectual and political French feminist writing see: Elaine Marks, 'Women and Literature in France', *Signs: Journal of Women in Culture and Society*, vol. 3, no. 4, summer 1978, pp. 832–842; and Carolyn Burke, 'Report from Paris: Women's Writing and the Women's Movement' in ibid., pp. 843–855.
12 'The Story of O' is discussed in Susan Griffin, *Pornography and Silence: Culture's Revenge Against Nature*, London, The Women's

Press, 1981, pp. 217–232. Jessica Benjamin, 'Master and Slave: The Fantasy of Erotic Domination' in *Desire: The Politics of Sexuality*, ed. Ann Snitow, Christine Stansell, Sharon Thompson, London, Virago, 1984. The issues raised are also discussed in *Against Sadomasochism: A Radical Feminist Analysis*, ed. Robin Ruth Linden, Darlene R. Pagano, Diana E. H. Russell, Susan Leigh Star, California, Frog in the Well, 1982.

13 Luce Irigaray, *This Sex Which Is Not One*, trans. Catherine Porter with Carolyn Burke, Ithaca, New York, Cornell University Press, 1985, p. 26.

14 Luce Irigaray, 'When Our Lips Speak Together', in *Signs*, p. 75.

15 Luce Irigaray, *This Sex Which Is Not One*, p. 25.

16 Barbara G. Walker, *The Women's Encyclopedia of Myths and Secrets*, San Francisco, Harper & Row, 1983, p. 414. Diana Collecott commented on reading this script, 'Notice also how Broumas loves the sound "O" in the poem "Rumpelstiltskin" for example "Grown women. Turning/ heliotropes to our own, our lovers' eyes." ' I should also note here the positive use Monique Wittig makes of the image of the circle in *The Oppoponax* and *Les Guérillères* where it is used as a mark of pleasure rather than of negation.

17 See Janice Raymond, *A Passion for Friends: Toward a Philosophy of Female Affection*, London, The Women's Press, 1986, for one account of these distinctions between lesbian women and women-identified women (pp. 16-18). Adrienne Rich's booklet, *Compulsory Heterosexuality and Lesbian Existence*, London, Onlywomen Press, 1981, offers her perspective which does not go unchallenged. See also 'On "Compulsory Heterosexuality and Lesbian Existence": Defining the Issues', by Ann Ferguson, Jacquelyn N. Zita and Kathryn Pyne Addelson, in *Signs: Journal of Women in Culture and Society* vol. 7. no 1, 1981, pp. 158-200.

18 Hélène Cixous, 'The Laugh of the Medusa', in *New French Feminisms: An Anthology*, ed. and intro. Elaine Marks and Isabelle de Courtivron, trans. Keith Cohen and Paula Cohen, Brighton, Harvester, 1981, p. 251.

11 'WITHIN THE FOLD OF PURPLE': H.D.'s ARGUMENT WITH FREUD

(Notes for pages 166–189)

1 H.D., *Tribute to Freud, Writing on the Wall, Advent*, Manchester, Carcanet Press, 1985 (*TF*) p. 70; and *Notes on Thought and Vision* (includes her essay 'The Wise Sappho') San Francisco, City Lights Books, 1982, p. 58.

2 Rachel Blau DuPlessis, 'For the Etruscans' (1979), in Elaine Showalter (ed.), *The New Feminist Criticism: Essays on Women, Literature and Theory*, London, Virago, 1986, p. 273.

3 Rachel Blau DuPlessis and Susan Friedman, ' "Woman is Perfect"': H.D.'s Debate with Freud', *Feminist Studies*, vol. 7, no. 3, fall 1981, p. 419.

4 Clare Buck, 'Freud and H.D. – bisexuality and a feminine discourse', *m/f*, no. 8, 1983, p. 56.

5 Juliet Mitchell, in 'Introduction I', *Feminine Sexuality: Jacques Lacan and the école freudienne*, eds. Jacqueline Rose and Juliet Mitchell, trans. Jacqueline Rose, London, Macmillan, 1982, p. 13.

6 Jacqueline Rose, 'Introduction II, ibid., p. 40.

7 Jacques Lacan, 'The Meaning of the Phallus', ibid., p. 82.

8 Luce Irigaray, 'This Sex Which Is Not One', in *This Sex Which Is Not One*, trans. Catherine Porter with Carolyn Burke, Ithaca, New York, Cornell University Press, 1985, p. 25.

9 Lacan, 'The Meaning of the Phallus', in *Feminine Sexuality*, p. 78.

10 Jacques Lacan, 'Of the Subject of Certainty', in *The Four Fundamental Concepts of Psychonalysis*, ed. Jacques-Alain Miller, trans. Alan Sheridan, Harmondsworth, Penguin Books, 1979. Lacan suggests that the female homosexual is still bound up with the father: 'it is in the desire of the father that the female homosexual finds another solution, that is, to defy the desire of the father'. Thus he can say that she has to show 'the father how one is, oneself, an abstract, heroic, unique phallus, devoted to the service of a lady' (pp. 38–9).

11 Teresa Brennan (ed.), *Between Feminism and Psychoanalysis*, London, Routledge, 1989, p. 4. In her introduction, Brennan highlights the fact that 'the ideally neutral phallus is presented in a one-sided masculine way'.

12 Luce Irigaray, 'When Our Lips Speak Together', trans. Carolyn Burke, *Signs: Journal of Women in Culture and Society*, vol. 6, no. 1, 1980, p. 72.

13 Jan Montefiore, *Feminism and Poetry: Language, Experience, Identity in Women's Writing*, London and New York, Pandora, 1987, p. 149.

14 Luce Irigaray, *This Sex Which Is Not One*, p. 31.

15 Margaret Whitford, 'Rereading Irigaray', in *Between Feminism and Psychoanalysis*, p. 108.

16 Sigmund Freud, 'The Infantile Genital Organisation: (An Interpolation into the Theory of Sexuality) (1923)', in *On Sexuality: Three Essays on the Theory of Sexuality and Other Works*, vol. 7, Harmondsworth, Penguin Books, 1977, p. 311. I should note here that despite these difficulties experienced when approaching Freud's theories of sexuality, his work has been of particular importance to later theorists of homosexuality and sexual difference. See pp. 52–55, for his discussion of bi-sexuality and 'psychical hermaphroditism'.

17 Rachel Blau DuPlessis and Susan Friedman, ' "Woman is Perfect"': H.D.'s Debate with Freud', op. cit., p. 422.

18 This particular pattern of colours and erotic imagery can be found repeatedly in H.D.'s work. Diana Collecott has referred me particularly to the volcanic/sexual imagery of the poem 'I Said', where

H.D. speaks of 'clusters of field-violet,/ (rill on rill of violets!/ parted and crested fire!)' (*CP* 322–325). In a recent article, Collecott explores earlier renderings of this poem, commenting that 'an early holograph version of these lines reads: "in the *crater* of Hymettus, rill on rill of violets – parted fire" ' (DC's italics), and suggests that 'we seem to be in the presence of metaphors for the female genitals rather than celebrations of an absent Greek landscape': Diana Collecott, 'What is not said: a study in textual inversion', in *Textual Practice*, vol. 4, no. 2, summer 1990, 'A Special Issue, Lesbian and Gay Cultures: Theories and Texts', guest ed. Joseph Bristow, p. 250.

19 Luce Irigaray, *Speculum of the Other Woman*, trans. Gillian C. Gill, Ithaca, New York, Cornell University Press, 1985, p. 83.

20 Lacan, 'The Meaning of the Phallus', in *Feminine Sexuality*, 75.

21 Claire Buck, commenting on this passage in 'Freud and H.D. – bisexuality and a feminine disexuality', sees this image as evoking 'an original moment prior to culture . . . since only in a mythical or imaginary register, prior to culture and the Symbolic can this "phallic woman" exist' (*m/f*, no. 8, 1983, p. 63). Buck decides that the 'figure of their reconciliation necessarily slips back into an Imaginary register and is produced as a phallicised woman: "that Lord become woman." ' Whitford's comments on the imaginary, in 'Rereading Irigaray' (pp. 117–121) does render DuPlessis' and Friedman's reading problematic. How is the imaginary to be articulated within the symbolic if it is unconscious? Does a female imaginary even exist? As Buck points out, this figure has to be articulated in the symbolic (which I suggest may well be 'mythic' – and future-oriented), and that even the bi-sexual woman must 'take up a position which is already sexed' (Buck, p. 63). Moreover, the image of the wo(man) who incorporates the male within herself, need not necessarily be seen as disavowing 'castration'. If the poet is seen as writing strategically or prophetically – she looks to the future effects of her writing, which Whitford suggests would be 'not something lurking in the depths of women's unconscious, but [might produce] a possible re-structuring of the imaginary by the symbolic which would make a difference to women' (Whitford, p. 117). Hence this woman whose 'arms are the waving of the young male' (*CP* 455) can be seen as a re-visionary figure, rather than as one hailing from 'an original moment prior to culture'. As such, this figure need not 'line up on one side or other of the sexual divide' (Buck, p. 64) in the same way that H.D. found herself required to do as a female writer, writing within the patriarchal symbolic. The use of the identifying metaphor thus allows H.D. to imagine a non-essentialist figurative representation in the symbolic which I see as having the potential to reach for 'a comprehensive unity striving to encompass hetero-geneity' (Buck, p. 63). Blau DuPlessis, in her adaptive response to Buck, sees the phallic woman as 'one of H.D.'s several interlocking solutions to claiming gender authority', and suggests that 'the attempt to represent female gender authority by our conventions of representation has to proceed according to familiar

metaphors and images': Rachel Blau DuPlessis, *H.D.: The Career of That Struggle*, Brighton, Harvester, 1986, p. 81.

22 Lacan, 'The Meaning of the Phallus, in *Feminine Sexuality*, p. 84.

23 Buck notes that Aphrodite 'is goddess of desire, sprung from the foam which gathered about the genitals of Uranus when Cronus castrated his father and threw them into the sea. The birth of desire is fixed therefore to the moment of castration' ('Freud and H.D.', p. 62).

24 Marina Warner, *Alone of All Her Sex: The Myth and the Cult of the Virgin Mary*, London, Picador, 1976, see illustration 6, p. 200.

25 Elizabeth Grosz, *Sexual Subversions: Three French Feminists*, Sydney, Allen & Unwin, 1989, p. 118.

26 Teresa Brennan, introduction, *Between Feminism and Psychoanalysis*, p. 13.

27 'Norman Holmes Pearson', on H.D.: An Interview,' conducted by L. S. Dembo, in *Contemporary Literature*, Special Issue on H.D., vol. 10, no. 4, autumn 1969, p. 444.

28 *H.D.: Tribute to Freud; Writing on the Wall, Advent*, p. 152. Rachel Blau DuPlessis and Susan Friedman have already explored this conflict in some detail so I will not pursue this further.

29 Margaret Whitford, 'Rereading Irigaray', in *Between Feminism and Psychoanalysis*, pp. 113–114. Whitford comments 'Now the real of the maternal body, in Lacanian terminology, means psychosis or foreclosure. So Laplanche and Pontalis, glossing Lacan, define foreclosure as follows: "Foreclosure consists in not symbolising what should have been symbolised." ' (Whitford's reference: Jean Laplanche and J. B. Pontalis, *The Language of Psychoanalysis*, translated by David Nicholson-Smith, London, Hogarth Press, 1973.)

30 Whitford, 'Rereading Irigaray', p. 115; Whitford cites Irigaray, *Speculum*, p. 84.

31 Lacan, 'The Meaning of the Phallus, in *Feminine Sexuality*, p. 84.

32 Margaret Whitford remarks that writers on Irigaray have encountered difficulties with the use of the term imaginary in dealing with it 'too summarily, by a precipitate celebration of the female imaginary, which bypasses the problem of its existence (whether it exists and what kind of existence it might have)'. She comments further: 'The imaginary can be described in more than one way. a) The female imaginary can be seen as the unconscious of western (male) thought – the unsymbolised, repressed underside of western philosophy. . . . b) [It is] something which does not yet exist, which still has to be created. . . . the female imaginary would be, not something lurking in the depths of women's unconscious, but a possible restructuring of the imaginary by the symbolic which would make a difference to women' ('Rereading Irigaray', p. 117).

33 Hélène Cixous, 'The Laugh of the Medusa', in *New French Feminisms: An Anthology*, ed. Elaine Marks and Isabelle de Courtivron, trans. Keith Cohen and Paula Cohen, Brighton, Harvester, 1981, p. 255.

12 'GOD CLAPS AND CLAPS/ HER ONE HAND'

(Notes for pages 190–202)

1 Title taken from a line of Olga Broumas' poem 'Innocence', in *Beginning With O*, New Haven and London, Yale University Press, 1977, p. 45.
2 Elly Bulkin, 'An Interview with Adrienne Rich', in *Conditions Two*, vol. 1. no. 2, October 1977, p. 57.
3 Susan Griffin, *Made from this Earth: Selections from her Writing 1967–1982*, London, The Women's Press, 1982, p. 274.
4 Susan Griffin, 'Notes on the Writing of Poetry', in ibid., p. 226.
5 Olga Broumas, 'Rumpelstiltskin', in *Beginning with O*, p. 64.
6 Jacques Lacan, 'From Love to the Libido', in *The Four Fundamental Concepts of Psychoanalysis*, ed. Jacques-Alain Miller, trans. Alan Sheridan, Harmondsworth, Penguin Books, 1979 (1973), p. 199.
7 Jacques Lacan, 'The Subject and the Other: Aphanisis', ibid., p. 203.
8 Jacques Lacan, 'From Love to the Libido', ibid., pp. 194–195.
9 Jacques Lacan, 'The Subject and the Other: Aphanisis', ibid., p. 218. Lacan says: 'Hence the division of the subject: when the subject appears somewhere as meaning, he is manifested elsewhere as "fading", as disappearance.'
10 Broumas, 'Innocence', *Beginning With O*, pp. 45–46.
11 Readers interested in following this up might look at Linda Hurcombe, *Sex and God: Varieties of Women's Religious Experience*, New York and London, Routledge & Kegan Paul, 1987. See also Charlene Spretnak, ed., *The Politics of Women's Spirituality: Essays on the Rise of Spiritual Power Within the Feminist Movement*, New York, Anchor Book, 1982.
12 Broumas, 'Innocence', *Beginning With O*, p. 45.
13 How far these 'small steeples' may be seen as phallic is a difficult question. I imagine a more conical design, volcano shape, wide at the base and squat! Short steeples surely can be imagined as breast shaped, even if rather sharp! Again this seems to me to be an appropriation of imagery traditionally considered as male, re-inscribing it in female terms. (What male would like his organ to be described as 'small'?) But perhaps it is more useful to place this image in the context of Cixous' account of bisexuality: 'Bisexuality: that is, each one's location in self (*repérage en soi*) of the presence – variously manifest and insistent according to each person, male or female – of both sexes, non-exclusion either of the difference or of one sex, and, from this "self-permission", multiplication of the effects of the inscription of desire, over all parts of my body and the other body.' Hélène Cixous, 'The Laugh of the Medusa', in *New French Feminisms: An Anthology*, ed. Elaine Marks and Isabelle de Courtivron, trans. Keith Cohen and Paula Cohen, Brighton, Harvester, 1981, p. 254. This is to argue that female specificity is not bound to traditional ideas of 'the feminine' and nor does it exclude characteristics currently considered as masculine. Openness and

receptiveness to the other means that the psyche is not exclusively
female. Again, this is a female specificity that is, paradoxically,
both/and rather than either/or.

14 Audre Lorde, *Zami: A New Spelling of My Name*, London, Sheba
Feminist Publishers, 1982, prologue.

15 Audre Lorde, 'Black Mother Woman', in *Chosen Poems: Old and
New*, New York and London, W. W. Norton & Co., 1982, p. 52.

16 I see Lorde as creating 'patterns for relating across our human
differences as equals' in this poem. See Audre Lorde, 'Age, Race,
Class, and Sex: Women Redefining Difference', in *Sister Outsider:
Essays and Speeches by Audre Lorde*, New York, The Crossing Press,
1984, p. 115.

17 Alicia Suskin Ostriker, *Stealing the Language: The Emergence of
Women's Poetry in America*, London, The Women's Press, 1987,
p. 188.

18 Ibid., p. 186.

19 Audre Lorde, 'My Words Will be There', in *Black Women Writers:
Arguments and Interviews*, ed. Mari Evans, London and Sydney,
Pluto Press, 1985, p. 261.

20 Johari M. Kunjufu: 'Ceremony', in *Black Sister: Poetry by Black
American Women, 1746–1980*, ed. Erlene Stetson, Bloomington,
Indiana University Press, 1981, p. 192.

21 Audre Lorde, in *Black Women Writers*, p. 264.

22 Audre Lorde, 'Recreation', in *The Black Unicorn: Poems*, New York,
W. W. Norton & Co., 1978, p. 81.

23 Audre Lorde, 'Uses of the Erotic: The Erotic as Power', in *Sister
Outsider*, p. 53.

24 Adrienne Rich, 'Poem XI' from 'Twenty-One Love Poems', *The
Dream of a Common Language: Poems, 1974–1977*, New York and
London, W. W. Norton & Co., 1978, p. 30.

25 Audre Lorde, 'Recreation', *The Black Unicorn*, p. 81.

26 Olga Broumas, 'Leda and Her Swan', in *Beginning with O*, p. 6.

27 Rich was researching *Of Woman Born* and reading many of the
founding texts of the women's spirituality movement at this time.
See especially her chapter 'The Primacy of the Mother'.

28 Vicki Noble, *Motherpeace: A Way to the Goddess through Myth, Art
and Tarot*, San Francisco, Harper & Row, 1983, pp. 25, 27. However,
Sally Gearheart and Susan Rennie, *A Feminist Tarot*, Massachusetts,
Persephone Press, 1981, first came out in 1976 and could have been
influential. Rich was later to distance herself from the more indi-
vidualist manifestations of the spirituality movement in the States.
See her interview with Margaret Packwood, in *Spare Rib*, February
1981, p. 14.

29 Adrienne Rich, 'Twenty-One Love Poems, Floating Poem', *The
Dream of a Common Language*, op. cit., p. 32.

30 Elly Bulkin, 'An Interview: "Andre Lorde and Adrienne Rich" ', in
Sister Outsider, p. 98.

31 Audre Lorde, 'Love Poem', in *Chosen Poems: Old and New*, p. 77.

32 Diana Collecott, 'What is not said: a study in textual inversion', in

Textual Practice, vol. 4, no. 2, summer 1990, 'A Special Issue, Lesbian and Gay Cultures: Theories and Texts', guest ed. Joseph Bristow, p. 247.

33 Audre Lorde, 'Dahomey', in *The Black Unicorn*, p. 11.

34 Audre Lorde *Zami*, prologue.

CONCLUSION

(Notes for pages 203–206)

1 Hélène Cixous, 'The Laugh of the Medusa', in *New French Feminisms: An Anthology*, ed. Elaine Marks and Isabelle de Courtivron, trans. Keith Cohen and Paula Cohen, Brighton, Harvester Press, p. 252.

SELECT BIBLIOGRAPHY

PRIMARY TEXTS

Broumas, Olga

Beginning With O, New Haven and London, Yale University Press, 1977.

H.D. (Doolittle, Hilda)

H.D.: Helen in Egypt, intro. Horace Gregory, New York, New Directions, 1961.
Notes on Thought and Vision (includes 'The Wise Sappho', an essay), San Francisco, City Lights Books, 1982.
H.D.: Collected Poems: 1912-1944, ed. Louis L. Martz, Manchester, Carcanet Press, 1984.
H.D.: Tribute to Freud, Writing on the Wall, Advent, foreword by Norman Holmes Pearson, Manchester, Carcanet Press, 1985.

Griffin, Susan

Pornography and Silence: Culture's Revenge Against Nature, London, The Women's Press, 1981.
Made from this Earth: Selections from her Writing 1967-1982, London, The Women's Press, 1982.
Woman and Nature: The Roaring Inside Her, London, The Women's Press, 1984.

Lorde, Audre

The Black Unicorn: Poems, New York, W. W. Norton & Co., 1978.
Chosen Poems: Old and New, New York and London, W. W. Norton & Co., 1982.
Zami, A New Spelling of My Name, London, Sheba Feminist Publishers, 1982.
Sister Outsider: Essays and Speeches by Audre Lorde, New York, The Crossing Press, 1984.

Plath, Sylvia

Collected Poems, ed. and intro. Ted Hughes, London, Faber & Faber, 1981.

The Journals of Sylvia Plath, ed. Ted Hughes and Frances McCullough, New York, Ballantyne Books, 1982.

Rich, Adrienne

Of Woman Born: Motherhood as Experience and Institution, London, Virago, 1977.

The Dream of a Common Language: Poems 1974-1977, New York and London, W. W. Norton & Co., 1978.

On Lies, Secrets and Silence: Selected Prose 1966-1978, London, Virago, 1980.

Compulsory Heterosexuality and Lesbian Existence, London, Only-women Press, 1981.

The Fact of a Doorframe: Poems Selected and New, 1950-1984, New York & London, W. W. Norton & Co., 1984.

Your Native Land, Your Life, New York and London, W. W. Norton & Co., 1986.

Blood, Bread and Poetry: Selected Prose, 1979-1985, London, Virago, 1987.

Time's Power: Poems 1985-1988, London, W. W. Norton & Co., 1989.

SECONDARY SOURCES

Articles from Newspapers

Plath, Aurelia, *New York Times*, 9 October 1979.

Articles from Journals

Adams, Parveen, 'Representation and Sexuality', *m/f*, no. 1, 1978, pp. 65-81.

Brown, Beverly and Adams, Parveen, 'The Feminine Body and Feminist Politics', *m/f*, no. 3, 1979, pp. 35-49.

Buck, Clare, 'Freud and H.D. - bisexuality and a feminine discourse', *m/f*, no. 8, 1983, pp. 53-66.

Bulkin, Elly, 'An Interview with Adrienne Rich', Part 1, *Conditions One* 1/1, April 1977; pp. 50-65, and Part 2, *Conditions Two*, 1/2, October 1977, pp. 53-65.

Carruthers, Mary, 'The Re-vision of the Muse: Adrienne Rich, Audre Lorde, Judy Grahn, Olga Broumas', *Hudson Review*, vol. XXXVI, spring 1983, pp. 293-324.

Cixous, Hélène, 'Castration or Decapitation?', trans. Annette Kuhn, in *Signs: Journal of Women in Culture and Society*, vol. 7. no. 1, 1981, pp. 36-55.

Collecott, Diana, 'Remembering oneself: the reputation and the later poetry of H.D.', *Critical Quarterly*, vol. 27, no. 1, spring 1985, pp. 7-22.

Collecott, Diana, 'What is not said: a study in textual inversion', *Textual Practice*, vol. 4, no. 2, summer 1990, 'A Special Issue, Lesbian and Gay Cultures: Theories and Texts', guest ed. Joseph Bristow, pp. 236-258.

Dallery, Arleen B., 'Sexual Embodiment: Beauvoir and French Feminism (*écriture féminine)*', *Women's Studies International Forum*, vol. 8, no. 3. 1985, pp. 197-202.

Dembo, L. S., 'Norman Holmes Pearson on H.D.: An Interview,' *Contemporary Literature: Special Issue on H.D.*, vol. 10, no. 4, autumn 1969, pp. 435-446.

DuPlessis, Rachel Blau, and Friedman, Susan, '"Woman is Perfect": H.D.'s Debate with Freud', *Feminist Studies*, vol. 7, no. 3, fall 1981, pp. 407-429.

Ferguson, Ann, Jaquelyn N. Zita, and Kathryn Pyne Addelson, 'On "Compulsory Heterosexuality and Lesbian Existence": Defining the Issues', *Signs: Journal of Women in Culture and Society*, vol. 7, no. 1, 1981, pp. 158-200.

Fox Keller, Evelyn, 'Gender and Science', *Psychoanalysis and Contemporary Thought*, 1, 1978, pp. 409-433.

Irigaray, Luce, 'When Our Lips Speak Together', trans. Carolyn Burke, in *Signs: Journal of Women in Culture and Society*, vol. 6, no. 1, 1980, pp. 66-79.

Kuhn, Annette, intro. to Hélène Cixous, 'Castration or Decapitation?', in *Signs: Journal of Women in Culture and Society* vol. 7, no. 1, 1981, pp. 36-55.

Lorde, Audre, and Rich, Adrienne, 'An Interview with Audre Lorde', *Signs: Journal of Women in Culture and Society*, vol. 6, no. 4, summer 1981, pp. 713-736.

McDaniel, Judith, 'The Transformation of Silence into Language and Action', *Sinister Wisdom* 6, summer 1978, pp. 4-25.

Marks, Elaine, 'Women and Literature in France', *Signs: Journal of Women in Culture and Society*, vol. 3, no. 4, 1978, pp. 832-842.

Montefiore, Jan, '"What Words Say": Three Women Poets Reading H.D.', in *Agenda: H.D. Special Issue*, ed. Diana Collecott, vol. 25, nos 3 and 4, autumn/winter 1987/1988, pp. 172-190.

Ruddick, Sarah, 'Maternal Thinking', *Feminist Studies* 6, no. 2, summer 1980, pp. 342-367.

Shaktini, Namaskar, 'Displacing the Phallic Subject: Wittig's Lesbian Writing', *Signs: Journal of Women in Culture and Society*, vol. 8, no. 1, 1982, pp. 29-44.

Zimmerman, Bonnie, 'The Politics of Transliteration: Lesbian Personal Narratives', *Signs: Journal of Women in Culture and Society*, vol. 9, no. 4, 1984, pp. 663-682.

GENERAL BIBLIOGRAPHY

Annas, Pamela J., *A Disturbance in Mirrors: The Poetry of Sylvia Plath*, London, Greenwood Press, 1988.

Bassnett, Susan, *Sylvia Plath*, London, Macmillan, 1987.

Beauvoir, Simone de, *The Second Sex*, trans. and ed. H. M. Parshley, Harmondsworth Penguin, 1981 (1949).

Brennan, Teresa, ed., *Between Feminism and Psychoanalysis*, London, Routledge, 1989.

Bundtzen, Lynda K., *Plath's Incarnations: Woman and the Creative Process*, Ann Arbor, University of Michigan Press, 1983.

Chodorow, Nancy, *The Reproduction of Mothering: Psychoanalysis and the Sociology of Gender*, Los Angeles, London, University of California Press, 1978.

Cixous, Hélène, *Vivre l'orange*, Paris, Editions des femmes, 1979.

Cixous, Hélène, 'The Laugh of the Medusa', in *New French Feminisms: An Anthology*, ed. Elaine Marks and Isabelle de Courtivron, Brighton, Harvester, 1981, pp. 245-267.

Cixous, Hélène, and Clément, Catherine, *The Newly Born Woman*, trans. Betsy Wing, intro. Sandra Gilbert, Manchester, Manchester University Press, 1986.

Cooper, Jane Roberta, *Reading Adrienne Rich: Reviews and Re-Visions, 1951-81*, Ann Arbor, University of Michigan Press, 1984.

Daly, Mary, *Gyn/Ecology: The Metaethics of Radical Feminism*, London, The Women's Press, 1979.

Daly, Mary, *Beyond God the Father: Towards a Philosophy of Women's Liberation*, Boston, Beacon Press, 1973; London, The Women's Press, 1985.

Derrida, Jacques, *Of Grammatology*, trans. and intro. Gayatri Chakravorty Spivak, Baltimore and London, The Johns Hopkins University Press, 1976.

Dinnerstein, Dorothy, *The Rocking of the Cradle and the Ruling of the World*, London, The Women's Press, 1987. First published as *The Mermaid and the Minotaur*, New York, Harper & Row, 1976.

DuPlessis, Rachel Blau, *Writing Beyond the Ending: Narrative Strategies of Twentieth Century Women Writers*, Bloomington, Indiana University Press, 1985.

DuPlessis, Rachel Blau, *H.D.: The Career of That Struggle*, Brighton, Harvester Press, 1986.

Eco, Umberto, *Semiotics and the Philosophy of Language*, London, Macmillan Press, 1984.

Eisenstein, Hester, and Alice Jardine, eds, *The Future of Difference*, Boston, G. K. Hall, 1980.

Evans, Mari, ed., *Black Women Writers: Arguments and Interviews*, London and Sydney, Pluto Press, 1985.

Freud, Sigmund, *The Interpretation of Dreams*, trans. and ed. James Strachey, vol. 4, Harmondsworth, Penguin Books, 1976.

Freud, Sigmund, *On Psychopathology: Inhibitions, Symptoms and Anxiety and Other Works*, trans. and ed. James Strachey, vol. 10, Harmondsworth, Penguin, 1983.

Freud, Sigmund, *On Sexuality: Three Essays on the Theory of Sexuality and Other Works*, trans. and ed. James Strachey, vol. 7, Harmondsworth, Penguin, 1977 (1905).

Freud, Sigmund, *Civilisation, Society and Religion*, trans. James Strachey, ed. Albert Dickson, vol. 12, Harmondsworth, Penguin, 1985.

Freud, Sigmund, *The Origins of Religion: Totem and Taboo, Moses and Monotheism and other Works*, trans. and ed. James Strachey, vol. 13, Harmondsworth, Penguin, 1985.

Friedman, Susan Stanford, *Psyche Reborn: The Emergence of H.D.*, Bloomington, Indiana University Press, 1981.

Gearheart, Sally, and Susan Rennie, *A Feminist Tarot*, Massachusetts, Persephone Press, 1981.

Gilbert, Sandra, and Susan Gubar, eds, *Shakespeare's Sisters: Feminist Essays on Women Poets*, Bloomington and London, Indiana University Press, 1979.

Green, Gayle, and Coppelia Kahn, eds, *Making a Difference: Feminist Literary Criticism*, New York, Methuen, 1985.

Grosz, Elizabeth, *Sexual Subversions: Three French Feminists*, Sydney, Allen & Unwin, 1989.

Grosz, Elizabeth, *Jacques Lacan: A Feminist Introduction*, London, Routledge, 1990.

Hanscome, Gillian & Virginia Smyers, *Writing For Their Lives: The Modernist Women 1910-1940*, London, Women's Press, 1987.

Harrison, Jane, *Themis: A Study of the Social Origins of Greek Religion*, London, Merlin Press, 1963.

Heyward, Carter, *Our Passion for Justice: Images of Power, Sexuality, and Liberation*, New York, The Pilgrim Press, 1984.

Homans, Margaret, *Women Writers and Poetic Identity: Dorothy Wordsworth, Emily Brontë, and Emily Dickinson*, Surrey, Princeton University Press, 1980.

Hunter Steiner, Nancy, *A Closer Look at Ariel: A Memory of Sylvia Plath*, intro. George Stade, London, Faber, 1974.

Hurcombe, Linda, *Sex and God: Varieties of Women's Religious Experience*, New York and London, Routledge & Kegan Paul, 1987.

Irigaray, Luce, *This Sex Which Is Not One*, trans. Catherine Porter and Carolyn Burke, Ithaca, New York, Cornell University Press, 1985 (1977).

Irigaray, Luce, *Speculum of the Other Woman*, trans. Gillian C. Gill, Ithaca, New York, Cornell University Press, 1985.

Jacobus, Mary, *Reading Woman: Essays in Feminist Criticism*, New York Columbia University Press, 1986.

Juhasz, Susanne, *Naked and Fiery Forms: Modern American Poetry by Women, A New Tradition*, New York and London, Harper & Row, 1976.

Kaplan, Cora, *Sea Changes: Essays on Culture and Feminism*, London, Verso, 1986.

Keohane, Nannerl O., Michelle Z. Rosaldo and Barbara C. Gelpi, eds, *Feminist Theory: A Critique of Ideology*, Brighton, Harvester, 1982.

Klein, Melanie, *Envy and Gratitude, and Other Works, 1946-1963*, London, The Hogarth Press and the Institute of Psychoanalysis, 1975.

Kristeva, Julia, *Desire in Language: A Semiotic Approach to Literature and Art*, ed. Leon S. Roudiez, trans. Thomas Gora, Alice Jardine and Leon S. Roudiez, Oxford, Basil Blackwell, 1981.

Kristeva, Julia, *Powers of Horror: An Essay on Abjection*, trans. Leon S. Roudiez, New York, Columbia University Press, 1982.

Lacan, Jacques, *Ecrits: A Selection*, trans. Alan Sheridan, London, Tavistock Publications, 1977, originally published in French by Editions du Seuil, 1966.

Lacan, Jacques, *The Four Fundamental Concepts of Psychoanalysis*, ed Jacques-Alain Miller, trans. Alan Sheridan, Harmondsworth, Penguin, 1979.

Lauter, Estella, *Women as Mythmakers: Poetry and Visual Art by Twentieth Century Women*, Bloomington, Indiana University Press, 1984.

Linden, Robin Ruth, Darlene R. Pagano, Diana E. H. Russell, and Susan Leigh Star, eds, *Against Sadomasochism: A Radical Feminist Analysis*, California, Frog in the Well, 1982.

McFague, Sallie, *Models of God: Theology for an Ecological, Nuclear Age*, London, SCM Press, 1987.

Marks, Elaine, and Courtivron, Isabelle de, eds, *New French Feminisms: An Anthology*, trans. Keith Cohen and Paula Cohen, Brighton, Harvester Press, 1981.

Martin, Wendy, *An American Triptych: Anne Bradstreet, Emily Dickinson, Adrienne Rich*, London, University of North Carolina Press, 1984.

Miles, Siân (ed.), *Simone Weil: An Anthology*, London, Virago, 1986.

Mitchell, Juliet, and Rose, Jacqueline, eds, *Feminine Sexuality: Jacques Lacan and the école freudienne*, trans. Jacqueline Rose, London, Macmillan, 1982.

Moi, Toril, *Sexual/Textual Politics: Feminist Literary Theory*, London, Methuen, 1985.

Moi, Toril, *Julia Kristeva: The Kristeva Reader*, Oxford, Basil Blackwell, 1986.

Monteith, Moira, ed., *Women's Writing: A Challenge to Theory*, Brighton, Harvester Press, 1986.

Montefiore, Jan, *Feminism and Poetry: Language, Experience, Identity in Women's Writing*, London and New York, Pandora Press, 1987.

Ostriker, Alicia Suskin, *Writing Like a Woman*, Ann Arbor, University of Michigan Press, 1983.

Ostriker, Alicia Suskin, *Stealing the Language: The Emergence of Women's Poetry in America*, London, The Women's Press, 1987.

Pope, Deborah, *A Separate Vision: Isolation in Contemporary Women's Poetry*, Baton Rouge and London, Louisiana State University Press 1984.

Raymond, Janice, *A Passion for Friends? Toward a Philosophy of Female Affection*, London, The Women's Press, 1986.

Segal, Lynne, *Is the Future Female? Troubled Thoughts on Contemporary Feminism*, London, Virago, 1987.

Sellers, Susan, ed., *Writing Differences: Readings from the Seminar of*

Hélène Cixous, Milton Keynes, Open University Press, 1988.

Showalter, Elaine, *The New Feminist Criticism: Essays on Women, Literature and Theory*, London, Virago, 1986.

Snitow, Ann, Christine Stansell, and Sharon Thompson, eds, *Desire: The Politics of Sexuality*, London, Virago, 1984.

Spretnak, Charlene, ed., *The Politics of Women's Spirituality: Essays on the Rise of Spiritual Power Within the Feminist Movement*, New York, Anchor Books, 1982.

Starhawk, *Dreaming the Dark: Magic, Sex and Politics*, Boston, Beacon Press, 1982.

Stetson, Erlene, ed., *Black Sister: Poetry by Black American Women 1746–1980*, Bloomington, Indiana University Press, 1981.

Stevenson, Anne, *Bitter Fame: A Life of Sylvia Plath*, Harmondsworth, Penguin, 1989.

Weed, Elizabeth, ed., *Coming to Terms: Feminism, Theory, Politics*, London, Routledge, 1989.

Wheedon, Chris, *Feminist Practice and Poststructuralist Theory*, Oxford, Basil Blackwell, 1987.

Wood Middlebrook, Diana, *Coming to Light: Women Poets in the Twentieth Century*, Ann Arbor, University of Michigan Press, 1985.

INDEX

abject 55, 62, 77
Anderson, Linda 52
Annas, Pamela J. 73

Barrett Browning, Elizabeth 66
Bassnett, Susan 82
Bergman, Ingmar 73
Beuscher, Ruth 52
biological difference 3, 10, 12, 21, 114, 116, 117, 133, 150, 153, 158, 162, 172, 203; determinism 142–143, 174, 188
Bishop, Elizabeth 11
bisexuality 115, 118, 121, 165, 167, 168, 172, 177, 179–180, 201
black women 23–33, 195; lesbian 194–202; mothers 195; lesbian poet 195, 197; African folklore 201
body 4, 10, 12, 13, 30, 50, 70, 90, 115, 140, 147, 149, 170, 173, 177–179, 198, 202–203; body language 50, 162, 186; castrated 127; erotic 161, 198–199; as ground of identity 21; infant 132; integrity of 97; knowledge of 34, 38, 43, 44; lesbian 157, 161, 193; maternal 116, 130, 189; as preceding language 20; sexual 69, 133, 162, 165, 184, 193; specificity of 114, 116, 178, 189; textual 126, 150, 185, 199; theology of 193; voice of 43; woman's/female 144, 150, 164–165, 167, 172, 177, 187–188;

wisdom of 200; writing the body 117–125, 143–145
Braidotti, Rosa 12, 13
Brennan, Teresa 114, 172–173, 180
Broumas, Olga 162, 198, 199–200; 'Snow White' 159; 'Artemis' 161; 'Rumpelstiltskin' 191; 'Innocence' 193–194
Buck, Claire 167

castration, castration complex 127, 152, 159, 163, 167, 168–169, 172, 175, 177–179, 188–189
censor, censorship 15, 19, 43, 49, 74, 96; inner 51, 115, 126, 191, 200, 205
Cixous, Hélène 3, 9, 23, 80, 85, 88, 111–125, 126, 165, 189
Clément, Catherine 9, 80, 88
Collecott, Diana 101, 159, 201

Dallery, Arlene 115
Daly, Mary 14, 44, 50
De Beauvoir, Simone 80, 130
desire and the erotic 3, 4, 20, 96, 116–118, 121, 149, 152, 158, 164, 177, 180, 190–203; dialectics of 112; economy of 178–179; field of 74; inscription of 115; to know 134; lesbian 178, 181–189; limitless 132; for the mother 96, 104, 105, 131, 132; object of 113, 163, 169, 180; for a source 121; thwarted 1
Dickinson, Emily 11, 66

234